"THESE ARE NOT DRUNKEN, AS YE SUPPOSE"

(Acts 2:15)

Ye shall know the Truth (Jesus) & the Truth
shall make you free.

Sincerely yours in Christ

Howard M. Ervin

June 4, 1972

"THESE ARE NOT DRUNKEN, AS YE SUPPOSE"

(Acts 2:15)

by

Howard M. Ervin

PLAINFIELD, NEW JERSEY

Table of Contents

"THESE ARE NOT DRUNKEN,
AS YE SUPPOSE"

(Acts 2:15)

PROLOGUE

"Truth Divorced From Experience..."

"Truth divorced from experience must always dwell in the realm of a doubt," remarked Henry Krause, distinguished Christian business man and industrialist. We were lingering over a between sessions lunch in the Pine Room of the Queen Charlotte Hotel in Charlotte, North Carolina. The regional convention of the Full Gospel Business Men's Fellowship was in session, and our conversation was centered on the supernatural manifestations of the Holy Spirit in our day. Our "table talk" had been interspersed with such concise maxims, so characteristic of the "word of wisdom." [1] But somehow this profound word, simply spoken, transcended the mood of the moment. An oft quoted scripture echoed a solemn admonition: "He that hath an ear, let him hear what the Spirit saith to the churches." [2] For Wisdom speaks ageless and universal Truth. It is the womb of revelation—the archetype of the divine mysteries of creation [3] and redemption. [4] This then was no platitudinous

---

[1] I Cor. 12:8. Unless otherwise noted, all Biblical quotations are from *The Holy Bible, American Standard Version* (New York: Thomas Nelson & Sons, Copyright 1929 by the International Council of Religious Education). Abbr. ASV.

[2] Rev. 3:22.

[3] Prov. 22:31.

[4] I Cor. 2:6ff.

cliché from my companion. The very cadence of his words carried the compelling self-authentication of Truth.

The first draft of this book was nearing completion. For months we had dredged the murky depths of recrimination and condemnation of the Pentecostal experience. Reactions, their emotional overtones disqualify the description responses, oscillated between scholarly detachment (?)—"I could not care less," and dogmatic hostility—"Its all of the Devil;" between institutional expediency—"Don't rock the boat," and ecclesiastical condescension—"Its not relevant to our task." But the elusive common denominator behind all these negative reactions resisted clear definition. Now here it was in all its lucid simplicity. "Truth divorced from experience must always dwell in the realm of a doubt."

The countenance of Truth, eroded by skepticism, was scarcely discernible in the numerous caricatures of the charismatic experience which we had read. Bishops hinted darkly at schizophrenia—the demogoguery of the shibboleth. Synods convened inquisitorial commissions. Church conventions adopted coercive resolutions—obviously liberty of conscience (?) is not to be construed as freedom of conduct! Psychologists, and fellow-travelers, with Olympian disdain, dismissed it with a caustic "religious hysteria" [5]—but to label is oft to libel. Linguists sampled tape recordings, and *ex cathedra* assured all and sundry that *glossolalia* [6] is not really language. Theologians, finding no congenial categories for it in their anti-supernatural Philosophies of Religion, scorned it as irrational. After all, the theological *avant garde* (?) has decreed that "God is dead"—or what

[5] The limitations of such judgments are illustrated in this paraphrase of David Roberts by Orville S. Walters, "Have Psychiatry and Religion Reached a Truce?" *Christianity Today*, X, 1 (Oct. 1965), 21. "The psychiatrist cannot adequately evaluate his patient's religious views without an understanding of religious experience, preferably at first hand."

[6] A technical term for "speaking in tongues". It is a compound of the Greek words *glossa*, "tongue" (hence, "language") and *lalia*, "speech".

is almost as puerile, "Deaf and dumb." New Testament lexicons expressed a preference for "religious ecstasy." Distinguished Bible versions followed suit with "ecstatic utterances" as a *bona fide* translation of "tongues-speech." Even
the exegetical literature wheezed an asthmatic skepticism—
its "corybantic" fantasies savoring more of mythology than
of theology. The whole heterogeneous edifice wore the pa-
tina of hoary doubt—"Yea, hath God said . . .?" [7] But the
attempt to interpret the charismatic manifestations of the
Holy Spirit without a charismatic experience is as fatuous
as the application of the "Christian ethic" apart from a regenerate dynamic.

These are turbulent waters for the timid or the uncommitted. Like surf on sand, definitions and categories assumed as fixed by one critic are effaced by another. The
phenomenal world may be measured, scrutinized, and ana-
lyzed with scientific detachment. Observations, analogies,
and correlations work with predictable probability, because
man has learned experientially many of the laws governing
his physical environment. Not so, however, in the spiritual
world. In the realm of supernatural reality, these same tech-
niques (observations, analogies, and correlations) without
an empirical frame of reference are something less than
educated guesses. And only a personal involvement can provide an empirical frame of reference. The Scriptures are
explicit on this point: "The unspiritual man does not receive the gifts of the Spirit of God, for they are folly to him,
because they are spiritually discerned." [8] Which is simply
another way of saying that understanding of spiritual truth
is predicated upon spiritual experience. The Holy Spirit

[7] Gen. 3:1.
[8] I Cor. 2:14. *The New Testament, Revised Standard Version* (New York:
Thomas Nelson & Sons, Copyright 1946 by Division of Christian Education
of the National Council of Churches in the United States of America). Abbr.
RSV.

does not reveal spiritual secrets to the uncommitted, and quite frankly, the Pentecostal experience is one of total commitment. The fundamental presupposition of this book is "Pentecostal" in its unqualified committment to the whole counsel of God. Etched into every line of it is the joyous awareness that *Jesus is alive!* It echoes the ancient Easter salutation: "He is risen, indeed!" "Jesus Christ *is* the same yesterday and today, *yea* and for ever." [9] Every charismatic manifestation of His Holy Spirit is a supernatural confirmation of this fact.

The basic material incorporated in this volume is the outgrowth of extensive speaking opportunities before conventions and chapter meetings of the Full Gospel Business Mens' Fellowship International, as an occasional instructor in charismatic seminars at the Oral Roberts University, School of Evangelism, as a panelist in ministers' and students' seminars on the charismatic renewal of the Church, and in churches and prayer groups in many parts of our nation and abroad. The bulk of the information contained in it, however, represents a lengthy and intensive teaching ministry to the congregation of the Emmanuel Baptist Church in Atlantic Highlands, N. J.

The wide diversity of audiences has afforded us some small insight into the spiritual barrenness that blights many areas of Christian life and witness. We have also been confronted repeatedly with the gnawing spiritual hunger of great numbers of professed Christians who are withering spiritually under the unrelenting diet of rationalism, humanism, scientism, and even dead orthodoxy which they are being offered. It is the growing awareness of the almost insuperable spiritual need of our churches that impells us to write this book at this time.

[9] Heb. 13:8.

The ambitions it embodies are modest indeed. It makes no pretense of being definitive, merely provocative. It is, in essence, an interpretation of the Biblical basis for the present charismatic renewal of the Church.

Some five years ago, after receiving the baptism in the Holy Spirit, I began to toy with the idea of writing some such book as this. Its scope, as projected then, was much more ambitious than the present effort. It was my hope that at some future date there would be both time and opportunity to thoroughly research this fascinating subject. However, the procession of days has stretched into weeks, months, and finally years without the hoped for opportunity presenting itself. Pastoral responsibilities, numerous speaking engagements, and increasing involvement in a charismatic ministry to the larger Body of Christ, have finally forced upon me the realization that I may never achieve my original goal. Conversely, the growing awareness of the pressing need for an explicit, and reasonably comprehensive statement of the case for the present charismatic quickening in many churches of all denominations becomes more insistent with the passage of time. It is this felt need that constitutes the justification (if such be needed) for adding one more to the growing list of publications discussing the Pentecostal experience. The thorough research and definitive statement of the subject still awaits someone with greater capabilities than mine, in addition to the time and resources to achieve such a goal.

Once the decision was made to write for publication the results of my own study and experience, the question of even minimal documentation became a pressing one. Lacking the facilities of a theological library, documentation, of necessity, has been confined almost exclusively to those resources available on an average pastor's bookshelves. Resources that are slender enough, to be sure, but nonetheless gratifying enough to suggest the wealth of untapped riches in the Church's theological heritage.

There remains now the happy responsibility of acknowledging my indebtedness to those who have helped to forward this project. The following, in order of mention, have read the manuscript in an earlier draft. The Rev. Michael Harper, founder of the Fountain Literature Trust of London, England; Mr. John Sherrill, senior editor of *Guideposts* magazine; the Rev. Oral Roberts, evangelist and founder-president of the Oral Roberts University of Tulsa, Oklahoma; the Rev. Dr. R. O. Corvin, dean of the Graduate School of Theology of the Oral Roberts University; and the Rev. Dr. John Rea. This final form of the manuscript owes much to their perceptive comments. I gladly acknowledge my indebtedness to them for their efforts so freely given in reviewing and criticising this manuscript. On points of disagreement, however, I have not hesitated to follow my own convictions, where I felt these were justified. Nevertheless, on many points, I have yielded to their mature, and weighty suggestions. Sole responsibility, however, for the final form and content of the book is mine.

Many thanks are due to Mrs. Nancy Lingo, one of our Spirit-filled Emmanuel fellowship, and to my daughter Gretchen for efficiently discharging the laborious task of typing multiple copies of the manuscript. It is also my privilege to acknowledge the prayerful support and encouragement of the congregation of my church, the Emmanuel Baptist Church of Atlantic Highlands, N. J., whose Spirit-filled fellowship has provided a "laboratory" where the practical consequences of the views expressed in this volume have been repeatedly tested. My thanks are due also to Mr. Demos Shakarian, founder and president of the Full Gospel Business Mens' Fellowship International, and to the directors and chapter presidents who have repeatedly extended to me the freedom of their convention platforms, where some of the ideas developed in this book were first crystallized. Last, but far from least, my appreciation for the enthusiastic encouragement of my wife, and our three daughters is imperfectly acknowledged in the dedication of this volume to them.

CHAPTER I

"Be Filled With the Spirit"

(Luke 1:15, 41, 67; 4:1)

"Be filled with the Spirit." [1] The translation of the
Geneva Bible (1560–62), sounds a little quaint, even stilted
in our ears. Yet it lends a dimension of freshness the word
"filled" has lost in our more modern translations. "Fulfilled" carries with it the overtone of complete realization,
or manifestation, neatly illustrated by the inversion of its
members. For example, "fulfilled" = "filled full," that is to
say, "filled to the level of overflowing."

What significance does this apostolic injunction have for
the average Christian? Is it merely rhetorical moralizing?
i.e., "be not drunken with wine, wherein is riot, but be
filled with the Spirit." Or is it perchance simply an arrest-
ing metaphor? Is it incidental to the Christian profession?
Or is it the very essence of Christian experience?

Let the reader take note of this, it is not stated as an
option. It is first of all an admonition. But more then that,
it is an opportunity to experience life abundant. It is a
divine imperative addressed to every Christian. It is not
merely the unique privilege of a spiritual clique, a remote
possibility attainable only by the exceptional soul—the spir-

[1] Eph. 5:18. *The New Testament Octapla,* ed. by Luther A. Weigle, (New
York: Thomas Nelson & Sons, 1946).

9

itual athlete. On the contrary, to "be filled with the Spirit"
is the privilege of every true Christian. The Spirit-filled
life is, in fact, the norm of Christian experience, and to the
interpretation of this proposition the rest of this book will
be devoted. Granted this premise, it is of considerable practical consequence to investigate the conditions, the nature
and the manifestations of the Spirit-filled life.

In the Biblical context, the Christian who has been filled
with the Holy Spirit is characterized by a supernatural enablement to witness for Jesus Christ. Peter, for example,
before the crucifixion quailed at the accusing taunt of a
serving maid: "Thou also wast with Jesus the Galilean." [2]
And when the accusation was repeated despite his denial,
vehemently he began "to curse and to swear, I know not the
man." [3] But after being filled with the Spirit of God at
Pentecost, this same vacillating disciple was, with his companion John, hailed before the same Sanhedrin that had
condemned Jesus to death. Confronting their interrogators
in the power and boldness of the Holy Spirit, Peter, as
spokesman for the two, courageously defended their action
in the healing of the lame beggar before the temple gate
called "Beautiful," saying: "in the Name of Jesus Christ of
Nazareth whom ye crucified, whom God raised from the
dead, even in him both this man stand before you whole." [4]
The effect of these words upon the council was electrifying
for, "when they beheld the boldness of Peter and John, and
perceived that they were unlearned and ignorant men, they
marvelled." [5]

The testimony of the believer, filled with the Spirit of
God, is confirmed by the manifestations of the Spirit's supernatural gifts. Philip, a Spirit-filled deacon and evangel-

[2] Matt. 26:69ff.
[3] Matt. 26:74.
[4] Acts 4:10.
[5] Acts 4:13.

ist, went down to the city of Samaria, "and proclaimed unto them Christ." [6] Centuries of bitter hostility between Samaritans and Jews was dissolved, "and the multitude gave heed with one accord unto the things that were spoken by Philip, *when they heard and saw the signs which he did.* For from many of those that had unclean spirits, they came out crying with a loud voice: and many that were palsied and that were lame were healed." [7] And it is this *charismatic dimension* that sets the Pentecostal experience apart from every other teaching on the Spirit-filled life.

Furthermore, the life of the Spirit-filled Christian overflows with supernatural gracements bestowed by the Spirit of God. By way of illustration, the men chosen by the apostolic community to dispense alms to the needy were men of "good reputation," [8] filled with "wisdom," [9] "faith," [10] "grace and power." [11] To the virtue of "faith" was added by the Spirit "hope and love," [12] while abounding "joy" [13] characterized the life and worship of the charismatic community.[14] This is not meant to imply that a Christian who has not had a charismatic encounter with the Divine Spirit is entirely devoid of these spiritual gracements. It is, rather, a testimony to the fact that *there is a charismatic quickening* of the "fruit" of the Spirit. The relationship of the "fruit" and the "gifts" of the Holy Spirit will be discussed at greater length later on.

[6] Acts 8:5.
[7] Acts 8:6, 7. Italics mine, H.M.E.
[8] *The New English Bible New Testament* (Oxford: University Press; Cambridge: University Press, Copyright 1961 by the Delegates of the Oxford University Press, and the Syndics of the Cambridge University Press). Abbr. N.E.B.
[9] Acts 6:3.
[10] Acts 6:5.
[11] Acts 6:8.
[12] I Cor. 13:13.
[13] Acts 8:38; 13:52.
[14] Eph. 5:19.

Thus the Biblical pattern of the Spirit-filled life is quite clear. However, such practical questions as these—"Is this Biblical pattern valid for today?" "Are Christians filled with the Holy Spirit today in the same manner as they were on the day of Pentecost?" "Do the 'gifts' of God's Spirit still manifest today as they did in apostolic days?"—have all too frequently been obscured by the "fallout" from theological polemics. In an effort to present factual and objective answers to these questions, our first recourse will be a critical examination of the scriptures relating to this truth. Contemporary experience illustrates, but only the Biblical record validates our conclusions. Whenever, therefore, contemporary witness to this experience is invoked, it will be subordinated to the positive judgment of the Scriptures. (Yet, in the final analysis, neither the application of exegesis nor of logic to the written Word can infuse our conclusions with the self-validation of personal experience. Paradoxically, it is the living experience of the truth of God's Word that authenticates our conclusions—for "Truth divorced from experience must always dwell in the realm of a doubt." Consequently, a critical evaluation of primary sources *within an empirical frame of reference* is indispensable for our understanding of the Biblical injunction, "Be filled with the Spirit.")

We begin our investigation with an examination of the occurrences of the phrase, "filled with the Spirit." This expression, whether as a verb phrase or a noun phrase, is found, with one exception, only in the books written by Luke.

There are four instances of the phrase, "filled with the Spirit," or its noun counterpart, "full of the Spirit," in the Gospel according to Luke. In the first reference, an angel revealed to Zacharias that his hitherto barren wife Elizabeth would bear a son to be called John. The prophecy specifically stated: "he shall be filled with the Holy Spirit, even from his mother's womb." [15] Thus was the Baptist to be uniquely endowed for his ministry as fore-runner of the Messiah.

Some months later, when Mary, the mother of Jesus, went to visit her kinswoman Elizabeth, it is recorded by Luke, that "the babe leaped in her (Elizabeth's) womb; and Elizabeth was filled with the Holy Spirit." [16] In recording this devout reminiscence, the evangelist unmistakeably implied that this preternatural activity of Elizabeth's unborn child in the presence of Mary, the mother of the coming Messiah, was evidence of the influence of the Holy Spirit upon her unborn child. The prophecy of the angel to her husband Zacharias—"he shall be filled with the Holy Spirit, even from his mother's womb"—was being literally fulfilled. Then at the birth of John, it is further recorded, that Zacharias himself "was filled with the Holy Spirit, and prophesied. . . ." [17]

It is of more than passing interest, in the light of what will be discussed later, that in two of the three instances cited, the "fulness" of the Holy Spirit is evidenced by *prophetic utterance* on the part of those filled with God's Spirit. In the case of Elizabeth when Mary her kinswoman entered her home and greeted her, she "was filled with the Holy Spirit; and she lifted up her voice with a loud cry, and said. . . ." [18] What follows in the narrative is a prophetic acknowledgement of Mary as the mother of "my Lord," equivalent to saying, Messiah. So also Zacharias, John's father, "was filled with the Holy Spirit," at the birth of his

15 Luke 1:15.
16 Luke 1:41.
17 Luke 1:67.
18 Luke 1:41, 42.

son, and he "prophesied." As there will be occasion to stress later on, *supernatural utterance* is the initial response to the "fulness" of the Spirit's presence and power.

Despite similarities, there are notable differences between the experiences described by Luke in his Gospel and those described by him in the book of the Acts, the fact notwithstanding that both accounts are by the same chronicler. The Gospel narrative breathes the atmosphere of Old Testament anticipation, while the record of the Acts is a recital of the Church's realization of these anticipations. In a sense, the former is premonitory, the latter explanatory. These instances were unique, and, in the nature of the case, unrepeatable.

The incarnation was a once-for-all event in the unfolding of God's redemptive purpose, and these experiences were an intrinsic part of this unrepeatable event. The Old Covenant was still in effect. The crucifixion and resurrection of Jesus had not yet ushered in the New Covenant. These were Old Testament saints whom Luke described as "filled with the Spirit" for a unique and special mission. Consequently, these examples, while informative, are not normative for Christian experience.

One last reference to the phrase in Luke's Gospel does have a bearing on the New Testament pattern of the "fulness of the Spirit." This relates the experience of Jesus Himself when the Holy Spirit descended upon Him in bodily form as a dove during His baptism by John in the river Jordan; e.g., "Jesus full of the Holy Spirit, returned from the Jordan. . . ." [19]

The descent of the Spirit upon Jesus at the outset of His public ministry was not only expressive of the Father's approbation—"Thou art my beloved Son" [20]—it was a testi-

[19] Luke 4:1.
[20] Luke 3:22.

mony to the personal presence and power of the Triune Godhead in Jesus' earthly ministry. As such, it was the prototype of the Pentecostal effusion of the Spirit upon the infant Church poised upon the threshold of its world-wide ministry in Jesus' name, and in the power and demonstration of the Holy Spirit. The book of the Acts traces in fuller detail the pattern and progress of the Church "filled with the Holy Spirit."

CHAPTER II

"Ye Must Be Born Again"

Before proceeding with the examination of the evidence in the book of the Acts, some preliminary theological presuppositions need statement and clarification. Certain events associated with the transition from the Old Covenant to the New Covenant have an immediate bearing upon our subject. It is no overstatement to say that an understanding of the interrelationship of these events is essential to a proper interpretation of the Biblical context of this experience.

For our point of departure in the consideration of these events, we begin with a post-resurrection experience of Jesus' disciples, sometimes erroneously identified with the Pentecostal "fulness" of the Spirit. The Fourth Evangelist related the circumstances of the event thus: "When therefore it was evening, on that day, the first day of the week, and when the doors were shut where the disciples were for fear of the Jews, Jesus came and stood in the midst, and saith unto them, Peace be unto you. And when he had said this, he showed unto them his hands and his side. The disciples therefore were glad, when they saw the Lord. Jesus therefore said unto them again, Peace be unto you: as the Father hath sent me, even so send I you. And when he had said this, *he breathed on them* (literally, "breathed into"),[1] and saith unto them, *Receive ye the Holy Spirit:*

[1] Greek *"enephusēsen, to breath upon, to breath into, to inflate."* Henry George Liddell & Robert Scott, *A Greek-English Lexicon* (7th ed.; New York: Harper & Brothers, 1889), p. 468.

whose soever sins ye forgive, they are forgiven unto them;
whose soever sins ye retain, they are retained." [2]

Observe the time, the resurrection day; and the setting, a
frightened, doubt-ridden group of Jesus' disciples huddled
behind locked doors, fearing imminent arrest as followers of
the recently crucified Nazarene. For them, hope had been
turned into mourning, expectation to despair by the events
of Gethsemane, Golgotha and the Garden Tomb—the mel-
ancholy circumference of memory constricted by despair.
The darkness of Gethsemane's betrayal, the awesome gloom
of Golgotha's "midnight at noon," the stygian embrace of
the rock-hewn tomb—brooding memory's legacy of grief
hued with apprehension and perplexity. Apprehension at
the recollection of His prophetic requiem over their Holy
City. "O Jerusalem, Jerusalem, that killeth the prophets,
and stoneth them that are sent unto her! how often would
I have gathered thy children together, even as a hen gather-
eth her chickens under her wings, and ye would not! *Behold your house is left unto you desolate.*" [3] For devout
Israelites such as they, the words had an ominous ring. Did
they betoken an impending national catastrophe?—perhaps
another "Babylonian Captivity"! How was this dirge to be
interpreted in the light of the longed for Messianic Kingdom? The threat to their theocratic hope but intensified
their perplexity.

During the Passion Week, when confronted with the in-
flexible rejection of His Messianic claims by Israel's leaders
—their repudiation of Him taut with a frustrated fury,
shortly to erupt in the mass denunciation, "crucify, crucify Him!" [4] Jesus pronounced solemn sentence of interdict
upon the ancient covenant nation: "Therefore say I unto

[2] John 20:19–23. Italics mine H.M.E.
[3] Matt. 23:37, 38. Italics mine H.M.E.
[4] Luke 23:21.

you, the kingdom of God shall be taken away from you, and shall be given to a nation bringing forth the fruits thereof." [5] This was a proclamation of far reaching importance for the interpretation of the transition from the Old to the New Covenant.

Thus Judaism refused fealty to her Messiah King. Her rejection was epitomized in the answer of her priests to Pilate's question: "Shall I crucify your King?" [6] To which they had responded: "We have no king but Caesar." [7] Categorically they rejected Him. And just as emphatically, "Great David's greater Son" [8] revoked Israel's theocratic status, and this is most significant for our study.

With the crucifixion of Jesus, the Old Covenant promulgated at Sinai ceased to be efficacious. Until the death of Messiah Jesus, His disciples were as much "saved" as Abraham, Issac, Jacob, Moses, Isaiah, Jeremiah, or any of the other Old Testament saints. Their relationship with, and access to, God were comprehended under the terms of the Old Testament Covenants. But the disciples had heard their Master pronounce judicial sentence of interdict against the nation of Israel. This could only mean one thing to them personally. Their covenant privileges and prerogatives must cease with those of the nation of which they were a part. They were to be suspended in favor of a "new nation." They had yet to learn that the "new nation" was the Church.[9] The old "theocracy" was to be superseded by the "new kingdom," [10] the *ekklēsia* of Christ. Hence, their bewilderment was compounded not only by the in-

[5] Matt. 21:43.
[6] John 19:15.
[7] *Ibid.*
[8] James Montgomery, "Hail to the Lord's Anointed," *Christian Worship, A Hymnal* (Philadelphia: The Judson Press, 1941), 257.
[9] I Peter 2:9.
[10] Rev. 1:6; 5:10.

creasing certainty of Jesus' death, but also by the portent of spiritual, as well as, temporal desolation of their beloved nation.

Their preoccupation with the idea of Israel's loss of "the kingdom" is brought into clearer focus when the edict of our Lord Jesus—*"the kingdom of God shall be taken away from you"*—is compared with the anxious question of the disciples addressed to their risen Master on the Mount of the Ascension: *"Lord dost thou at this time restore the kingdom to Israel?"* [11] The urgency of their query is underscored by the circumstances under which they asked it.

At such a time, and under such circumstances, one may justifiably assume that there were scores of unanswered questions they would have wanted to ask Him. Why then is such priority given to this one question? It is the only one recorded for posterity out of this last earthly conversation between Jesus and His personal followers. The context suggests the answer.

During the forty days of post-resurrection appearances, our Lord taught them further "the things concerning the kingdom of God." [12] Apparently no additional revelation of the details of Israel's future restoration was given to them at that time. Only the cryptic answer to their question: "It is not for you to know times or seasons"—that is, for the restoration of Israel's theocratic status—"which the Father hath set within his own authority. But ye shall receive power when the Holy Spirit is come upon you: and ye shall be my witnesses . . . unto the uttermost part of the earth." [13] Details of such a restoration must await the fuller revelation promised to the apostles as a ministry of the Holy Spirit, who, when He came, would "declare unto you the

[11] Acts 1:6. Italics mine H.M.E.
[12] Acts 1:3.
[13] Acts 1:7, 8.

things that are to come." [14] It is the still future "restoration," which the apostle Paul declared was contingent upon the appointed time when "the fulness of the Gentiles be come in; (i.e., to the Church) and so all Israel shall be saved." [15] Thus, by inspiration of the Holy Spirit, he foretold the future conversion of Israel, for "Israel a Christian nation, Israel a nation a part of the Messianic kingdom is the content of his thought." [16]

However, before this will take place, the Church must accomplish its world-wide, age-long ministry of evangelization to the whole world—to both Jew and Gentile. Therefore, cryptic though Jesus' answer to their question must appear —"But ye shall receive power when the Holy Spirit is come upon you: and ye shall be my witnesses . . . unto the uttermost part of the earth"—His reply, nevertheless, contained in germ the fuller answer given later to Paul by revelation.

In essence, Jesus said that Pentecost is a part (and an indispensable part) of the answer to their question. True, His answer would not be understood by them beforehand. Only when it became a vital part of their own experience did the answer to their question begin to unfold. In the very act of evangelizing the nations, they were setting the stage for Israel's eventual restoration.

A concrete illustration of this fact is found in Peter's discourse to the curious multitude in the temple, after the healing of the crippled beggar before the gate, "Beautiful." Calling for personal repentance as the precondition, he continued; "and that he may send the Christ who hath been appointed for you, even Jesus: whom the heaven must receive until the times of restoration of all things." [17]

[14] John 16:13.
[15] Rom. 11:25, 26.
[16] James Denney, *St. Pauls Epistle to the Romans, The Expositor's Greek Testament,* ed. by W. Robertson Nicoll, II (Grand Rapids: Wm. B. Eerdmans, n.d.), 683.
[17] Acts 3:20, 21.

In conformity with the mission strategy outlined by the Lord Himself, the evangelization of the world was to begin with Jerusalem and Judaea, then branch out to Samaria, and finally radiate throughout the whole world. The evangel His disciples were commissioned to proclaim was individual repentance and a personal acceptance of Jesus by faith. Clearly Peter, and we may logically conclude the whole Church too, had grasped something of the implications in His answer to their question, when after Pentecost, they committed themselves without reservation to the implementation of His "Great Commission."

We digress at this point to note parenthetically, that if Jesus implied in His answer to the disciples' question that full knowledge of these things was veiled to Him before His ascension, then this limitation of knowledge was removed after His glorification. Certainly, John the Revelator stated this unequivocally: "This is the revelation given by God to Jesus Christ. It was given to him so that he might show his servants what must shortly happen." [18] After His ascension, all self-imposed limitations of His incarnation[19] were removed, and the Father gave to His Son knowledge of details to reveal to His Church. Consequently, Jesus' teaching before His ascension, "the things concerning the kingdom of God," omitted details concerning Israel's future relationship to the kingdom in a national sense. These details were supplied by the Holy Spirit after His descent upon the Church, beginning with Pentecost.

What is most important for the immediate discussion is that their question clearly indicated their awareness that the rejection of Israel, the termination of its theocratic status—announced by Jesus before His crucifixion—*was already in effect before His ascension.*

18 Rev. 1:1 N.E.B.
19 His *kenosis*, cf. Phil. 2:5f.

With the suspension of Israel's theocratic status, the way was cleared for the inauguration of the "new nation." The disciples of Jesus, passing from life under the Mosaic Covenant to the New Covenant of our Lord and Saviour Jesus Christ, were not exempted from the conditions of that New Covenant. They too must meet the pre-conditions for entering the "new nation": "Except a man be born anew, he cannot see the kingdom of God." [20] Admission to the New Covenant community was thus, in our Lord's own words, clearly defined, for one "cannot enter into the kingdom of God" unless, and until "one be born of water and the Spirit." [21]

Without the "new birth" no man can either "see" or "enter" the kingdom of God. The incredulous reaction of Nicodemus to these words of Jesus—"How can a man be born when he is old? can he enter a second time into his mother's womb, and be born?" [22]—is explained by A. T. Robertson thus: "Nicodemus was probably familiar with the notion of rebirth for proselytes to Judaism for the Gentiles, but not with the idea that a Jew had to be reborn." [23]

This concept of an individual spiritual "rebirth" marked an advance over their previous experience with, and relationship to God under the Old Testament economy. True, the benefits of Christ's atonement are retroactive to the Old Testament saints, as for example, it is written: "Abraham put his faith in God, and that faith was counted to him as righteousness." [24] However, whatever quality of spiritual experience is deduced from this for the Old Testament believers (and one has but to read Old Testament passages like the moving penitential Psalm 51 to realize how deep

[20] John 3:3.
[21] John 3:5.
[22] John 3:4.
[23] *Word Pictures in the New Testament*, V (New York: Harper & Brothers, c. 1932), 45.
[24] Rom. 4:3, N.E.B.

and personal was this experience), we must recognize its incompleteness. The writer of the epistle to the Hebrews, after calling the roll of Old Testament heroes of the faith, concluded by saying: "And these won a glowing testimony to their faith, but they did not then and there receive the fulfillment of the promise." [25] Concerning which A. C. Kendrick remarked: "They lived and died in the hope, but not the possession, of the spiritual blessings vouchsafed to the days of the manifested Messiah and of the better Covenant." [26] Contrast with Peter's affirmation that "he has granted to us his precious and very great promises" whereby the New Testament believers "become partakers of the divine nature." [27]

Before Christ's death and resurrection, His disciples, along with all the Old Testament believers, were "saved by faith" looking forward to the ultimate reality of His atoning death and resurrection. After His resurrection all the benefits of the atonement, which had been theirs by anticipation, became theirs in experience. This was consummated by their personal identification by faith with Jesus Christ in His resurrection life.

Inasmuch as His death and resurrection are events in history, so also their participation in His resurrection life was effected at a specific point in history. It is of this that Peter wrote in these words: "Praise be to the God and Father of our Lord Jesus Christ, who in his mercy gave us *new birth* into a living hope *by the resurrection of Jesus from the dead.*" [28] His resurrection is the source of our spiritual re-

---

[25] Heb. 11:39. *The New Testament in Modern English,* trans. by J. B. Phillips, *The New Testament in Four Versions,* Christianity Today Edition (New York: The Iverson-Ford Associates, c. 1963). Abbr. N.T.M.E.

[26] *Commentary on the Epistle to the Hebrews, An American Commentary on the New Testament,* ed. by Alvah Hovey (Philadelphia: The American Baptist Publication Society, 1889), p. 164.

[27] II Peter 1:4.

[28] I Peter 1:3, NEB. Italics mine H.M.E.

generation, and it is a personal participation by faith in His resurrection life that constitutes the experience of the "new birth."

The apostolic community was no exception to the rule ennunciated by Jesus. They too must be "born anew" of the Holy Spirit, in order to enter the New Covenant community of our Lord and Saviour Jesus Christ. The "new nation," to whom "the kingdom" is now committed, is not a homogeneous ethnic group. It is an election of God's grace "out of every nation and of *all* tribes and peoples and tongues," [29] who have "washed their robes, and made them white in the blood of the Lamb." [30]

[29] Rev. 7:9.
[30] Rev. 7:14.

CHAPTER III

"Receive Ye the Holy Spirit"

(John 20:19–23)

"Ye must be born again!" When were the disciples of Jesus "born anew"? In other words: When did they pass from the sphere and influence of the Old Covenant to the privileges and responsibilities of the New Covenant?

Some have assumed that this took place before the crucifixion, when Jesus said to them, "but rejoice that your names are written in heaven." [1] Others have seen in Peter's confession of the deity of Jesus—"Thou art the Christ, the Son of the Living God" [2]—evidence that he was born again. But all such suggestions ignore the fact that the covenant of Sinai was still in force. True there is no past, present, or future in the mind of God who lives in an eternal now. But on the plane of time and space there is a definite chronological unfolding of the divine purposes, for God Himself is the Author of times and seasons, of "days and years." [3] The New Covenant had not then been promulgated. Even our Lord Jesus was born subject to the conditions of the Old Covenant; for in the words of Scripture: "when the fulness of time came, God sent forth His Son, born of a woman,

---

[1] Luke 10:20.
[2] Matt. 16:16.
[3] Gen. 1:14.

25

born under the law, that we might receive the adoption of sons." [4]

The foregoing assumptions are, therefore, really anachronistic. They imply that Jesus' disciples entered the New Covenant while their Lord, according to the flesh, was still under the provisions of Sinai's legal Covenant. This, of course, cannot be true, for "The abolition of the law, the rescue from bondage, was a prior condition of the universal sonship of the faith." [5] This "prior condition" was only effected by the death and resurrection of Jesus Christ. It is only by identification with Him in His death and resurrection that we are enabled to "walk in newness of life." [6]

Still others have equated the outpouring of the Holy Spirit at Pentecost with the beginning of the New Covenant. It is this assumption that underlies the oft-repeated cliche, "Pentecost is the birthday of the church." This is tantamount to saying, that the disciples of Jesus were "born anew" by the descent of the Holy Spirit on that day.[7] This in turn has led to the spiritually enervating assumption that all believers are, therefore, automatically "filled with the Spirit" at conversion.

As a matter of fact, none of these views quite squares with the Biblical evidence. There remains, however, a fruitful avenue of investigation yet to be explored. Its starting

---

[4] Gal. 4:4, 5.

[5] J. B. Lightfoot, *Saint Paul's Epistle to the Galatians* (London: Macmillan and Co., 1896), p. 168.

[6] Rom. 6:4.

[7] For an exposition of this view see G. Campbell Morgan, *The Acts of the Apostles* (New York: Fleming H. Revell Company, 1924), pp. 28, 29. "But here upon the day of Pentecost, that which happened was not merely the renewal of the life of these men; it was the imparting to them of a new germ of life, a new principle of life, something they never had before . . . there was given to them the life of Christ, the Incarnate One; so that there came to these men that which made them one with Him and with each other, and constituted their membership in the Church of the first-born."

point is the passage from John's Gospel already cited, viz., John 20:19–23.

Fundamental to the interpretation of this passage is the acknowledgment that the deeds, no less than the words, of Jesus have didactic significance. In other words, the Master taught by His acts—visual education—as well as by His words. Note then that having entered the upper room where His followers were gathered together, He first allayed their quite natural apprehensions, saying, "Peace be unto you." [8] Next He exposed the wounds of His passion in His hands and side, inviting their inspection. Thus He authenticated for them the fact of His bodily resurrection from the dead. Such concrete evidence was needed, since they were loath to accept the testimony of those who were first to see Him after His resurrection.[9] Yet faith in His resurrection is a pre-condition of salvation, "because if thou shalt confess with thy mouth Jesus *as* Lord, and shalt believe in thy heart that God raised him from the dead, thou shalt be saved." [10] To which may be added the corroborative testimony of Peter: "Praise be to the God and Father of our Lord Jesus Christ, who in his mercy *gave us new birth* into a living hope *by the resurrection* of Jesus Christ from the dead." [11]

With faith in His resurrection powerfullly stimulated by this tangible evidence, they were prepared for what followed next: "And when he had said this, he breathed on them, and saith unto them, Receive ye the Holy Spirit." [12] In the exposition of this passage, the meaning of Jesus' words must be weighed in their relation to His action in "breathing on them." Some interpreters have seen this as

---

[8] In the light of the context—"for fear of the Jews," vs. 19—the traditional greeting, *shalom lakem,* meant more than simply, Hello!

[9] Mark 16:14; Luke 24:41.

[10] Rom. 10:9.

[11] I Peter 1:3, NEB. Italics mine, H.M.E.

[12] John 20:22.

"a symbolic act with the same word used in the LXX when
God breathed the breath of life upon Adam (Gen. 2:7)." [13]
This act of breathing upon His disciples "was meant to convey the impression that his own very Spirit was imparted to
them." [14] Yet in a fuller sense, it was much more than merely emblematic, for the natural sense of the expression implies that "some gift was offered and bestowed then and
there." [15] The universal and natural symbol of life is breath,
and "in the Bible it is used as a symbol of divine life." [16]
Thus by direct impartation Jesus infused His disciples with
"that divine life which man never *acquires,* which God
alone can give." [17]

This experience was not simply a promise, an anticipation of the greater effusion to be poured out upon them at
Pentecost. The word here translated "receive" (*labete*) is an
aorist imperative,[18] which "cannot *merely promise* a recep-

---

[13] Archibald Thomas Robertson, *Word Pictures in the New Testament,*
V, 314.

[14] Marcus Dods, *The Gospel of St. John, The Expositor's Greek Testament,* ed. by W. Robertson Nicoll, I (Grand Rapids: Wm. B. Eerdmans,
n.d.), 865.

"He breathed on them, '*enephusēse;*' the same word is used in Gen. ii.7
to describe the distinction between Adam's 'living soul,' *breathed* into him
by God, and the life principle of the other animals."

[15] A. Plummer, *The Gospel According to St. John, The Cambridge Bible
for Schools and Colleges* (Cambridge: at the University Press, 1923), p. 362.

[16] Lyman Abbott, *An Illustrated Commentary on the Gospels* (New York:
A. S. Barnes & Company, 1906), p. 230.

"God breathes into man the breath of life (Gen. 2:7); in the vision of
Ezekiel the wind breathes on the dry bones and clothes them with life
(Ezek. 37:9, 10); in Christ's conversation with Nicodemus the life-giving
power of God is compared to the breath of wind (ch. 3:8); and it is significant of the extent to which this symbol underlies Scripture that the Greek
word used for spirit is the one also used for wind, which is poetically
represented as the breath of God."

[17] *Ibid.*

[18] H. E. Dana & Julius R. Mantey, *A Manual Grammar of the Greek
New Testament* (New York: The Macmillan Company, 1955), p. 300.

"The aorist Imperative in Commands. When the aorist imperative is
used it denotes summary action—'an action that is either transient or
instantaneous . . . or to be undertaken at once' (W. 313)."

tion belonging to the *future,* but expresses a reception actually present." [19] The force then of this verb in the aorist tense, imperative mood is "receive right here and now;" [20] thereby "implying that the recipient may welcome or reject the gift: he is not a mere passive receptacle." [21] What Jesus bestowed on them, and they received, "is not a simple promise, *but neither is it the fulness of the Spirit* . . . As by Pentecost He will initiate them into His ascension, so by breathing on them now He associates them with His life as the Risen One." [22]

The resurrection day, therefore, marks the beginning of the new creation. As in the old creation, man received life by the breath of God, so in the new creation, redeemed man receives new spiritual life—literally a "new birth"—by the breath of God the Son. It is this breath of the risen Son of God that is not only the source, but also the pledge of that eternal life [23] bestowed on all who "believe on the son." [24]

There is one objection to this view that requires an answer. This is the proposition that John 20:19–23 "is Pentecost itself, so far as it was known to the evangelist." [25] In support of this view, it is claimed that "this scene is for John almost certainly the counterpart of Pentecost; for . . . he 'telescopes' Resurrection, Ascension, and Pentecost into one event of 'glorification.' " [26] But the same writer concedes

[19] Heinrich A. W. Meyer, *Critical and Exegetical Hand-Book to the Gospel of John,* trans. by William Urwick (5th German ed.; New York: Funk & Wagnalls, 1884), p. 532.

[20] Dana & Mantey, loc. cit, "When the aorist imperative is used it denotes summary action."

[21] Plummer, *op. cit.,* p. 362.

[22] F. Godet, *Commentary on the Gospel of St. John, Clark's Foreign Theological Library,* 4th series, LVI, trans. by S. Taylor & M. D. Cusin, III (Edinburgh: T. & T. Clark, 1900), 321. Italics mine H.M.E.

[23] Chr. Wordsworth, *The New Testament of our Lord and Saviour Jesus Christ,* I (7th ed.; London: Rivingtons, 1870), 321.

[24] John 3:36.

[25] Baur's view according to Godet, *op. cit.,* p. 321.

[26] G. H. C. Macgregor, *The Gospel of John, The Moffatt New Testament Commentary* (New York: Harper and Brothers, cir. 1928), p. 365.

that there are "occasional hints . . . of the survival of the point of view of the Synoptists, who regard Resurrection, Ascension, Parousia, as three events distinct in space and time." [27]

Behind such an exegesis lies Form Criticism's unhistorical assumption of the "free creation and flow of tradition," [28]— the hypothesis of independent and often contradictory sources of the Biblical narratives. A cogent rebuttal to such a hermeneutic is the recognition of the regulative influence of the apostles themselves upon the Biblical tradition. The visit of Paul to Jerusalem to confer with those "who were of repute," [29]—among whom James, Peter, *and John* are singled out for special mention [30]—illustrates the point, that "There was an authoritative source of information about the facts and doctrines of Christianity in the apostolic collegium in Jerusalem. . . ." [31] It cannot be conceded, therefore, that John in his account of the resurrection day makes a concession to the more primitive (?)[32] tradition of the Synoptists, which he preserved in "form," but spiritualized

---

Cf. also, Wilbert F. Howard, *The Gospel According to St. John*, "Exegesis," *The Interpreter's Bible*, ed. by George Arthur Buttrick, et. al., VIII (Nashville: Abingdon-Cokesbury Press, c. 1952), 796. "This gift of the Spirit could be bestowed only after the glorification (i.e., the resurrection) of Christ, according to the view of the evangelist."

[27] Macgregor, *op. cit.*, p. 360.

[28] Clark H. Pinnock, "The Case Against Form Criticism," *Christianity Today*, IX, 21 (July 1965), 12, 13.

[29] Gal. 2:1 ff.

[30] Gal. 2:9. Italics mine H.M.E.

[31] Pinnock, *op. cit.*, p. 12.

[32] William Foxwell Albright, *From Stone Age to Christianity* (2nd ed.; Garden City: Doubleday Anchor Books, Doubleday & Company, Inc., 1957), p. 383.

Cf. his appraisal of C. C. Torrey's thesis of an Aramaic original for the Gospels. "Torrey concludes that all the Gospels were written before 70 A.D. and that there is nothing in them which could not have been written within twenty years of the Crucifixion."

The Dead Sea Scrolls have been thought to point to an early date for John's Gospel. Cf. George A. Turner, "A Decade of Studies in John's Gospel," *Christianity Today*, IX, 5 (Dec. 1964), 5. 6.

to such an extent that he virtually denied its "substance." [33]

John was present with the rest of the apostles on the day of Pentecost, and it is hardly likely that the dramatic events of that day should be confused in his mind with the equally noteworthy happenings on the resurrection day. The Holy Spirit, or Paraclete, is presented in Jesus' farewell discourse "as practically equivalent to the presence of the risen exalted Jesus—His alter ego (xiv. 16–18; xvi. 7)." [34] In point of fact, John stated clearly Jesus' ascension as the pre-condition of the coming of the Holy Spirit: "It is expedient for you," said Jesus, "that I go away; for if I go not away, the Comforter will not come unto you; but if I go, *I will send him unto you.*" [35] Manifestly then, John looked beyond the resurrection to the ascension of Jesus for the coming of the promised Holy Spirit. It is in His absence that He is to send the Comforter to them, a clear reference to the Pentecostal effusion of the Spirit poured out by Jesus after His ascension.[36] The facts of the case are succinctly stated by A. Plummer as follows: "There was therefore a Paschal as distinct from a Pentecostal gift of the Holy Spirit, the one preparatory to the other." [37]

The passage in John 20:19–23 is, therefore, of crucial importance to an understanding of the Holy Spirit's ministry to the Church. It is not a record of a "Johanine Pentecost." Rather it marks the transition from the terms of the Old Covenant to those of the New Covenant. As God imparted life by breathing His breath into man on the day of the former creation, so also, Jesus imparted new spiritual life to His followers by breathing the Holy Spirit into them on the

[33] Macgregor, quoting Scott, *op. cit.,* p. 362.
[34] R. H. Strachan, *The Fourth Gospel Its Significance and Environment* (3rd ed.; London: Student Christian Movement, 1941), p. 288.
[35] John 16:7. Italics mine H.M.E.
[36] Acts 2:33.
[37] *Op. cit.,* p. 362.

day of the new creation. Thus did His disciples enter the
New Covenant through the "new birth." The "new nation," whose responsibility it now became to "bring forth
the fruits" of the kingdom of God, thus displaced the old
theocracy, Israel. The stage was now set for the acting out
of the next scenes in the divine drama of redemption.

It is essential to note further, that the transition from
Judaism to Christianity was accomplished before the book
of Acts opens. The Acts does not contain such a transitional
phase. There is no "second offer" of the kingdom to Israel
nationally in its pages, for the transition from Judaism to
Christianity involved not only Israel's rejection of Jesus as
her Sovereign, but also Messiah's rejection of Israel as the
theocratic nation—a rejection consummated in the crucifixion of Jesus. Therefore, when the disciples preached the
gospel in the Acts, they were not addressing the "Good
News" to Israel corporately. They addressed the gospel to
them as Jews, individually and ethnically. To miss this distinction is to miss an important point in Peter's quotation
of the prophecy of Joel: "And it shall be, that *whosoever*
shall call on the name of the Lord shall be saved." [39] Observe closely, that the appeal in the passage is to individuals,
not to a corporate entity.

Thus, beginning with this, the first public proclamation
of the gospel by the Church, the appeal is directed to individual Israelites, not to the Jewish nation corporately. The
apostle Paul quoted this same verse in a context that places
this interpretation beyond a reasonable doubt. He explicitly
divested it of any exclusively national application. This is
all the more noteworthy, since it occurs in a context in
which he dealt at length with the mystery of Israel's rejection, and ultimate restoration: "For there is no distinction
between Jew and Greek: for the same *Lord* is Lord of all,

[39] Acts 2:21. Italics mine, H.M.E.

and is rich unto all that call upon him: for, whosoever shall call upon the name of the Lord shall be saved." [40] Characteristically, Paul declared that the "whosoever" of the gospel does not distinguish between Jew and Gentile.

The "whosoever" in Acts 2:21 and Romans 10:13 forms a trilogy with the "whosoever" in John 3:16: "For God so loved the world, that he gave his only begotten Son, that whosoever believeth on him should not perish, but have eternal life."

[40] Rom. 10:12, 13.

CHAPTER IV

"The Promise of the Father"

(Luke 24:49; Acts 1:4)

The Gospel of Luke closes with the promise: "And behold, I send forth *the promise of my Father* upon you: but tarry ye in the city until ye be clothed with power from on high." [1] The book of the Acts opens with a reaffirmation of this identical promise, for "being assembled together with them, he charged them not to depart from Jerusalem, but to wait for *the promise of the Father,* which said he, ye heard from me: for John indeed baptized with water; but ye shall be baptized in the Holy Spirit not many days hence." [2] To what does *the promise* refer? The context makes it clear that it is "the baptism in the Holy Spirit." More precisely: "The promise is the Spirit," [3] Himself, who has been "spoken of in prophetic oracles:" [4] for, "The Holy

---

[1] Luke 24:49. Italics mine, H.M.E.

[2] Acts 1:4, 5. Italics mine, H.M.E.

[3] Alexander Balmain Bruce, *The Synoptic Gospels, The Expositor's Greek Testament,* I (Grand Rapids: Wm. B. Eerdmans, n.d.), 651.

[4] *Ibid.,* "Is. xliv.i, Joel ii.28." Cf., also Ezek. 36:27; 39:29.

Cf., also H. K. Luce (ed.), *The Gospel According to St. Luke, The Cambridge Bible for Schools and Colleges* (Cambridge: The University Press, 1936), p. 255.

" 'What was the promise referred to? One would expect a direct reference to something in the Gospel. If so it must be the prophecy of John the Baptist, 'He shall baptize you with the Holy Spirit and with fire' . . . Otherwise it must be thought that the reference is to various passages in the O.T., which promised the gift of the Spirit' (Lake, p. 106)."

34

Spirit is the divine promise par excellence." [5] It is the same "promise of the Spirit" [6] we receive through faith, the same "Holy Spirit of promise" [7] in whom we are sealed, now poured forth in Pentecostal fulness.

Immediately upon the Pentecostal effusion of the Holy Spirit, Peter, interpreting the significance of the event in the light of Jesus' crucifixion, resurrection, and ascension, said: "Being therefore by the right hand of God exalted, and having received of the Father *the promise of the Holy Spirit* he hath poured forth this, which ye see and hear." [8] He is not here referring to the work of the Holy Spirit in conversion and regeneration, the "new birth". For the things "which ye see and hear" *can only be understood in the light of the supernatural and charismatic phenomena accompanying the Spirit's descent:* for example, "the rushing of a mighty wind," [9] "tongues parting asunder like as of fire," [10] they "began to speak with other tongues, as the Spirit gave them utterance." [11]

In reply to the conscience stricken inquiry of the bystanders who heard him speak, Peter stated the conditions for the reception of *the promise:* "Repent ye, and be baptized every one of you in the name of Jesus Christ unto the remission of your sins: and ye shall receive *the gift of the Holy Sprit.* For to you is *the promise,* and to your children, and to all that are afar off, even as many as the Lord our God shall call unto him." [12] Here again the apostle Peter de-

[5] F. Godet, *A Commentary on the Gospel of St. Luke, Clark's Foreign Theological Library*, 4th series, trans. by M. D. Cusin, II (Edinburgh: T. & T. Clark, 1878), 361.

[6] Gal. 3:14.

[7] Eph. 1:13.

[8] Acts 2:33. Italics mine H.M.E.

[9] Acts 2:2.

[10] Acts 2:3.

[11] Acts 2:4.

[12] Acts 2:38, 39. Italics mine H.M.E.

scribed the Pentecostal "gift of the Holy Spirit" as "the promise" that is, *"The promise made by Jesus (1:4)* and foretold by Joel (verse 18)." [13] Each reference to *the promised gift of the Holy Spirit* in Luke's Gospel and the Acts must be understood in the light of the outpouring of the Holy Spirit at Pentecost, and the supernatural and charismatic phenomena accompanying it.

It should now be self-evident, that "the promise of my Father," [14] "the promise of the Father," [15] "the promise of the Holy Spirit," [16] and the promised "gift of the Holy Spirit," [17] are all allusions to the Pentecostal experience [18] Jesus described as being "baptized in the Holy Spirit." [19] The difference in terminology here between Jesus and Luke may be resolved in one of two ways, although, in the final analysis, the distinction between them is so slight, they are for all practical purposes one and the same. One, Luke either regarded the terms, *baptized in the Holy Spirit* and *filled with the Holy Spirit,* as synonymous: or two, he used them interchangeably as related aspects of the same experience. Suffice it to say, that *the baptism in the Holy Spirit* results in one being permeated by, and filled to overflowing with, the presence and power of the Holy Spirit Himself.

It should be pointed out that Luke recorded the phrase, *baptized in the Holy Spirit,* only twice in the Acts. First in the passage already noted in Acts 1:5, and again in Acts 11:16. In the latter instance, Peter quoted these words of Jesus to those, "that were of the circumcision" [20] in the

---

[13] Robertson, *Word Pictures in the New Testament,* III, p. 36.
[14] Luke 24:49.
[15] Acts 1:4.
[16] Acts 2:33.
[17] Acts 2:38, 39.
[18] Acts 2:4.
[19] Acts 1:5
[20] Acts 11:2.

church at Jerusalem, who contended with him for breaking the legal taboo and entering the ceremonially unclean confines of the house of the Gentile centurion, Cornelius. He reminded them of "the word of the Lord, how he said, John indeed baptized with water; but ye shall be baptized in the Holy Spirit." [21] In every other place where Luke, the historian, made reference to the Pentecostal *baptism in the Holy Spirit,* he employed such phrases as, "the Holy Spirit comes upon," [22] "filled with the Holy Spirit," [23] "received the Holy Spirit," [24] "the Holy Spirit fell upon," [25] and "was poured out the gift of the Holy Spirit." [26]

A fundamental point of disagreement among interpreters is the question of the repetition and continuity of the Pentecostal *baptism in the Holy Spirit.* Was it, as some affirm, a once-for-all event in the Church's experience?—a sort of cosmic shove to get things rolling. Or is it a personal experience that can, and does recur in the lives of successive generations of believers? To those involved in the present charismatic dialogue, this issue is often sharply drawn. It is axiomatic to charismatic Christians that *the baptism in the Holy Spirit* did not expire with Pentecost, nor even with the close of the Apostolic Age. They believe it is the birthright of every Christian, and represents the Biblical norm for the Spirit-filled life. On the other hand, there are those who categorically affirm that "The baptism of the Holy Spirit which it was our Lord's prerogative to bestow was, strictly speaking, something that took place once for all on the day of Pentecost when He poured forth 'the promise of

[21] Acts 11:16.
[22] Acts 1:8; 19:6.
[23] Acts 2:4, 31; 9:17.
[24] Acts 8:17.
[25] Acts 8:39 alternate manuscript reading to be discussed in Chapter XII.
[26] Acts 10:45.

the Father' on His disciples and thus constituted them the
new people of God." [27]

The foregoing assertion, that *the baptism in the Holy
Spirit* was "something that took place once for all on the
day of Pentecost," is often repeated, but none the less erroneous. For instance, some ten years after the Jerusalem
Pentecost (circa A.D. 40),[28] Peter visited the home of the
Roman centurion, Cornelius, in Caesarea. He, with his now
believing household, received "the gift of the Holy
Spirit." [29] Confronted with the consequent hostility of certain of the Jewish believers in Jerusalem, who objected
strenuously to Peter's transgression of the ban on fraterniza-
tion with Gentiles, he fended off their accusation by saying
in part; "and as I began to speak, the Holy Spirit fell on
them, even as on us at the beginning." [30] Obviously Peter
was thus alluding to their own *baptism in the Holy Spirit*
on the day of Pentecost. The very language used to describe
both the outpouring of the Holy Spirit in Jerusalem at
Pentecost, and the pouring forth in Caesarea of the Holy
Spirit, more than a decade later, coupled with the charismatic phenomena evident in both cases, places the claim
beyond cavil, that Pentecost was indeed repeated in the

[27] F. F. Bruce, *Commentary on the Book of the Acts, The New International Commentary on the New Testament,* ed. by F. F. Bruce (Grand
Rapids: Wm. B. Eerdmans, 1964), p. 76.

It should be pointed out that there is no baptism of the Holy Spirit.
The preposition *en* is best understood with the locative = "in". The Holy
Spirit is the "medium" in which the baptism takes place, after the analogy
of baptism in water. The Holy Spirit does not do the baptizing, for Jesus
is the Baptizer.

Furthermore, the disciples entered the New Covenant on the Resurrection day when they became "the new people of God," and not as above
on the day of Pentecost.

[28] Philip Schaff, *History of the Christian Church,* I (New York: Charles
Scribner's Sons, 1887), 220.

[29] Acts 10:45.

[30] Acts 11:15.

house of Cornelius. Some have even called it "the Gentile Pentecost."

However, *the baptism in the Holy Spirit* bestowed upon Cornelius and his household is not the only recurrence of the Pentecostal experience in the Acts. As already demonstrated, the phrase "the gift of the Holy Spirit," is one of several synonymous designations used by Luke for the Pentecostal baptism. Cornelius, and his household, received "the like gift" [31] of the Holy Spirit as the first disciples at Pentecost. Peter stressed the identical nature of the two experiences, as shown above. So also the Samaritans "received the Holy Spirit . . . the gift of God," [32] when Peter and John laid their hands upon them. Each of these instances constitutes a repetition of the Pentecostal "gift [33] of the Holy Spirit," in charismatic fulness, that Peter said is *the promise* to all that are afar off [34] even as many as the Lord our God shall call unto him." [35] Manifestly God is still calling, the gospel is still preached to all men, and the promise is still in effect.

[31] Acts 11:17.

[32] Acts 8:17, 20.

[33] F. F. Bruce, *The Acts of the Apostles* (Grand Rapids: Wm. B. Eerdmans, 1960), p. 98.

Acts 2:38 (*"dorean"*) "free gift": used of the Holy Spirit viii, 20; x. 45; xi. 17."

[34] Certainly far more than Diaspora Judaism is intended, as the "all flesh" of Acts 2:17 indicates. Cf. Robertson, *Word Pictures in the New Testament,* III, 36. "the horizon widens and included the Gentiles. Those 'afar off' from the Jews were the heathen (Is. 49:1; 57:19; Eph. 2:13, 17). The rabbis so used it."

[35] Acts 2:39.

CHAPTER V

"Baptized Into One Body"

(I Cor. 12:13)

The "Pentecostal" significance of the phrases "the gift of the Holy Spirit," and "the promise of the Father," as used in the book of the Acts, is clearly established in each context. Unequivocally Peter stated that "the gift of the Holy Spirit" is synonymous with "the promise" of the Father extended "to all that are afar off, even as many as the Lord our God shall call unto Him." However, dogmatic presuppositions constrain many interpreters to ignore, or to blur, this evidence for the repetition and continuity of the Pentecostal baptism in the Holy Spirit in the experience of subsequent generations of converts to the Christian faith. "The gift of the Holy Spirit," "the promise of the Father" and the "baptism in the Holy Spirit" are arbitrarily identified by them with conversion and regeneration. The Biblical basis for this identification is supposedly found by them in Paul's words: "For in one Spirit were we all baptized into one body,[1] whether Jews or Greeks, whether bond or free, and were all made to drink of one Spirit." [2]

[1] *en heni Pneumati hēmeis pantes eis sōma.* Cf., G. G. Findlay, *St. Paul's First Epistle to the Corinthians, The Expositor's Greek Testament,* ed. by W. Robertson Nicoll, II (Grand Rapids: Wm. B. Eerdmans, n.d.), 890. *"en* defines the *element* and *ruling influence* of the baptism, *eis* the relationship to which it introduces."

[2] I Cor. 12:13.

This identification of the "baptism in one Spirit" in I Cor. 12:13 with conversion and regeneration, consequently prompts the somewhat rhetorical question, "But are not all believers baptized in the Spirit into Christ's Body, the Church?" The obvious implication being, "Of course they are." If this be true, then they have been "baptized in the Spirit" at the moment of their conversion. Therefore, "the baptism in the Holy Spirit" is conterminous with the "new birth."

All too frequently the question is asked defensively to parry the implication that the Pentecostal experience is something subsequent to the experience of conversion and regeneration. However, when this question is asked in a contemporary frame of reference, it must be pointed out that it is being posed in a context of Christian experience considerably different from the one in which, and to which Paul wrote. Such a question has currency only where the activity of the Holy Spirit is considered terminal in conversion and regeneration. Hence the oft quoted cliche: "We received all there is to have of the Holy Spirit in conversion and the "new birth."

From the proposition that Paul's words—"in one Spirit were we all baptized into one body"—refer to the activity of the Holy Spirit in regeneration (a "baptism in the Spirit" common to all believers), it is advocated as a truism that every believer has been "baptized in the Spirit" *in a Pentecostal sense* at conversion. The truth, or error, of such deductions rests upon the meaning of Paul's words in their context, and in their relation to the references to "the baptism in the Spirit" found in the Gospels and in the Acts. It will be well to keep this in mind as the various interpretations of the Apostle's words are investigated. To emphasize this admonition, we would pose the following question at the outset of our investigation of various interpretations of this verse. If Paul did equate "the baptism in the Spirit" in I Cor. 12:13 with regeneration, can it be argued from this fact that the same phrase means the same thing in the Gospels and in the book of the Acts? Can one thus legitimately normalize other occurrences of this phrase by considering Paul's use here as definitive?

Several interpretations have been proposed for this mooted passage. The first of these to be considered here refers the entire verse to Christian baptism under two separate metaphors—"being immersed in the Spirit, and made to drink of the Spirit as a new elixir of life." [3] In favor of this view are the aorist passive indicatives—"were we all baptized," and "were all made to drink"— which bespeak a definite event in past time; the former, "the outward badge . . . the symbol of an inward change already wrought in them by the Holy Spirit." [4] It may be objected to this view that neither figure of speech refers to "the outward symbol of an inward change," namely water baptism; but both figures speak of inward spiritual realities in the experience of the Christian.

According to the second interpretation, the first figure is referred to Christian baptism, the latter to the partaking of the Lord's Supper. However, the aorist indicatives designate a definite past event, and not a repeated act, as in the partaking of the Lord's Supper. Furthermore, "drinking the Spirit" is an inept figure of speech for the Eucharist.

A third interpretation translates the preposition *en*, "in," as an instrumental, for example, "*with, or by means of,* one

[3] Archibald Robertson & Alfred Plummer, *A Critical and Exegetical Commentary on the First Epistle of St. Paul to the Corinthians, The International Critical Commentary,* ed. by Samuel Rolles Driver, Alfred Plummer, & Charles Augustus Briggs (2nd ed.; Edinburgh: T. & T. Clark, 1963), p. 272.

[4] Robertson, *Word Pictures in the New Testament,* IV, 17.

Spirit were we all baptized into one body." Merrill F. Unger, an exponent of this view, remarks that "the reference is patently that of the very common instrumental use of *en,* meaning 'with,' or 'by means of'." [5] But A. T. Robertson, the New Testament grammarian, pointedly questioned the instrumental use of *en* in the phrase "baptize in the Holy Spirit." [6] He, in fact, advanced the sweeping observation "that all the N. T. examples of *en* can be explained from the point of view of the locative." [7]

Some Pentecostal advocates have seized upon this interpretation in an attempt to cut the "Gordian Knot" in I Cor. 12:13. They stress the difference between a supposed baptism *by* the Spirit (i.e., the Spirit does the baptizing), and the baptism *in* the Spirit of which Jesus is the administrator. (Cf., Acts 2:33 where Jesus "poured forth" the Holy Spirit upon the waiting Church, and the sound of the mighty wind from heaven which "filled all the house where they were sitting," in the same manner, "As a bath is filled with water,

5 *The Baptizing Work of the Holy Spirit* (Findlay, Ohio: The Dunham Publishing Co., c. 1962), p. 80.

6 *A Grammar of the Greek New Testament in the Light of Historical Research* (Nashville: Broadman Press, c. 1934), p. 590.

7 *Ibid.* In the light of Dr. Robertson's definitive study, Dr. Unger's contention must be rejected, viz., "it is proper to say 'baptism *with* the Spirit' or 'baptism *by* the Spirit,' but not 'baptism *in* the Spirit'." *Loc. cit.*, p. 79.

Two additional facts militate against this contention.

(1) In the Synoptic Gospels Jesus is the Baptizer, the Holy Spirit is the sphere or medium in which the candidate is baptized. The Holy Spirit is not the Baptizer. John the Baptist testified: "I indeed baptize you in water unto repentance: but he that cometh after me is mightier than I, whose shoes I am not worthy to bear: *he shall baptize you in the Holy Spirit* and in fire" (Matt. 3:11; Cf. also Mk. 1:8; Lk. 3:16).

(2) In Acts 1:5, Jesus compared the baptism in the Spirit with baptism in water. "John indeed baptized in water; but ye shall be baptized in the Holy Spirit not many days hence." In John's baptism, John was the administrator, the water was the sphere or medium in which the baptism took place. By analogy then, Jesus is the Baptizer, and the Spirit is the sphere or medium in which the baptism takes place. In none of these instances is the Holy Spirit the instrument of the baptism referred to.

that they might be baptized with the Holy Ghost in fulfillment of Acts 1:5").[8]

According to these apologists, the baptism *by* the Spirit, which places the believer in Christ's Body, is synonymous with regeneration, and the baptism *in* the Holy Spirit by Jesus is equated with the Pentecostal enduement.

A fourth suggestion regards the baptism in the Spirit in I Cor. 12:13 as the sign, or seal of one's prior membership in the Body of Christ.[9] Support for this thesis is adduced from the interpretation of the preposition *eis,* "into (one body)," as "with reference to one body." This resultant translation reads thus: "For in *one* Spirit we were all baptized with reference to (the) *one* Body, whether Jews or Greeks, whether slaves or free; yea, we all were given to drink *one* Spirit."

This view equates both figures of speech with the Pentecostal baptism in the Spirit. That is to say, the believer enters into relationship with the Body of Christ in conversion, and this subsequent baptism "with reference to the Body," "marks us out, or seals us as members of the one and the same Body." [10] Stress is also laid upon the claim that Jesus is the one who joins believers to His Body at conversion, and this membership in the Body of Christ is prior to the baptism in the Spirit.

Support for this interpretation is drawn analogically from water baptism "unto repentance," by calling attention to the fact that repentance precedes water baptism. Thus Biblical baptism is not "for the purpose of repentance," but "on the basis or ground" [11] of a prior repentance.

---

[8] Robertson, *Word Pictures in the New Testament,* III, 21, quoting Canon Cook.

[9] Called to my attention in a personal correspondence by a colleague, Dr. John Rea.

[10] *Ibid.*

[11] Robertson, *Word Pictures in the New Testament,* III, 35.

Attractive as this view may seem at first glance, there are certain problems it does not solve. For instance, it may be objected on theological grounds, that if the baptism in I Cor. 12:13 is identical with the Pentecostal baptism, then it is vulnerable to the accusation that those who have not had a Pentecostal baptism do not have the seal of their membership in Christ's Body. Paradoxically, they have the membership, without the seal of this relationship.

The most cogent objection to this view, though, derives from grammatical considerations. On these grounds, the translation of the preposition *eis* as "with reference to," is almost certainly erroneous, because, "The usual idiom with *eis* was undoubtedly with verbs of motion when the motion and the accusative case combined with *eis* ('in') to give the resultant meaning of 'into,' 'unto,' 'among,' 'to,' 'towards,' or 'on,' 'upon,' according to the context." [12] The translation of the usual idiom with *eis* thus gives no support to the translation "with reference to the body."

Consistent with this fact is the judgment, that "The spirit is the element in (*en*) which the baptism takes place, and the one body is the end to (*eis*) which the act is directed." [13] The weight of J. H. Thayer's scholarship also endorses this interpretation of the use of the preposition *eis* "to indicate effect: *eis hen sōma,* to unite together into one body by baptism." [14] The interpretation "with reference to" was anticipated, and rejected, almost a century ago by Thomas Charles Edwards who wrote in part: *"eis hen sōma,* not 'in reference to one body,' but 'into one body'." [15]

The fifth, and last suggestion to be considered here sees

---

[12] Robertson, *A Grammar of the Greek New Testament in the Light of Historical Research,* p. 593.

[13] Robertson & Plummer, *op. cit.,* p. 272.

[14] *A Greek-English Lexicon of the New Testament* (New York: American Book Company, 1889), p. 94.

[15] *A Commentary on the First Epistle to the Corinthians,* 2nd ed., (New York: A. C. Strong & Son, 1886), p. 325.

in the first figure of speech the spiritual reality symbolized in Christian baptism, i.e., life in the Spirit; while the second alludes "to the outpowering of spiritual gifts after Baptism," that is to say, as a result of the Pentecostal effusion. It should be noted that the baptism in the Spirit in I Cor. 12:13 is not the same as the baptism in the Spirit at Pentecost. The former places one in the body of Christ, the Church. The latter is for power manifested in charismatic witnessing.

If it be objected, that the identification of the baptism in the Spirit in the Corinthian passage with conversion and regeneration—as distinct from the Pentecostal baptism in the Spirit—contradicts the "one Baptism" of Eph. 4:5, this objection loses its force when Eph. 4:5 is seen in its historical context. If the suggestion is correct (and there is much to commend it), that this epistle was written as a corrective to incipient Gnostic heresies, then "one Lord" is in contrast to the Gnostic series of aeons; "one faith" is one way of salvation for all, not "faith" for the vulgar, but a sophisticated "gnosis" for the Gnostic initiate; "one baptism" is the one Christian ordinance in contrast with additional Gnostic initiatory rites.[16]

I Cor. 12:13 stresses two aspects of the Christian's relationship to the Holy Spirit. To be "baptized in the Spirit" is to be placed in the sphere of the Holy Spirit, that is at conversion; while "being given to drink of the Spirit" places the Spirit's fulness within the believer. This fulness of the Spirit is normally attested by charismatic manifestations— a subject to be developed later.

It follows then that inasmuch as the believer is placed in the mystical Body of Jesus at conversion (with its concomitant "new birth"), Paul therefore used the idiom "baptized in the Spirit" as synonymous with this event.

[16] Robertson, *Word Pictures in the New Testament*, IV, 535.

It is faulty methodology, however, to read this usage back into the book of Acts, and, on this basis, to assert that Jesus (and Peter) used this phrase with exactly the same meaning. They apparently did not, as a critical comparison demonstrates. Nor can it be argued, that because Paul used this idiom for conversion, therefore, every believer's experience of the "new birth" is tantamount to a Pentecostal enduement with the Spirit. The fact that Paul added, "and were all given to drink of one Spirit," indicates that more than regeneration is involved in the Holy Spirit's full-orbed operations.

If it be objected, on the other hand, that this introduces ambiguity into the use of the phrase, "baptized in the Spirit," it must be pointed out that such ambiguities are inherent in language usages, and that it is the task of exegesis to unravel such equivocal terminology. For instance, we do not use words univocally (i.e., in one sense only), but we commonly use them equivocally (i.e., with more than one meaning in different contexts). Compare, for example, the English word "ball," which may be either a spherical toy, or a party, or in colloquial usage, any enjoyable "good time," depending on the context. The context is decisive for the final meaning of any word or phrase, and not the dictionary definition.

Apropo of this discussion, attention needs to be called to a phenomenon in Luke's choice of words to describe the Pentecostal experience. In the Acts, Luke used the words "baptized in the Spirit," only twice (Acts 1:5; 11:16), and each time as a quotation of the words of Jesus. It seems obvious that Luke himself deliberately avoided the word "baptism," and referred to the experience by a variety of synonymous expressions. For example, the disciples were "filled with the Holy Spirit" at Jerusalem. The converts in Samaria "received the Holy Spirit," while upon the household of Cornelius at Caesarea, "the gift of the Holy Spirit was poured out." Yet in each instance, the Pentecostal experience is thus described.

Was it because of current ambiguities in the use of the phrase, "baptized in the Spirit," that Luke used various circumlocutions to identify the Pentecostal experience as distinct from conversion and regeneration? We cannot know for certain, but Luke's close association with Paul, and the latter's influence upon his life, must be taken into consideration in any analysis and synthesis of the various examples of the phrase "baptized in the Spirit." Did Paul's use of the phrase as practically identical with the "new birth" prompt Luke to avoid it when describing the Pentecostal effusion of the Spirit subsequent to regeneration? Suffice it to say here, that by whatever name it is designated in the book of the Acts, the Pentecostal 'baptism in, i.e., fulness of the Spirit" is not confounded with the Holy Spirit's activity in conversion. Rather the "new birth" is prerequisite to the former.

In Jerusalem,[17] Samaria,[18] Damascus,[19] the baptism in the Holy Spirit was separated from conversion and regeneration by an appreciable interval of time. On the other hand, the immersion in the Spirit was immediately attendant upon the conversion of the Ethiopian eunuch (as a variant reading suggests),[20] Cornelius and his household,[21] and the twelve former disciples of John the Baptist Paul met at Ephesus.[22] In the latter instances, conversion and the baptism in, that is to say, fulness of the Spirit are almost simul–

[17] Acts 2:1–4.
[18] Acts 8:4ff.
[19] Acts 9:1ff.
[20] Acts 8:39.
[21] Acts 10:44.
[22] Acts 19:1–6.

taneous, yet, nonetheless, distinct administrations of the Holy Spirit. (In passing, may we call attention to a paradox in the attitude of some theologians who affirm that the Ephesian epistle of Paul is normative for Church doctrine, but who deny that the Ephesian experience of Paul's converts—"the Holy Spirit came on them; and they spake with tongues and prophesied"—is now normative for Christian experience.)

In the book of the Acts, conversion and its attendant regeneration—symbolized by water baptism—and the baptism in the Holy Spirit belong together as "two sides of one great act, whereby men are brought into the Church, the Body of Christ." [23] They are what a colleague, Dr. Charles Farah, has aptly termed a "unit whole." The significance of these two baptisms is not, however, identical. They are still "two sides" of the Spirit's ministrations. They represent a progression in the spiritual experience of the individual believer.

The cogency of this interpretation may be tested by answering two questions. First, within the context of their own experience, how would the churches to which Paul wrote interpret his words, "For in one Spirit were we all baptized into one body . . . and were all made to drink of one Spirit"? In Jerusalem, Samaria, Caesarea, and Ephesus, and by clear inductive reasoning, at Corinth also, they had been converted and regenerated, and then subsequently baptized in/filled with the Holy Spirit. The operation of the Holy Spirit's supernatural "gifts" in their midst—tongues, prophecy, healings, exorcisms—testifies to the fact that they knew the enduement with power that follows the baptism in/filling with the Holy Spirit. In fact, the apos-

[23] A. C. Winn, *Acts of the Apostles, The Layman's Bible Commentaries* (London: SCM Press Ltd., c. 1960), p. 107.

tolic Christians were commanded by Jesus not to leave Jerusalem [24] until they had received the Holy Spirit's enduement
with power. Clearly then, their "new birth," received on
that first Easter day was not all they were to expect from the
Holy Spirit of promise.

The second question is this: In the light of his own experience, what did Paul mean in I Cor. 12:13? The answer
is obvious. One need but to remember that Paul was converted on the Damascus road (a fact to be explored further
in another place), and three days later in Damascus he was
filled with, i.e., baptized in the Holy Spirit when Ananias
laid his hands upon him in the Name of Jesus. It is readily
apparent then, that the Spirit's activity in conversion and
regeneration was not terminal in Paul's experience. His
baptism in = filled with the Holy Spirit followed his conversion by three days.

[24] Acts 1:4.

CHAPTER VI

"Ye Shall Be My Witnesses"

(Acts 1:8)

The charismatic nature of the Pentecostal baptism in the Holy Spirit is implicit in the purpose for which it is given. Jesus said; "ye shall receive power *(dunamis)*, when the Holy Spirit is come upon you: and ye shall be my witnesses both in Jerusalem, and in all Judaea and Samaria, and unto the uttermost part of the earth." [1] All agree that the purpose of the Pentecostal enduement with the Holy Spirit— "ye shall be my witnesses . . . unto the uttermost part of the earth"—has not yet been accomplished. Jesus' commission is still in effect, and by parity of reasoning, so is the charismatic enduement with power given to realize this purpose.

Inasmuch as the human faculty preëminently used in witnessing is the power of speech, it need come as no surprise, nor should it jar our aesthetic sense of propriety, that on the day of Pentecost the Spirit's fulness was manifested in supernatural utterance; for, "they were all filled with the Holy Spirit, and began to speak with other tongues, as the Holy Spirit gave them utterance." And in each subsequent recital of the experience of believers being baptized in/ filled with the Spirit, whether explicitly or implicitly stated,

[1] Acts 1:8.

the initial manifestation of the Holy Spirit's power and presence is supernatural speech in other tongues.

This is unquestionably the thorniest question in any discussion of the Pentecostal experience. Sooner or later it evokes the question: Must everyone speak in tongus to be filled with the Spirit? What the questioner means is this. There are a lot of wonderful Christians who must be Spirit-filled, but they do not speak with tongues. Why then should I? (But ought not one who is open to all that God has for them ask instead: How can I be filled with the Holy Spirit, and know experimentally the gifts of the Holy Spirit?)

Perhaps an understanding of the *rationale* of tongues would obviate the objections to it. Speech is a unique manifestation of personality. It is, in fact, one of the most distinctly personal things men do. It is rightly regarded as evidence of personality. It is not accidental to personality. It is rather indispensable to human personality. The perceptive comment of Eduard Thurneysen is a welcome emphasis of this very fact: "Only the fact that man can speak and does speak makes him man . . . In the last analysis, the mystery of speech is identical with the mystery of personality, with the image of God in man." [2]

God is also personal, *and as a Person manifests Himself in speech*. This is the predicate of all revelation; for, "God, having of old spoken unto the fathers in the prophets by divers protions and in divers manners, hath at the end of these days spoken unto us in his Son." [3] In the divine Personality, speech is not extrinsic, it is intrinsic. It was by speech that God created the world.[4] Jesus is called by John the Evangelist, "the Word" incarnate, and this Word is

---

[2] *A Theology of Pastoral Care*, trans. by Jack A. Worthington, et. al. (Richmond: John Knox Press, 1963), p. 103.

[3] Heb. 1:1, 2.

[4] Gen. 1:3ff.

God.[5] The writer of the epistle to the Hebrews categorically affirmed that the Son "upholds all things by the word of his power." [6] Furthermore, the expression, "the Spirit said . . ." [7] has often been invoked by orthodox theologians as evidence of the Holy Spirit's personality. Speech and personality are inseparable in the Deity.

It is an article of the Church's faith, that God can and does speak to His people in their own languages, but such communication is always limited by two human factors. When God addresses Himself to man (or conversely, when man addresses himself to God) in the languages man has learned, their communication is limited; (one) by the thought categories in which the individual structures his thoughts; and (two) by the vocabulary with which one is conversant. By the way of contrast, when the Spirit-filled Christian prays or speaks in tongues, he is speaking a language he has never learned. The vocabulary he uses is controlled by the Holy Spirit. It may be one language, or many languages, at the Spirit's discretion, and all restrictions of vocabulary and thought categories are surpassed. It was thus that Paul described his own experience of glossolalia: "For if I pray in a tongue," said he, "my spirit prayeth, but my understanding is unfruitful." [8] Nor did the Apostle depreciate this, for he added: "What is it then? I will pray with the spirit (i.e., in tongues as the Spirit gives utterance), and I will pray with the understanding also (i.e., in the languages he had learned): I will sing with the spirit (i.e., in tongues), and I will sing with the understanding also (i.e., in the languages he knew)." [9]

Jesus promised His disciples power when the Holy Spirit

[5] John 1:1.
[6] Heb. 1:3.
[7] Acts 8:29; 13:2.
[8] I Cor. 14:14.
[9] I Cor. 14:15.

came upon them, *and the first distinctively personal manifestation of the Spirit's power was supernatural utterance in
other languages.* Thus the Holy Spirit demonstrated His
sovereignty over the organs of human communication involved in fulfilling their responsibility as witnesses.
Tongues are the unique charismatic manifestation of the
divine Spirit's presence and power on the day of Pentecost.
Every other charismatic manifestation of the Holy Spirit
can be paralled before Pentecost, with the exception of
tongues. They were, and are, the normative evidence of the
Pentecostal *dunamis* in the lives of Christians.

A closing word is indicated here to clarify the relationship of the tongues at Pentecost with Peter's quotation from
the prophecy of Joel wherein prophecy is the distinctive
feature of the outpouring of God's Spirit "upon all flesh." [10]
Was it simply a loose accommodation, dictated by homiletical expediency, of the ancient seer's words to the Pentecostal
phenomenon? Or was there a more precise link between
Joel's "prophesying" and Pentecost's "tongues"? The answer is suggested by the Greek word translated in our English versions of Acts 2:4 as "utterance." In the Septuagint
translation of the Old Testament this very word is "used
not of ordinary conversation, but of the utterance of prophets." [11] Peter apparently interpreted the tongues at Pentecost as prophetic utterance in other tongues.[12] In this sense,
the tongues were a literal fulfillment of Joel's words: "I

---

[10] Acts 2:17.

[11] R. J. Knowling, *The Acts of the Apostles, The Expositor's Greek
Testament,* II (Grand Rapids: Wm. B. Eerdmans, n.d.), pp. 4, 5.

"Ver. 4. *apophtheggesthai*—a word peculiar to Acts, cf. v.14 and xxvi.25;
in the LXX used not of ordinary conversation, but of the utterances of
prophets; cf. Ezek. xiii.9, Micah v.12, I Chron. xxv.1, so fitly here: (cf.
apophthegmata, used by the Greeks of the sayings of the Wise and phi-
losophers, and see also references in Wendt)."

[12] This same aspect will be referred to again in the exposition of I Cor.
14:6.

will pour forth of my Spirit upon all flesh: And your sons and your daughters shall prophesy." [13] When the apostolic community spoke in tongues, "as the Spirit gave them utterance," on the day of Pentecost, they were speaking supernaturally languages they had not previously learned. To them it was tongues, but to the bystanders who heard and understood them speaking in their dialects,[14] they did not hear tongues, they heard prophecy. They heard them extol, not "the mighty works of God," [15] but "the magnificence of God" [16] with prophetic ardor. It was this same manifestation of praise in tongues that occurred later in the house of the Roman centurion, Cornelius, when "they heard them speak with tongues and magnify God."

[13] Acts 2:17.

[14] Acts 2:6.

[15] Acts 2:11.

[16] N.T.M.E. Cf., also William F. Arndt, and F. Wilbur Gingrich, trans. of Walter Bauer, *A Greek-English Lexicon of the New Testament and Other Early Christian Literature* (Chicago: The University of Chicago Press, 1957), p. 497.

"*Megaleios* . . . in our literature only substantively. *to m.* greatness, sublimity."

A. T. Robertson and W. Hersey Davis, *A New Short Grammar of the Greek New Testament* (New York: Harper & Brothers, 1933), p. 205.

Gk. *ta megaleia*—"The articular neuter adjective is often used in the same sense as an abstract. . . ."

CHAPTER VII

"An Abiding Enduement"

(Acts 2:4; 4:8; 9:17; 13:9)

In the foregoing discussion, sufficient has now been said to formulate the normative pattern of the baptism in the Holy Spirit. By way of recapitulation, the following five propositions may be affirmed, with reasonable confidence, as regulative of this experience. Each has been derived from the historical accounts of the various groups, and individuals whose baptism in the Spirit has been recorded in the book of Acts. Since it is only in the historical narratives of the Acts that this Spirit-baptism is recorded in its details, such a formulation must depend entirely upon these historical records.

The allusions to the baptism in, or filling with the Spirit in the epistles interpret didactically the significance, and subsequent manifestations of the Holy Spirit in the lives of Spirit-filled/baptized Christians. The epistles do not record the initial experience, they pre-suppose it. Consequently, a normative pattern for the baptism in the Holy Spirit cannot be derived from these sources. Nowhere, for instance, in the epistles is one told how to be filled with the Spirit of God. It is assumed that the readers already know this. We must turn to the book of Acts for this vital information. Accordingly, any reconstruction of the circumstances, and details of the baptism in the Spirit must be derived from the records of those who experienced this baptism.

In the first place, John the Baptist's baptism supplied the type for the baptism in the Spirit. Jesus linked the two, when He said, "for John indeed baptized with water; but ye shall be baptized in the Holy Spirit not many days hence." [1] As the baptism of John placed one in the medium of water, so the baptism of Jesus places the candidate in the sphere of the Spirit.

Secondly, Jesus is Himself the administrator of this Spirit-baptism. John the Baptizer testified of Him, "he shall baptize you in the Holy Spirit and *in* fire." [2] To this Peter added confirmatory testimony, when, in his Pentecostal sermon, he said: "Being therefore by the right hand of God exalted, and having received of the Father the promise of the Holy Spirit, he hath poured fourth this which ye see and hear." [3] In Jerusalem, as in Casarea, the effusion of the Spirit was mediated without the laying on of hands. In every case, though, the administrator of the baptism in the Holy Spirit is the Lord Jesus Himself.

In the next place, the baptism in the Holy Spirit is not synonymous with conversion and the 'new birth." Rather, it is subsequent to conversion and regeneration. This proposition will be discussed at greater length in Chapter XIII.

Fourthly, the normative evidence of this baptism is a charismatic manifestation of the Holy Spirit's personality and power, for "they were all filled with the Holy Spirit, and began to speak with other tongues, as the Spirit gave them utterance." Tongues-speech, as the evidence of the baptism in, or filling with the Holy Spirit, is explicitly stated as occurring in Jerusalem, Casarea, and Ephesus.

[1] Acts 1:5.
[2] Matt. 3:11; Mark 1:8; Luke 3:16; John 1:33.
[3] Acts 2:33.

This will be discussed more fully, along with the implicit evidence for this premise, in Chapter XII. It has already been pointed out, that in I Cor. 12:13 those who were baptized in the Spirit were given to drink of the Spirit's charismatic fulness.

And in the last place, the baptism in the Holy Spirit is synonymous with being filled with the Spirit. Jesus, speaking prophetically of the Pentecostal baptism in the Spirit, said, "ye shall be baptized in the Holy Spirit not many days hence." [4] Luke, in recording the circumstances of the event, wrote, "And they were all filled with the Holy Spirit." [5] It is no homiletical extravagance to conclude, therefore, that there is no other pattern for being filled with the Holy Spirit taught in the Bible. The Christian who would claim his birth-right, and be Spirit-filled must submit himself as a candidate to Jesus the Baptizer, and permit Him to baptize him in the Holy Spirit—with or without the laying on of hands of those already baptized in His Spirit. It is a full surrender involving obedience [6] to our Triune God in every area of life, surrendering even the "untamed" member, the tongue,[7] to the sovereign manifestation of the Holy Spirit's person and power. Baptized in the Spirit, filled with the Spirit—it is one and the same experience. The cliche, "one baptism, but many fillings," cannot, therefore, be true. If there is one baptism in the Spirit, there is one filling with the Spirit. The assertion, "Repeated fillings with the Holy Spirit are necessary to continuance and increase in power," [8] is Scripturally unfounded. It is at variance with the pattern of the baptism shown in the book of

[4] Acts 1:5.
[5] Acts 2:4.
[6] Acts 5:32.
[7] James 3:8.
[8] R. A. Torrey, *The Person and Work of the Holy Spirit* (London: James Nisbet & Co., Limited, 1910), p. 212.

the Acts. Rather than being repeatedly refilled, the Biblical pattern and provision is a state of constant fulness with the Holy Spirit.

The discussion has now come around full circle to the point at which we digressed from this theme in Chapter II. The way is now prepared to discuss the significance of Luke's use of the phrase, "filled with the Spirit," in the book of the Acts.

In Acts 2:1–4, the first baptism in the Holy Spirit is described. As an abiding consequence of this baptism, the disciples "were all filled with the Spirit." Here the Greek word "filled *(eplēsthēsan)*" is the aorist tense. It is what grammarians call the *ingressive aorist*. This use of the aorist tense is described thus by two New Testament scholars: "The action signified by the aorist may be contemplated in its beginning. This use is commonly employed with verbs which signify a state or condition, *and denote entrance into that state or condition.*" [9] The significance of the ingressive aorist, used to describe the inception of the baptism in the Spirit on the day of Pentecost, must be underscored here. Baptized in the Spirit by Jesus, they entered "into that state or condition" of fulness of the Spirit. It was not a transitory experience that needed to be repeated. Instead it was an abiding state or condition of fulness into which they entered. The same use of the aorist occurs in Acts 4:31 with the same meaning. This will be referred to again in the exposition of that verse.

Shortly after the Pentecostal experience, Luke had occasion to elaborate upon the effect of the Spirit's fulness in the life of Peter. Brought before the ruling council of the Jewish nation, they demanded that he tell them the nature of the "power," of the identity of the "name" [10] whereby

9 Dana & Mantey, *op. cit.*, p. 196. Italics mine H.M.E.
10 Acts 4:7.

the lame man at the temple gate called Beautiful had been healed.[11] Luke prefaced Peter's reply with the explanatory comment, "Then Peter, filled with the Holy Spirit, said unto them. . . ."[12] The grammatical form of the word "filled" in this place is an aorist passive participle. It is used here as a circumstantial participle,[13] which, in the aorist and perfect tenses, is customarily used to express "antecedent action relative to the main verb."[14] The force of this idiom may be clarified by translating thus: "Then Peter, who had been filled with the Holy Spirit, said. . . ." It is no mere rhetorical flourish to ask at what prior time Peter had been filled with the Holy Spirit? The obvious answer is on the day of Pentecost, when he, with the one hundred and twenty in the upper room, was baptized in the Spirit by the ascended Jesus, and entered into the state, or condition of being filled with the Spirit.

It was a Spirit-filled Peter who was the human instrument in the healing of the lame man at the temple gate. It was to this abiding fulness of the Holy Spirit that he referred when he said to the lame beggar, "Silver and gold have I none; but what I have, that give I thee. In the name of Jesus Christ of Nazareth, walk."[15] It was a Spirit-filled Peter who then preached in the temple courts, was arrested, imprisoned, and finally arraigned before the Sanhedrin because of his evangelistic activities. And there, "Peter (still)

[11] Acts 3:1ff.

[12] Acts 4:8.

[13] Henry Lamar Crosby, and John Nevin Schaeffer, *An Introduction to Greek* (New York: Allyn and Bacon, 1928), p. 65.

"A participle, when used without the article and in agreement with a noun or pronoun expressed or implied, is called the *circumstantial participle.* It may denote *time, manner, means, cause, condition, concession,* or any *attendant circumstances* of an action."

[14] Dana & Mantey, *op. cit.,* p. 230.

[15] Acts 3:6.

filled with the Holy Spirit" boldly answered his interrogators in the power of the same Spirit.

Precisely the same grammatical construction occurs in Acts 13:9. Paul, in preaching to the proconsul Sergius Paulos at Paphos, was hindered by the diabolical antagonism of the sorcerer, Bar Jesus. Confronting his antagonist, Luke said of the Apostle, that "Paul, filled with the Holy Spirit, fastened his eyes on him, and said. . . ." Here, as in Acts 4:8 above, the word "filled" is a circumstantial participle in the aorist tense, passive voice. Once again, it expresses action antecedent to that of the main verb. Here also, a more precise translation would read: "But Saul, who is also called Paul, who had been filled with the Holy Spirit, fastened his eyes on him, and said. . . ." Again the issue is focused more sharply by asking: When was Paul filled with the Holy Spirit? The answer, according to the Acts, is when Ananias laid his hands upon him in the name of Jesus, and said, "Brother Saul, the Lord, *even* Jesus, who appeared unto thee in the way which thou camest, hath sent me, that thou mayest receive thy sight, and be filled with the Holy Spirit." [16]

The Biblical sources thus indicate that Peter and Paul each entered the state, or condition of being Spirit-filled when Jesus baptized them in His Spirit—Peter on the day of Pentecost, Paul (Saul) later in Damascus; Peter through the spontaneous effusion of the Spirit by Jesus, Paul through the laying on of Ananias' hands. For both, it was an abiding enduement with power by the Holy Spirit to make them effectual witnesses for Jesus. It was not a sort of "on again, off again, gone again" type of experience.

[16] Acts 9:17.

CHAPTER VIII

"They Were All Filled With the Holy Spirit"

(Acts 4:31)

The next recorded use of the phrase, "filled with the Spirit," occurs in Acts 4:31 in these words: "And when they had prayed, the place was shaken wherein they were gathered together; and they were all filled with the Holy Spirit, and they spake the word of God with boldness." Though the account of the experience is condensed, there is justification for believing that the pattern of the baptism in the Holy Spirit already outlined was fulfilled in this case also. The similarities with the account of the events on the day of Pentecost are succinctly stated by a distinguished Biblical scholar in these words: "The description here is reminiscent of the description of what happened on the day of Pentecost, both in the external signs of the Spirit's advent and in the prayerful attitude of the disciples when He came. . . ." [1] While agreeing wholeheartedly with this judgment, we must dissent from the conclusion drawn, that "while this was a fresh filling of the Spirit, it could not be called a fresh baptism." [2] Why not? inasmuch as baptism in, and filling with the Holy Spirit are practically synonymous in the Acts. However, the real point here is that this was,

[1] F. F. Bruce, *Commentary on the Book of Acts*, p. 107.
[2] *Ibid.*

62

in all probability, not a "fresh filling" (or refilling, to use a popular terminology) of those baptized in the Spirit at Pentecost. Rather, this was the occasion of the filling with, or baptism in the Holy Spirit of the converts won to saving faith in Christ Jesus since Pentecost. Two exegetical considerations lend support to this inference.

In the first place, there is a deeply meaningful variation in nuance between Acts 4:31 and Acts 2:2. In the latter place, Luke wrote: "And suddenly there came from heaven a sound as of the rushing of a mighty wind, and it *filled* all *the house where they were sitting."* [3] Note now, that in Acts 4:31 Luke preserved a subtle distinction in the description of these events, when he wrote: "And when they had prayed, *the place was shaken wherein they were* gathered together." [4] One's understanding of Acts 4:31 will be influenced, to a considerable degree, by their understanding of *ton oikon,* "the house," in Acts 2:2, and *ho topos,* "the place," in Acts 4:31. If they were merely synonymous, one could dismiss the contrast on stylistic grounds alone. Granted, that "the place where they were gathered together" could mean a house. In that case *ho topos* and *ton oikon* would be synonyms. But two facts argue strongly, that they are not used synonymously here. One, *topos,* "place," is used in New Testament Greek as a synonym for *chora,* "a tract of unbounded land," and for *chorion,* "a parcel of (enclosed) ground." [5] Two, Acts 4:4 places the number of new

---

3 Italics mine, H.M.E.

4 Italics mine H.M.E.

5 Joseph Henry Thayer, *A Greek-English Lexicon of the New Testament,* p. 628.

"Syn. *topos* 1, *chora, chorion: topos place,* indefinite; a portion of space viewed in reference to its occupancy, or as appropriated to a thing; *chora region, country,* extensive; yet unbounded; *chorion parcel of ground* (Jn. iv.5), circumscribed; a definite portion of space viewed as enclosed or complete in itself; *topos* and *chorion* (plur., R.V. lands) occur together in Acts xxviii.7."

converts at about five thousand men, not counting the women. When Peter and John were released from custody by the Sanhedrin, it is said, that "they came to their own company." [6] Did "their company" mean only the initial group of disciples present at Pentecost? Or were the new converts included? The context suggests that "their company" now included not only the original Pentecost group, but also new converts. This is implied in the comment, that the words *"tous idious,* their own company" is "not necessarily limited to their fellow-Apostles . . . but as including the members of the Christian community." [7] Even more explicit is the opinion, that "Their own people as in John 1:11; 13:1; Acts 24:23; I Tim. 5:8; Tit. 3:14, is not merely the apostles" but "(all the disciples)." [8] Additional confirmation is supplied by Acts 4:32: "And the multitude of them that believed were of one heart and soul." [9] The *plēthous,* "multitude," in this verse finds its antecedent in the *polloi,* "many," (i.e., "the number of the men came to be about five thousand)," in verse 4. It is to this larger group that Luke referred in Acts 4:31.

Such an increase in the numbers of the Christian community argues for the need of the larger meeting area suggested by *topos,* "place," in Acts 4:31. Paul's later experi-

---

[6] Acts 4:23.

[7] R. J. Knowling, *The Acts of the Apostles, The Expositor's Greek Testament,* II (Grand Rapids: Wm. B. Eerdmans Company, n.d.) p. 132.

"Ver. 23 *tous idious:* not necessarily limited to their fellow-Apostles (so Meyer, Blass, Weiss), but as including the members of the Christian community (Overbeck, Wendt, Hilgenfeld, Zockler), cf. xxic.23, John xiii.1, I Tim. v.8 and also of one's fellow-countrymen, associates, John 1:11, 2 Macc. xii.22."

[8] Robertson, *Word Pictures in the New Testament,* III, p. 54.

[9] Heinrich Meyer, *Critical and Exegetical Hand-Book to the Acts of the Apostles,* trans. from 4th German ed., by Paton J Gloag, (New York: Funk & Wagnalls, 1883), p. 96.

It is a violation of the context to say of vs. 32, that "the multitude of believers are *contrasted with these,*" i.e., "their own company," vs. 23. Vs. 24 stresses their unity.

ence at Phillipi, where he found "a place of prayer" [10] by the side of a river, reflects an established Jewish custom, and provides an illustrative parallel. The customary *topos proseuchēs,* "place of prayer," of the Jews may well have supplied the pattern for such a Christian gathering place apart from the Temple and the synagogues of Jerusalem. Josephus quoted a decree of those of Halicarnassus, guaranteeing the right of the Jews "to make their prayers at the seashore, according to the customs of their forefathers." [11] These *proseuchai* were described by Epiphanius "as places of a semi-circular form *(theatrodeis),* without roofs, and outside the cities." [12] There is an explicit allusion to such a place in I Macc. 3:46 as follows: "And they gathered themselves together, and came to Mizpah, over against Jerusalem; for in Mizpah there had been aforetime a place of prayer [*topos proseuchēs*] for Israel." [13]

The second of the exegetical reasons supporting the conclusion, that Acts 4:31 refers to the filling with, i.e., baptism in the Holy Spirit of new converts added to the Church since Pentecost, hinges upon the form of the word "filled," *(eplēsthēsan).*" In Acts 2:4 and 4:31, the identical form is used. As already pointed out, Luke used the *ingressive aorist* in Acts 2:4 to describe the experience of the disciples on the day of Pentecost. It bears repeating here, that "This use is commonly employed with verbs which signify a state or condition." It is, therefore, analogically sound reasoning to interpret Luke's use of the aorist tense as ingressive in Acts

---

[10] Acts 16:13.

[11] William Whiston, *The Works of Flavius Josephus, Antiquities of the Jews,* XIV, 10 (Hartford: S. S. Scranton Co., 1905), p. 434.

[12] Quoted by Chr. Wordsworth, *op. cit.,* I, 119.

[13] R. H. Charles, (ed), *The Apocrypha and Pseudepigrapha,* I (Oxford: The Clarendon Press, 1963), 78. Cf. also III Macc. 7:20, "and having dedicated a place of prayer [*topon proseuches*] on the spot where they had held their festival, they departed unharmed, free, and full of joy." *Op. cit.,* I, 173.

4:31 also, thereby describing the entrance of subsequent converts to Christianity into the state or condition of being filled with the Holy Spirit.

On the other hand, the burden of the proof rests with those who deduce another meaning from the aorist tense in Acts 4:31. For example, the interpretation that this passage represents a refilling with the Holy Spirit of those present at Pentecost arbitrarily assumes the sense of repeated action in the verb "filled," i.e., "they were all filled again." But the aorist tense does not convey the iterative sense. If this were what Luke intended to say, there are other tenses that would have conveyed this meaning. For instance, he could have used an iterative imperfect, but not the aorist, which represents the action of the verb as "punctiliar (point action)." [14]

It is the use of the word "all" that has proven a stumbling block to many in the interpretation of this verse, (i.e., "they were all filled with the Holy Spirit"). Recognition of the force of the aorist tense in Acts 4:31 mitigates this objection. If it be objected that the ingressive use of the aorist cannot be pressed in this verse, a related use of the aorist tense reinforces what has already been said. The use of the tense here may be regarded as a dramatic aorist.[15] "This idiom is a device for emphasis. It is commonly used of a state *which has* just been realized. . . ." [16]

It is in the following sense that the comprehensive "all" may be reconciled with the view propounded here. The original band of disciples had entered the state or condition of being filled with the Spirit on the day of Pentecost. They were still filled with the Holy Spirit. Note that in the

---

[14] Robertson and Davis, *op. cit.*, p. 295.

[15] Dana & Mantey, *op. cit.*, p. 199. Robertson agreed with Moulton that in the dramatic aorist, "we have probably to do . . . with one of the most ancient uses of the aorist."

[16] *Ibid.*, p. 198. Italics mine H.M.E.

same context,[17] probably earlier the same day, *a Spirit-filled Peter* stood before the Sanhedrin to answer for his conduct in the healing of the lame man, and his consequent proclamation of the gospel in the Temple precincts. As already shown, this was not a new filling with the Holy Spirit for Peter. Rather the idiom used refers to Peter's prior filling with the Spirit at Pentecost. This was also true of the rest of those present who had been filled with the Spirit of God at Pentecost. But now the converts won to Christ through their Spirit-filled witness were also introduced into the same state or condition by this fresh effusion of the promised Holy Spirit. It was no longer the unique privilege of those present at Pentecost, for now "all" were inducted into the Spirit's fulness. The Spirit-filled state "has now been realized" [18] by all the Christians.

For those who read Acts 4:31 as a refilling with the Holy Spirit of the apostolic band, the pointed reference to Peter's status of being "filled with the Spirit" in Acts 4:8 is an anomaly. What happened to Peter's Spirit-filled experience between the events recorded in Acts 4:8 and Acts 4:31? Was a fulness added to fulness? (Can one be filled "fuller" then "full"? But this is merely a play upon words.) Or did Peter somehow lose the fulness of the Spirit he exemplified in his appearance before the ruling council of Judaism? If so, then it is in order to ask, how? when? and why? and until these questions are adequately answered, it is futile to claim that Peter was refilled with the Holy Spirit in Acts 4:31. No matter how one looks at the facts, Peter's experience in Acts 4:8 abridges the comprehensive force of the "all" in Acts 4:31; and if this exception be admitted for Peter, it cannot consistently be denied in the case of the rest of the disciples present with Peter on the day of Pentecost.

[17] Acts 4:8.
[18] Dana & Mantey, *op. cit.,* p. 199.

CHAPTER IX

"And the Converts Were Filled...
With the Holy Spirit"

(Acts 7:55; Acts 13:9; Acts 13:52)

In the next occurence of the phrase, "filled with the Spirit," there occurs a grammatical usage of considerable importance for this inquiry: "But he [Stephen], being full of the Holy Spirit looked up steadfastly into heaven, and saw the glory of God, and Jesus standing on the right hand of God, and said, Behold, I see the heavens opened, and the Son of Man standing on the right hand of God." [2] Here the phrase, "being full of the Holy Spirit," is a participle used with a predicate noun. It is the present participle of the verb *huparchō*, meaning "to exist." It is "a widely used substitute in Hellenistic Greek for *einai*," [3] the present infinitive of the verb "to be." This form of the verb *huparchō* may be translated, *"who is, since he is,"* [4] thereby attributing one's present state, or experience, to antecedent causes. For instance, this usage is illustrated in Acts 3:2: "And a certain man that was [*huparchōn*] lame from his mother's womb. . . ." [5] The participle construction here alludes to the ante-

1 Acts 13:52, N.E.B.
2 Acts 7:55.
3 Arndt, Gingrich, Bauer, *op. cit.*, p. 845.
4 *Ibid.*, p. 846.
5 Cf. also Acts 22:3.

cedent lameness of the man. He did not become lame that day. He had been lame for a long time, and was still lame, which is precisely the intent of the participial phrase in this place.

The same grammatical construction occurs again in Acts 17:24: "The God that made the world and all things therein, he, being [*huparchōn*] Lord of heaven and earth . . ." God did not at that moment become Lord of heaven and earth—or what is even more bizarre, become Lord again. He is the Lord beause He always has been the Lord. These illustrations make it abundantly clear that this participle construction refers to the antecedent existence of some present matter of fact.

What light does this grammatical detail throw upon Stephen's experience? A great deal, indeed, for it "shows," said Wordsworth, "his antecedent spiritual state." [6] Stephen was no more refilled with the Holy Spirit at this time than that the lame man became lame that day, or that God became Lord again, at the moment spoken of in the texts above. Rather the idiom used refers to his filling with the Spirit at some prior time. This is further attested by the context.

In the Acts 6:3, "seven men of good report, full of the Spirit and of wisdom" was the pre-condition set by the Apostles for the choice of the first seven "deacons," or "almoners," of the Church. Verse 5 adds, "and they chose Stephen, a man full of faith and the Holy Spirit." Stephen was not filled again with the Spirit at this time to discharge these responsibilities. Men already "full" of the Spirit were chosen to fill this office. Stephen *had been* filled with the Spirit of God on a prior occasion, he *was* full of the Spirit when he was chosen as a deacon, and he *continued* to

[6] Wordsworth, *op. cit.*, I. 73.

be filled with the Holy Spirit right up to the moment that
he sealed his testimony by martyrdom.

Parenthetically, it is appropriate to note that the two
preceding uses of the phrase, "full of the Holy Spirit," [7] are
noun phrases. Another instance of the same kind reports
the identical experience of Barnabas, "for he was a good
man, and full of the Holy Spirit and of faith." [8]

In each instance, the genitive phrases, "of the Spirit and
of faith," qualify the subject which it "defines by attributing a quality or relationship to the noun it modifies." [9] In
every case, those who were filled with the Spirit entered
into an abiding *charismatic* relationship with the Third
Person of the Triune Godhead. These examples also show
that the charismatic fulness of the Spirit is complimented
by (though not contingent upon) abiding gracements of the
Divine Spirit, e.g., "wisdom, faith, good reputation, and
personal integrity." These spiritual endowments are epitomized in Stephen's case as "grace and power," that is to
work "great wonders and signs among the people." [10]

Attention has already been directed to Paul's confrontation with the sorcerer, Elymas, at Paphos. When this magician sought to impede Paul's testimony to the local consul,
it is recorded, that "Paul, filled with the Holy Spirit, fastened his eyes on him," [11] rebuked him and predicted his
impending blindness as the stroke of Divine judgment upon
him. In the preceding discussion of this passage, it was
pointed out, that the grammatical construction used in the
phrase, "filled with the Holy Spirit," pointed to a prior
time in the experience of Paul when he had been filled with
the Spirit. It is self-evident that this event took place in

[7] Acts 6:3, 5.
[8] Acts 11:24.
[9] Dana & Mantey, *op. cit.*, p. 74.
[10] Acts 6:8.
[11] Acts 13:9.

Damascus when Ananias "entered into the house; and lay-ing his hands on him said, Brother Saul, the Lord, even Jesus, who appeared unto thee in the way which thou cam-est, hath sent me, that thou mayest receive thy sight, and be filled with the Holy Spirit." [12]

The form of the verb, "be filled," in this place is an aor-ist, subjunctive, passive (*plēsthēis*). It is used in a final purpose clause [13] to express the purpose of the principle verb. Applied to this passage, it means that Ananias was sent to fulfill the two-fold purpose of the Lord Jesus for Saul (Paul), viz., that his vision be restored, and that he be filled with the Holy Spirit. This use of the final purpose clause removed the results from the realm of contingency, or even possibility. It was the fixed purpose of our Lord, and Ananias was simply the human instrument. Neither of these places countenances any assumption that Paul was re-filled with the Spirit. Rather, the use of the aorist tense in Acts 9:17, to describe his filling with, i.e., baptism in, the Holy Spirit, is reminiscent of the ingressive use of the aorist tense in Acts 2:4 and 4:31. In all three places, the aorist tense is used to relate the experience in its inception for those who had not previously entered the state of being filled with the promised Holy Spirit.

The only example in the book of Acts of the phrase, "filled with the Holy Spirit," that could be pressed to sub-stantiate a theology of repeated refillings with the Spirit is Acts 13:52. This reads: "And the disciples were filled with joy and with the Holy Spirit." In this text, the word trans-lated "were filled" (*eplērounto*) is the imperfect tense, pas-sive voice of *pleroō*.[14] Granted that the imperfect tense in Greek may be construed to describe repeated action in past

[12] Acts 9:17.
[13] Dana & Mantey, *op. cit.*, p. 283.
[14] There is no essential difference in meaning between *pimplēmi* in Acts 4:31 and *pleroō* in Acts 13:52.

time, the iterative use of the imperfect tense.[15] If the verb, "were filled," be understood as an iterative use of the imperfect, two choices are open to the interpreter. One, it may be translated, "And the disciples were being filled *again* and *again* with joy, and with the Holy Spirit." This sense could then be adduced to substantiate the teaching of repeated refillings with the Holy Spirit. However, even if it be taken as an iterative imperfect, such an interpretation is neither mandatory, nor consistent with the evidence of collateral passages dealing with this subject, as we have already seen.

The second choice open to us is then to translate it thus: "And the disciples were being filled *one after another* with joy, and with the Holy Spirit." And this is exactly the interpretation of the translators of the *New English Bible* which reads: "And *the converts* were filled with joy and with the Holy Spirit." [16]

This may be graphically illustrated by the use of the iterative imperfect of the word "baptize" (*ebaptizonto*), in Matt. 3:6, e.g., "and they were baptized of him (i.e., of John, the Baptist) in the river Jordan." Obviously, John was not baptizing the same candidates over and over again. Instead he was baptizing (iterative imperfect) *the converts one after another.*

Not all commentators are agreed, however, that the word, "were filled," in Acts 13:52 is an iterative imperfect. Some authorities regard it as the descriptive imperfect (durative), also called the progressive imperfect.[17] A. T. Robertson, for example, translated it, "they kept on being filled." [18] This

---

[15] Dana & Mantey, *op. cit.*, p. 188. "The iterative imperfect . . . may be used to describe action as recurring at successive intervals in past time."

[16] Italics mine, H.M.E.

[17] Dana & Mantey, *op. cit.*, p. 187. Cf., also A. T. Robertson, *A Grammar of the Greek New Testament in the the Light of Historical Research,* pp. 838, 883, 884.

[18] Robertson, *Word Pictures in the New Testament,* III, 203.

too is, in essence, the translation of the *New American Standard Bible* version which renders the passage: "And the disciples were continually filled with joy and with the Holy Spirit." [19] It is also the reading adopted by J. B. Phillips: "And the disciples continued to be full of joy and the Holy Spirit."

The weight of the evidence is, therefore, decidedly against interpreting Acts 13:52 in favor of the doctrine of repeated re-fillings with the Holy Spirit. It may be concluded from this examination of the evidence in the book of Acts, that there is no Biblical support for the theological formulation, "one baptism, but many fillings." Instead, the evidence points unmistakably to one crisis baptism in the Holy Spirit, whereby the candidate is filled with the Spirit, and inducted into a continuously Spirit-filled life and witness. Anything less than this is a compromise with the Scriptural norm.

[19] *New American Standard Bible, New Testament,* (Nashville: Broadman Press, c. The Lockman Foundation, 1963), Abbr. N.A.S.N.T.

CHAPTER X

"Be Continuously Filled With the Spirit"

(Eph. 5:18)

A final use of the phrase, "filled with the Spirit," is found in Ephesians 5:18: "And be not drunken with wine, wherein is riot, but be filled with the Spirit." Here the word, "filled (*plērousthe*), is the present tense, imperative mood, and passive voice. Once again, the interpreter is confronted with a choice, for the present imperative when used in commands means either continuous or repeated action.[1]

If the sense of repeated action (the iterative present) is adopted, the clause would read: "be filled again and again with the Spirit." This then would lend support to a view of repeated fillings with the Holy Spirit. On the other hand, if it is interpreted as a continuous (durative) present, the sense then is, "be continuously filled with the Spirit." In favor of the latter view, it may be urged that this is consistent with all prior uses of the phrase, "filled with the Spirit." Against this contention, however, it can be argued that prior usage can yield here only inductive probability. It cannot be completely definitive of the meaning of the phrase in this verse. The problem can only be settled by interpreting this phrase in its context, for neither the tense

[1] Dana and Mantey, *op. cit.,* p. 300.

nor the "significance of the verbal idea" offers a final solution.[2]

The sense in which the verb "be filled" is understood is affected by the antithetical parallelism in this verse between, "be not drunken with wine," and "be filled with the Spirit." This antithesis is not a contrast "between the *instruments* but between the *states*—between two elevated states, one due to the excitement of wine, the other to the inspiration and enlightenment of the Spirit." [3] The verb translated "be not drunken," in the first member of the parallelism, is also a present imperative, used here with the negative particle *mē* meaning "not." When the present imperative is thus used in prohibitions, "the present tense is properly used for expressing continued action." [4] As a matter of record, Robertson found that in a study of the present imperative, and the aorist subjunctive reprectively, in prohibitions, "The present imperative was found to be *regularly durative.*" [5] Therefore, since the present imperative in the the first member of the parallelism ("be not drunken with wine") is a continuous (durative) present, consistency dictates that the present imperative in the second half of the parallelism ("but be filled with the Spirit") be interpreted as a continuous present also. It may be more precisely translated thus: "Stop being continuously drunken with wine [6] . . . but be continuously filled with the Spirit."

Since the continuous (durative) idea is grammatically and contextually preferable to the iterative (repeated) sense of

[2] Dana and Mantey, *op. cit.,* p. 206. Rules for the interpretation of tense: "the *basal function of the tense,* the *relation to the context,* and *the significance of the verbal idea.*"

[3] Salmond, *op. cit.,* III, 363.

[4] Dana and Mantey, *op. cit.,* p. 301. Italics mine H.M.E.

[5] A. T. Roberston, *A Grammar of the Greek New Testament in the Light of Historical Research.* p. 890. Italics mine H.M.E.

[6] Dana & Mantey, *op. cit.,* p. 301. "A prohibition in the present imperative demands that action then in progress be stopped."

the verb, "be filled," it follows that this passage does not teach repeated refillings with the Holy Spirit.

One further question in relation to the phrase, "filled with the Spirit," remains to be resolved. The observant reader, as well as the student of New Testament Greek, will have noticed that two different words for "filled" have been used in the verse studied. The first word, *pimplēmi* or its variant *plētho,* is used in Acts 2:4; 4:8, 31; 9:17; and 13:9. However, *it was used only in the aorist tense,* and this is noteworthy. The second word, *plēroō,* was used twice, once in Acts 13:52 *in the imperfect tense,* and once in Eph. 5:18 *in the present tense.*

The basic definition of both words is the same, i.e., "to fill full." In addition, the second word (*plēroō*) has a secondary, or derived meaning, viz., "to complete or consummate," [7] in an absolute sense.[8] Entirely erroneous conclusions may, on occasion, be inferred from this derived meaning of the word. Any assumption that the filling with the Spirit referred to in Eph. 5:18 is qualitatively different from that described in the book of Acts, because *plēroō* is used rather than *pimplēmi,* is a completely fallacious inference. The implication, expressed or implied, that Eph. 5:18 means "go beyond the fulness of the Spirit received when you were baptized in the Spirit to a new, or absolute fulness of the Spirit," is likewise in error.

It is significant that the Cremer,[9] Thayer,[10] and Arndt, Gingrich, Bauer,[11] Greek Lexicons of the New Testament all list Eph. 5:18 under the primary meaning of the word

[7] Thayer, *op. cit.,* p. 518.
[8] Hermann Cremer, *Biblico-Theological Lexicon of New Testament Greek,* trans. by E. W. Simon and William Urwick (Edinburgh: T. & T. Clark, 1872), p. 519.
[9] *Ibid.,* p. 518.
[10] Thayer, *op. cit.,* p. 517.
[11] Arndt, Gingrich, Bauer, *op. cit.,* p. 677.

plēroō. None of these authorities ascribes the secondary meaning, "to perfect or consummate," to the use of the word in Eph. 5:18—and for a good grammatical reason.

The word used most frequently in the Acts, *pimplēmi* or *plēthō,* has a defective tense system in the New Testament, and related Christian literature. It is used only in the aorist tense, active and passive, and the future tense, passive voice. When the Biblical writers felt the need of another tense to convey a specific shade of meaning, they borrowed from the more complete tense system of *plēroō,* or, as in the case of Acts 7:55, used a comparable idiom. For instance, in this latter passage. Luke used a circumlocution for the unused present of *pimplēmi.* He achieved the same meaning by using the present participle of *huparchōn,* "being," and the predicate noun *plērēs,* "full." Again, in Acts 13:52, he filled out the incomplete tense system of *pimplēmi* with the imperfect tense borrowed from the word *plēroō.* So also in Eph. 5:18, lacking the present tense of *pimplēmi,*[12] Paul, or his scribe, simply used the present tense of *plēroō* to convey the same meaning of *plimplēmi.*

The choice, therefore, of *plēroō* in Eph. 5:18 was dictated by *grammatical,* and not by *theological* considerations. The use of one of these verbs over the other, in these foregoing instances, implies no difference in the degree or quality of the Spirit's fulness. It is fallacious theologizing to infer, on such specious grounds, that the baptism in the Holy Spirit does not result in a complete fulness of the Spirit in the Christian's life and witness.[13]

[12] Robertson, *A Grammar of the Greek New Testament in the Light of Historical Research,* p. 317.

[13] *Contra* Harold J. Sala, *An Investigation of the Baptizing and Filling Work of the Holy Spirit in the New Testament Related to the Pentecostal Doctrine of "Initial Evidence",* Unpublished Doctor of Philosophy dissertation, Bob Jones University, Greenville, South Carolina, 1966. This study was called to my attention after the manuscript of my own book was completed.

On the other hand, this does not affirm the opposite extreme. The baptism in the Holy Spirit is not a short cut in the Spirit's ministry of sanctification. Rather, the "Pentecostal" fulness of the Spirit opens one's understanding to the limitless vistas of spiritual potential set before every Christian. In a word, it is not a culmination of the Holy Spirit's activity, a sort of spiritual status symbol. Rather, it is a door into a charismatic dimension of limitless growth into the likeness of our Lord and Saviour, Jesus Christ.

CHAPTER XI

"One Baptism, Many Fillings" (?) [1]

To distinguish, as some do, an initial filling with the Holy Spirit, which one receives by the baptism in the Holy Spirit, from subsequent re-fillings with the Spirit, is, in our judgment, a doctrine neither stated nor implied in Scripture. It is supported by a series of deductions from an extra-Biblical definition of what constitutes the fulness of the Spirit.

For example, in explanation of this teaching, a highly respected colleague defined it for me thus: "the fulness of the Holy Spirit is much more than a charismatic outflow or empowering . . . the fruit of the Spirit is coordinate with the *charismata* as evidence of the Spirit's control of ones life." But this definition we deem wrong on both counts.

As for the first part of this definition, we reply that our Lord Jesus defined the limits of the baptism in = fulness of, the Spirit, as a charismatic empowering. Acts 1:8 makes this conclusion unmistakable: "But ye shall receive power (and the context makes it abundantly clear that He was referring to charismatic manifestations of this power), when the Holy Spirit is come upon you: and ye shall be my witnesses. . . ."

The subsequent evidence of the book of the Acts supports this view. In Acts 2:4, the disciples were filled with

1 Torrey, *op. cit.*, p. 212.

the Holy Spirit, and "began to speak with other tongues, as the Spirit gave them utterance." In this instance the fulness of the Spirit was evidenced by a charismatic outflowing of His personality in supernatural speech. Shortly after the Pentecostal enduement with the Spirit, a Spirit-filled Peter stood before the council of the Jewish nation, and boldly witnessed for Jesus. The lame man, healed at the temple gate, was exhibit A at the inquiry. Here also, *the evidence of the Spirit's fulness in the life of Peter was a charismatic miracle,* and *a charismatically charged witness.*

Similarly, a Spirit-filled Paul countered the attempts of the sorcerer Elymas, to divert the procounsul Sergius Paulus from the preaching of the Gospel, by pronouncing sentence of blindness upon the magician. In this instance also, the fulness of the Spirit was characterized by *a charismatic empowerment* of *word* and *deed.* So too, the events in Acts 4:31, when the place where the Christians were gathered together shook under the Spirit's activity, they were filled with the Holy Spirit, and they spoke the word with boldness—*all are charismatic manifestations.* The martyrdom of Stephen is further evidence of the charismatic nature of the Spirit's fulness, for in I Cor. 13:13 Paul listed *martyrdom with the charismatic manifestations* of tongues, prophecy, etc.

In the case of the Church's first "deacons," they were "men of good report, full of the Spirit and of wisdom" (Acts 6:3). Stephen especially was singled out from among them as one "full of grace and power," who "wrought great wonders and signs among the people" (Acts 6:8). Barnabas too is distinguished as "a good man, and full of the Holy Spirit and of faith." In each of these instances, the genitive phrases, "full of the Spirit" and "full of wisdom, full of faith," modify the noun by attibuting certain qualities to it. It is noteworthy, that "wisdom" and "faith" are not fruits of the Spirit. They are *charismatic empowerings* for service.

Only in Acts 13:52 is the fruit of the divine Spirit mentioned as a concomitant of the Spirit's fulness: "And the disciples were filled with joy and with the Holy Spirit." Here too, the context is one of charismatically empowered witness (cf. vs. 49). As we will show in greater detail in Chapter XX, the "fruit" of the Spirit is evidence of the "new birth," for "fruit" is a consequence of life in the Spirit. The "fruit of the Spirit" is not evidence of the baptism in/fulness of God's Spirit. It is the precondition of that fulness, for the "new birth" is a prior condition to the baptism in the Spirit. Manifestly, many Christians have shown the "fruit of the Spirit," in marked degree, who have never known the charismatic manifestations of the Spirit's power; nor is this a paradox, for "fruit" may be cultivated.

The further assumption, therefore, that "the fruit of the Spirit is coordinate with the *charismata* as evidence of the Spirit's control of one's life," arises from a confusion of the Spirit's sanctifying work with His charismatic empowering for service. But the sanctifying work of the Spirit is not contingent upon a charismatic experience. It proceeds independently of the charismatic manifestations of the Spirit's presence and power.

A lapse in the manifestations of the Spirit's "fruits" cannot justifiably be interpreted as a loss of the Spirit's "fulness." For example, Stephen was "full of faith and of wisdom," which are not "fruits" but charismatic enablings of the Holy Spirit. Yet in his denunciation of the Sanhedrin ("ye stiffnecked and uncircumcised in heart and ears" (Acts 7:51), he transgressed a spiritual principle later endorsed by Paul in similar circumstances. For, when rebuked for his own outburst at the unjust punishment meted out to him at the command of the High Priest, Paul acknowledged: "it is written, Thou shalt not speak evil of a ruler of thy people" (Acts 23:5). Was this passionate outburst on Stephen's part against the High Priest (Acts 7:1),—and the ruling council of his people (Acts 6:12),—extenuated though it was by the insufferable provocation to which he had been subjected—evidence that he had lost the Spirit's fulness?

By analogy, there are those who would argue that when Paul and Barnabas engaged in angry controversy over Mark (Acts 15:39), that this is evidence that they had forfeited the fulness of the Holy Spirit in their lives. Consistency would demand that the same be said of Stephen. But Scripture records that though he too was "a man subject to like passions" (James 5:17 KJV), it was the fulness of the Spirit that gave him supernatural courage to accept the martyrs crown. And if this can be said of Stephen, the same can be said of Paul and Barnabas. Human fraility is not *ipso facto* evidence that one has lost the fulness of the Spirit of God.

To carry the discussion one step further, Peter reacted incredulously to the vision of the sheet let down from heaven full of beasts and creeping things (Acts 10:1ff), even reacting against the divine command to "kill and eat." Years of religious training asserted itself when he ejaculated, "Not so Lord." Such a reflex reaction is a far cry from wilfull and premeditated disobedience. It cannot, therefore, be deduced that he ceased to be filled with the Holy Spirit because of this remark. If, as some suggest, Peter lost the Spirit's fulness as a consequence of his involuntary remark, then we ask: When? and How? was he *subsequently refilled* with the Spirit? Any answer to this question rests upon sheer speculation. Yet he went straightway to Caesarea, and there witnessed in the power of the Holy Spirt to Cornelius, and the Spirit of God fell in charismatic fulness upon this Gentile household. It was a *Spirit-filled* Apostle who produced these results.

Without belaboring the point further, certain conclusions may be reiterated. The obvious error in this premise, and its consequent deductions, is shown by its inner contradictions. If the continuing fulness of the Holy Spirit is contingent upon human fraility, then the fulness of the Spirit ceases to be a gift of grace, and becomes a product of human merit. If the fulness of the Spirit is initially a free gift of grace, but continuous fullness is conditioned by cultivation of the fruits of the Spirit, then one's power as witness ought to be in direct ratio to their cultivation of the Spirit's fruit. To argue that because Barnabas and Paul came to an angry disputation over Mark's default, or that because Peter in a momentary vacillation dissembled before the Judaizers in Galatia (Gal, 2:11-14), that they therefore lost the Spirit's fulness in their lives implies that they also lost their effectiveness as witnesses. But these are not facts of exegesis. They are the logical fall-out from an *a priori* theological assumption relating to the nature of the fulness of the Spirit.

Proponents of this theory have overlooked an important facet of the discussion that further militates against their view. While Scripture does not coordinate the fruits of the Spirit with the *charismata* as evidence of the fulness of the Spirit, Paul does equate *quenching* the Spirit with wilfull depreciation of the Holy Spirit's supernatural gifts: e.g., "Stop quenching the Spirit, stop despising prophesyings" (I Tess. 5:19-20). It is not, therefore, neglect of the fruits of God's Spirit, but contempt for His gifts that restricts Him.

This does not deny that the practical consequences of the Holy Spirit's influence in the life of the Christian are reflected in holy impulses and aspirations conducive to conforming the believer to the image of Christ. We do deny, however, that the attainment, and maintenance, of a certain degree of sanctification is indispensable to the Spirit's abiding fulness in us. The charismatic fulness of God's Spirit is called "the gift of the Holy Spirit." Grace and works of human merit are just as incompatible in the Pentecostal experience as they are in the Salvation experience.

It has been our personal observation that this teaching of an initial filling with subsequent refillings with the Holy Spirit has been a source of paralysis to the life and witness of many Spirit-filled Christians. In multiplied scores of charismatic services, defeated albeit Spirt-filled Christians have come to the altars requesting prayer for a refilling with the Holy Spirit. Their testimony runs something like this: "I recived the baptism in the Holy Spirit 'X' number of years ago. But I have lost the love, the joy, the peace I once knew. Pray that the Holy Spirit will fill me again."

Having been taught that the absence of any of the above gracements is evidence that they have lost the Spirit's fulness, their only recourse is to seek and to tarry for a "refilling"—and as often to go away disappointed. Such dispirited people go from one service to the next, looking for the right evangelist or Bible teacher to lay his hands upon them, and pray them full of the Spirit again. If the desired joy, peace, emotional response (or whatever else they have come to identify in their own minds as evidence of the fulness of the Spirit) is not forthcoming, they go away saddened, sometimes disillusioned, to await the next evangelist, pastor, or Bible teacher. This is a travesty of Jesus' promise, "Ye shall receive power after that the Holy Spirit is come upon you and ye shall be my witnesses." The real tragedy is this, that these very people have been endued with power, but refuse to believe it, or to act upon it, because they have been taught otherwise. So they sit forlornly by rather than moving obediently in Spirit-filled witness to a lost humanity, trusting the Spirit to manifest Himself sovereignly and charismatically whenever and wherever they bear witness to Jesus as Saviour and Lord.

Perhaps the real source of the difficulty is in the innate penchant of the human mind to pictorialize the Holy Spirit's fulness in spacial and quantitative terms, as though He were a measurable quantity. He is, however, a Person, infinitely loving, steadfast, forgiving, more anxious to bless then we are to accept His blessings. Time after time, we have counselled with doubt ridden Christians, explaining this simple, yet transcendent fact to them. We have encouraged them to believe, that if they have been baptized in the Spirit they are filled with the Spirit. They need but to "stir up the gift" which is in them. We have further counselled them to yield to Him again, just as they did when Jesus baptized them in the Holy Spirit, and as they worshipped Him to yield their tongues to His inexpressibly personal self-manifestation "in other tongues." In the natural realm, it is the *overflow* that brings blessing. Repeatedly, it has been our joy to see such Christians delivered from the bondage of stultifying dogma, which had convinced them that they could do nothing effective for Jesus unless, and until they were refilled with the Holy Spirit—with whatever manifestations they had been taught to expect as evidence of this refilling.

Is this an over simplification of the theological subtleties we have been discussing? Of course not! Was it not just such counsel Paul offered to his hard pressed young protege Timothy, when he wrote: "stir up the gift (*charisma*) of God, which is in thee *through the laying on of my hands*" (II Tim. 1:6). In our opinion, the "gift" to which Paul here referred is not the "gift" (*dorea*, Acts 2:38) of the Holy Spirit *per se*, but the "gift" (*charisma*) that accompanied Timothy's baptism in the Spirit through *the laying on of*

Paul's hands, namely, utterance in other tongues. For so it was also in the experience of his Ephesian converts, when Paul *"laid his hands upon them,* (and) the Holy Spirt came on them; and they spake with tongues and prophesied" (Acts 19:6).

We may push the discussion one step further by asking, what, if any, Scriptural provision is made for maintaining a Spirit-filled experience? Paul's answer in Ephesians 5:18 and 19 is simple and direct, that is to say, by charismatic worship: "continue to be filled with the Spirit; speaking one to another in psalms and hymns and spiritual songs." (The reader is urged to turn to the Supplement to Chapter XVI for a discussion of Paul's use of *pneumatikos,* "spiritual," especially the exegetical note there on this very passage.)

The effect of such charismatic worship—specifically, tongues-speech—is alluded to by Paul in I Cor. 14:5, e.g., "He that speaketh in a tongue *edifieth himself.*" He, furthermore, acknowledged its value in his own experience, saying: "If I pray in a tongue my spirit prayeth . . . ;" "I will pray with the spirit (i.e., in tongues) . . . ;" "I will sing with the spirit (i.e., in tongues) . . . ;" "I thank God, I speak with tongues more than you all. . . ."

The baptism in the Holy Spirit is not *per se* an emotional experience, nor can the continuing fulness of the Spirit be equated with one's transitory emotional experiences, or lack of them—an all too common fallacy on both sides of the charismatic dialogue. We have argued from Scripture that the baptism in, and fulness of the Spirit are synonymous; and furthermore, that a charismatic dimension is evidence of the Holy Spirit's fulness. Consistency dictates then that the continuing manifestations of this charismatic dimension are abiding evidence of the Spirit's fulness in Christian experience. Consequently, the nurture of these charismatic manifestations "edifies," that is to say, maintains the charismatic flow of the Holy Spirit's fulness. Nor have we improved upon Paul's simple formula: "stir up the gift of God, which is in thee through the laying on of my hands."

CHAPTER XII

The Pattern of Pentecost

"Verily, verily, I say unto you, he that believeth on me, the works that I do shall be do also; and greater works than these shall he do; because I go unto the Father." [1] By prophecy and promise, the normal Christian life is charismatic. In walk, in witness and in worship, the normal Christian church is a charismatic community. It is, in a word, "Pentecostal," for the source of its charismatic enablings is a personal Pentecost.

The normative pattern of the baptism in the Holy Spirit was summarized in five propositions in Chapter VII. Of the five statements deduced there, the first two are self-evident, the fifth has already been discussed in detail. Now an exposition of the Biblical evidence for the third and fourth propositions will be offered.

The third proposition restated says, that the baptism in the Holy Spirit is not synonymous with conversion and the "new birth." It is subsequent to regeneration. The fourth says, that the normative evidence of the baptism in the Holy Spirit is a charismatic manifestation of the Holy Spirit's personality and power. In a word, the initial evidence of the "Pentecostal" baptism in the Spirit is "tongues as the Spirit Himself gives utterance."

[1] John 14:12.

I. *Pentecost—Acts 2:1-4*

The evidence for Acts 2:4 has been given in sufficient detail to justify only a brief recapitulation here. The disciples of Jesus were "born again" on the resurrection day when He breathed on them and said, "Receive ye the Holy Spirit." Some fifty days later, "when the day of Pentecost was now come," the promised "gift of the Spirit" was poured out by our ascended Lord upon those gathered in the upper room. This was the baptism in the Holy Spirit prophesied by John, and promised by Jesus. In consequence of this Spirit-baptism, "they were all filled with the Holy Spirit," and in evidence of His overflowing presence, "began to speak with other tongues, as the Spirit gave them utterance."

Clearly then, the activity of the Holy Spirit in their regeneration was separated from their baptism in the Spirit by an interval of some seven weeks. Furthermore, when they were baptized in the Spirit, the initial manifestation of His abiding presence and power was speech in other tongues. In fact, His initial self-manifestation is uniformly "speech," and appropriately so; for the promised power of the Holy Spirit is fittingly manifested first in the organ preeminently associated with witnessing, namely, the tongue. And this is in complete accord with the purpose of the "Pentecostal" enduement as announced by Jesus: "but *ye shall receive* power, when the Holy Spirit is come upon you: and *ye shall be my witnesses* . . . unto the uttermost part of the earth."

II. *The Second Jerusalem "Pentecost"—Acts 4:31*

The "Pentecostal" effusion of the Spirit was repeated again a short time later, according to Acts 4:31. In the interim, the number of converts had increased to about five thousand men. These were now numbered among the company of believers comprising the growing Church. Subsequent to their conversion, they too were filled with the Holy Spirit. The sequence of events is clear thus far, and though tongues are not explicitly mentioned, attendant circumstances prompt the inference that they were part of the total pattern.

When Peter and John were released from custody by the Sanhedrin, their recital of the duress and threats to which they had been subjected initiated a prayer meeting of the whole Church to meet the challenge. Their prayer contained a three-fold request. *One,* "grant unto thy servants to speak thy word with all boldness." [2] i.e., in the face of threatened persecution, the full fury of which was soon to explode in the stoning of Stephen, the first Christian martyr. *Two,* "while thou stretchest forth thy hand to heal," [3] especially significant since it was the healing of the lame man at the gate of the temple, and the resultant evangelistic success of Peter and John that brought them into collision with the Sanhedrin. *Three,* "and that signs and wonders may be done through the name of thy Holy Servant Jesus." [4]

Then followed the second outpouring of the Holy Spirit, as at Pentecost, for (1) "the place was shaken wherein they were gathered together;" (2) "they were filled with the Holy Spirit," and (3) "they spake the word of God with boldness." [5] Even a superficial perusal of the ensuing context validates the judgment, that, "They were thus endued both with courage to declare the word of God *and with miraculous power for confirming its truth.*" [6]

[2] Acts 4:29.
[3] Acts 4:30.
[4] *Ibid.*
[5] Acts 4:31.
[6] Horatio B. Hackett, *A Commentary on the Acts of the Apostles, An American Commentary on the New Testament,* (Philadelphia: American Baptist Publications Society, 1882). p. 72. Italics mine H.M.E.

In response to their entreaty, there was an immediate divine manifestation, for "the place was shaken wherein they were gathered together; and they were all filled with the Holy Spirit." This was followed by a subsequent enablement, for "they spake the word of God with boldness," and confirmatory signs and wonders were done by the Apostles,[7] at the hands of Stephen,[8] and by Phillip.[9] The whole context is a charismatic one. Great "signs" (*semeia*, "miracles"), and "wonders" (*terata*, "prodigies"), exorcisms and healings—in such a charismatic context, it is more consistent to affirm, than to deny, that the initial "Pentecostal" charism of tongues were in evidence among these *semeia*, "signs," and *terata*, "wonders." These were among the "signs" intended to confirm the preaching of the gospel according to Mark 16:17-20.[10] Verse 20 concludes thus: "And they went forth, and preached everywhere, the Lord working with them, and confirming the word by the signs that followed." Whether or not one accepts the authenticity of this much debated passage, Acts 8:6 explicitly corroborates the confirmatory function of these charismatic signs, e.g., "And the multitude gave heed with one accord unto the things that were spoken by Philip, when they heard, and saw the signs which he did." Paul adds the weight of his testimony in these words: "Wherefore tongues are for a sign, not to them that believe, but to the unbelieving." Tongues were among the "signs" both *heard* and *seen* in Jerusalem, Caesarea, Ephesus, and Corinth. It is, therefore, an inference consistent with an oft repeated pattern to suggest that they too spoke in tongues when filled

[7] Acts 5:12.
[8] Acts 6:8.
[9] Acts 8:6, 7.
[10] The authenticity of the traditional ending is not really at issue here, for it at least represents a very ancient understanding, current within the Church, of its charismatic life and ministry.

with the Spirit according to Acts 4:31. It is a reflection of an
a priori bias against tongues *per se* to insist that the Pentecostal pattern of the baptism in the Holy Spirit was interrupted short of tongues simply because they are not mentioned explicitly in this place.

III. *The Samaritan "Pentecost"—Acts 8:14-17*

The next recorded manifestation of the Pentecostal effusion of the Spirit is recorded in Acts 8. The martyrdom of
Stephen triggered the first general persecution of the fledg-
ling Church. It resulted in the dispersion of all but the
Apostles from Jerusalem. Phillip, one of the seven "deacons," chosen because he was "full of the Spirit and wisdom," went down to the city of Samaria and preached
Jesus. Revival was the result as the "winds" of the Spirit
swept over the people, "And the multitudes gave heed with
one accord unto the things that were spoken by Phillip,
when they heard, and saw the signs which he did. For
from many of those that had unclean spirits, they came out,
crying with a loud voice: and many that were palsied, and
that were lame, were healed . . . But when they believed
Phillip preaching good tidings concerning the kingdom of
God and the name of Jesus Christ, they were baptized, both
men and women." [11] The sequence of events gives clear evidence that these Samaritans had become Christians in the
fullest sense of the word. They believed on Jesus, and were
baptized in the water by Phillip. This is obviously an instance of believer's baptism predicated, as it is, upon saving
faith in Christ, the prior condition for the "new birth."
These Samaritan converts thus experienced the regenerative work of the Holy Spirit in their lives.

The implications in the sequel need to be underscored
here, for "when the apostles that were at Jerusalem heard

[11] Acts 8:6, 7, 12.

that Samaria had received the word of God, they sent unto them Peter and John: [12] who, when they were come down, prayed for them, that they might receive the Holy Spirit: for as yet it (He) was fallen upon [13] none of them, only they had been baptized into the name of the Lord Jesus. Then laid they their hands on them, and they received the Holy Spirit." [14]

The order of the events parallels the pattern of the baptism in/filling with the Holy Spirit already deduced. First, saving faith in Jesus Christ, with its concomitant "new birth," followed by believer's baptism in water, the symbol of this regenerative experience. Then some time later—i.e., the time necessary for news of the revival to travel from Samaria to Jerusalem, and for the Apostles there to send two of their number to Samaria to investigate—Peter and John came down, and, "They laid their hands on them, and they received [15] the Holy Spirit." It is noteworthy here

[12] Robertson, *Word Pictures in the New Testament*, III, 106. "The sending of Peter and John was no reflection on Phillip, but was an appropriate mission since 'many Christian Jews would be scandalized by the admission of Samaritans' (Furneau). If Peter and John sanctioned it, the situation would be improved."

[13] From the verb *epipipto*, "to fall upon, to recline, to come upon." Cf., also Acts 8:16, 39 marginal reading; 10:44; 11:15. Arndt, Gingrich, Bauer, *op. cit.*, p. 297, "fall upon something, approach someone impetuously." The word implies the external origin of the Holy Spirit's operation. He falls upon from without, before He wells up from within. One cannot be filled until they have been immersed in Him.

[14] Acts 8:14-17.

[15] One might ask, how? or in what sense the work of the Holy Spirit in regeneration differs from His activity in the baptism? In the "new birth" we first receive Jesus Christ as personal Saviour and Lord, and from Him we receive the "authority", i.e., privilege *"to be"* or *"to become"* something: e.g., "to all who did receive him . . . he gave the right to become children of God . . . the offspring of God Himself" (John 1:12, 13 NEB; cf. I Peter 1:23). In the baptism in the Spirit we receive power (*dunamis*) "to do." The "new birth" is an ontological change in our nature, the baptism in the spirit is the "gift of the Spirit" in supernatural enablement for service. This empowerment, or *dunamis* is "power in operation, in action; not merely *power capable of action, but power in action*." Cremer, *op. cit.*, p. 200.

that Peter and John did not baptize again these Samaritan
converts in water before laying their hands upon them for
the reception of the Spirit, as Paul did later with the disciples of John the Baptist, whom he met at Ephesus. Obviously, these two representatives of the apostolic "synod" at
Jerusalem were satisfied that these Samaritan disciples were
"saved," in consequence of the Holy Spirit's regenerative
work accomplished through Phillip's preaching of the word.

The accompanying episode is in one sense cryptic, yet
nonetheless illuminating, for, "when Simon saw that
through the laying on of the apostles' hands the Holy Spirit
was given, he offered them money, saying, Give me also
this power, that on whomsoever I lay hands, he may receive
the Holy Spirit." [16] Signs and great miracles, including healings and exorcisms,[17] were performed by Phillip without
producing this result upon Simon the sorcerer, and so
arousing his cupidity. The question remains to be answered:
What did Simon "see" that convinced him that these Samaritan Christians had received the Holy Spirit through the
laying on of the hands of Peter and John? It is said that,
"a man convinced against his will is of the same opinion
still," and this is not the intent of the present author. However, for the unbiased enquirer, as well as the charismatic
Christian, there is considerable value in the answers given
to this question by scholars who cannot be accused of a
"Pentecostal" bias. The more so since their views cannot be
discounted as a "Pentecostal" apologetic.

Writing of what Simon "saw," Adam Clarke characterized it thus: "By hearing these speak with different tongues
and work miracles." [18] Heinrich Meyer's opinion is that

[16] Acts 8:18, 19.
[17] Acts 8:7, 13.
[18] Adam Clarke, *The New Testament of our Lord and Saviour Jesus
Christ, a Commentary and Critical Notes*, I, (New York: T. Mason, & G.
Lane, 1837), 741.

"The communication of the Spirit was visible . . . in the gestures and gesticulations of those who received it, perhaps also in similar phenomena to those which took place at Pentecost in Jerusalem." [19] The American editor of Meyer's Commentary, William Ormiston, appealed to Calvin's comment in the following vein: "Calvin on verse 16 writes: 'Surely Luke speaketh not in this place of the common grace of the Spirit, whereby God doth regenerate us, that we may be his children; but of those singular gifts, wherewith God would have certain endued at the beginning of the gospel to beautify Christ's kingdom." [20] To this Ormiston adds his own comment thus: "By the *Holy Ghost* we do not understand the regenerating and sanctifying agency of the Holy Spirit in the conversion and renewal of the soul; but the impartation of such a presence of the Holy Spirit as is accompanied with supernatural gifts; the miraculous influences of the Spirit, which were manifested by speaking with tongues, or other visible tokens." [21] N. B. Stonehouse is quoted to the same effect by F. F. Bruce, that the Spirit's operation here is subsequent to the "new birth:" "The prior operation of the Spirit in regeneration and faith is not in view here." [22] Bruce's own view is equally unambiguous, for he says: "The context leaves us in no doubt that their reception of the Spirit was attended by external manifestations such as had marked His descent on the earliest disciples at Pentecost." [23] The terse comment of A. T. Robertson is in the same vein: "This participle (second aorist active of *horaō*) shows plainly that those who received the

[19] Meyer, *Critical and Exegetical Handbook to the Acts of the Apostles*, p. 171.

[20] *Ibid.*, p. 180. The exception to Calvin's view urged here is that the Scriptures do not limit the baptism in the Spirit to a select few in the apostolic age.

[21] *Ibid.*, p. 180.

[22] F. F. Bruce, *Commentary on the Book of the Acts*, footnote, p. 181.

[23] *Ibid.*, p. 181.

gift of the Holy Spirit spoke with tongues." [24] Equally suc-
cinct and direct is the remark of F. J. Foakes-Jackson: "The
gift is manifested openly, possibly (though this is not
stated) by *Glossolalia*." [25]

Thus an analysis of the context justifies the conclusion
that these Samaritans received the baptism in the Holy
Spirit after their conversion, with the probable evidence of
speaking in tongues.

IV. *The Ethiopian Eunuch's "Pentecost"—Acts 8:38*

The normative Biblical pattern of the baptism in the
Spirit is reflected again in a curious marginal reading on
Acts 8:9. In place of the accepted reading, "the Spirit of the
Lord caught away Phillip," several manuscripts and Church
Fathers read, "The Spirit of the Lord fell upon the eunuch,
and the angel of the Lord snatched away Phillip." This
variant reading probably arose, according to Henry Alford,
"from a desire to conform the results of the eunuch's baptism to the usual method of the divine procedure." [26] This
is simply reiterating the fundamental premise of this study,
viz., *there is a normative pattern in the Spirit's* activity;
(1) in converson and its attendant regeneration (symbolized
by water baptism), and (2) the baptism in the Holy Spirit
subsequent to conversion.

This is also categorically spelled out in the declaration,
that "the much more important effect of the longer reading
is to make clear that the Ethiopian's baptism i.e., in water
was followed by the gift of the Spirit. However, even with
the shorter reading it is a safe inference that he did receive
the Spirit." [27] If one may "safely" infer this from the shorter

---

[24] Robertson, *Word Pictures in the New Testament,* III, 107.
[25] Cf., Knowling, *op. cit.,* p. 227.
[26] Henry Alford, *The Greek Testament,* II (5th ed.; Cambridge: Deighton,
Bell, and Co., 1865), 96.
[27] F. F. Bruce, *Commentary on the Book of the Acts,* p. 190.

reading, then it is equally valid to infer from the studied conformity of the longer reading "to the usual method of the divine procedure," that the entire pattern of the Pentecostal enduement with power is implied—including the evidence of *glossolalia*. Surely the context suggests that the Ethiopian's immediate reaction to the effusion of the divine Spirit was vocal, for "he went on his way rejoicing." However, A. T. Robertson's comment in another context is appropriate at this point: "One will believe here as the facts appeal to him." [28]

V. *Paul's "Pentecost"—Acts 9:1-19*

The personal Pentecost of Saul (Paul) is related in Acts 9:1-19. The facts are simply related. Paul met Jesus in a "theophany" while journeying to Damascus with warrants from the high priest at Jerusalem for the arrest of the Christians residing there. Escorted into the city, blinded as a result of this encounter with the living Son of God, he spent the next three days and nights in fasting and prayer. Meanwhile, the Lord appeared in a vision to a disciple, Ananias, probably one of the local community of believers, whom He commissioned to go to Paul, and to minister to him as "a chosen vessel." Reluctantly the former agreed, and verse 17 recounts how, "Ananias departed, and entered into the house; and laying his hands on him said, Brother Saul, the Lord, even Jesus, who appeared unto thee in the way which thou camest, hath sent me, that thou mayest receive thy sight, and be filled with the Holy Spirit." From the preceding context, it is clear that Ananias knew who Saul was, and that he had come to Damascus to persecute the Christians there. He would never, therefore, have entered Saul's presence and addressed him as, "Brother Saul," unless he had been reassured that Saul was, in very truth,

---

[28] Robertson, *Word Pictures in the New Testament*, III, 342.

a "Brother in Christ." [29] Saul must have become a Christian, in the fullest sense of the word, before Ananias came in to him. Can anyone sincerely doubt but that he was saved in his encounter with the glorified Saviour outside the city of Damascus?

If the narrative is clear and direct, so also are the conclusions to be drawn from it. It was in the Damascus road encounter that the "persecutor" of the Church became a disciple of Christ Jesus. He was "saved," and three days later he was healed of his blindness and "filled with," that is to say "baptized in" the Holy Spirit when Ananias laid his hands upon him in the name of Jesus. Here too, the pattern is consistent. First, conversion and its concomitant "new birth," and after that "filled with the Holy Spirit."

In passing, it should be noted that this is the second instance wherein the "Pentecostal" enduement was mediated through the laying on of hands by those who had themselves been filled with the Spirit. In this case, it is also noteworthy that the human instrument was not an apostle. He was simply a believer. The emphasis is not upon the human instrument, but upon the divine Administrator; for indeed, "Ananias laid his hands on Saul, but it was the power of Christ that in the same moment enlightened his eyes and filled him with the Holy Spirit." [30] It was not apostolic prerogative, but the authority of our Saviour's Name that validated the laying on of his hands. Jesus commissioned believers to perform a number of signs in His name, including "laying their hands upon the sick" [31] for their healing. This is precisely what Ananias obediently did, and Jesus both healed Saul (Paul) and filled him with His Spirit. It is a kind of exegetical "double vision" that would try to

[29] Robertson, *Word Pictures in the New Testament*, III, 121.
[30] F. F. Bruce, *Commentary on the Book of the Acts*, p. 201.
[31] Mark 16:18.

divorce the laying on of believer's hands for healing, from the laying on of their hands for the reception of the Spirit of promise.[32]

It is sometimes urged at this point, that Paul did not speak in tongues when he was filled with the Spirit. At least, it is not specifically mentioned in the text. On this basis, it is deduced, that the Pentecostal pattern of the baptism was interrupted short of utterance in other tongues, therefore others too may be baptized in the Spirit without manifesting tongues as evidence. However, before such a judgment can be accepted as definitive, Paul's own testimony must be considered, for he wrote: "I thank God, I speak with tongues more than you all." [33] Whether he spoke in tongues immediately or later is of little consequence to the major premise here. As the record consistently bears witness, there is a causal sequence and connection between being filled with/baptized in the Holy Spirit and speaking with tongues. Here the onus of proof rests with those who would dispute this causal sequence. It is a reasonable assumption then to affirm that Paul too spoke with other tongues when he received the Pentecostal gift of the Holy Spirit.

VI. *The Roman "Pentecost"—Acts 10:44-46*

Some ten years after Pentecost, Peter was summoned to the home of a Roman centurion, Cornelius by name. In spite of his exclusive Jewish scruples, allayed in part by a divine vision, he left Joppa for Caesarea, and there proclaimed to Cornelius and his household the promised

---

[32] Knowling, *op. cit.*, II, 237. To say, as Knowling does, that Ananias laid his hands on Paul, "not as bestowing the Holy Ghost (for see context), but as recovering from his blindness," ignores the immediate, and the larger context.

[33] I Cor. 14:14.

"words whereby thou shalt be saved." [34] Cornelius was, in all probability, "a God-fearing proselyte" [35] in relationship with the synagogue, through which he may have acquired the knowledge of Jesus' life that Peter assumed.[36] Jesus' baptism, miracles, crucifixion, resurrection—all are touched on by him. Apparently this is a summary of a much more detailed discourse.

The call to decision was pressed upon the Roman in the following words: "To him bear all the prophets witness, that through his name every one that believeth on him shall receive remission of sins." [37] The order of events sketched by Peter closely paralleled the sequence given by Jesus Himself: "Thus it is written, that the Christ should suffer, and rise again from the dead the third day; and that repentance and remission of sins should be preached in his name unto all the nations, beginning from Jerusalem." [38] Crucifixion, resurrection, repentance and remission of sins are plainly delineated, for decision, to be intelligent, must be rooted in an apprehension of Truth. Significantly, the commission in Luke's gospel closes with the words: "And behold, I send forth the promise of my Father upon you." [39] As previously noted, *"The promise of the Father" refers to the Pentecostal gift of the Holy Spirit*, which Peter declared prophetically on the day of Pentecost is not only for Jewish converts, but "to all that are afar off, *even* as many as the Lord our God shall call unto him." [40] Consistent with the pattern given in the Gospel according to Luke, as Peter preached, and Cornelius and his household received the

[34] Acts 11:14.
[35] Knowling, *op. cit.,* II, 251.
[36] Acts 10:1-11:48.
[37] Acts 10:37.
[38] Luke 24:46-47.
[39] Luke 24:49.
[40] Acts 2:38.

word with saving faith, Jesus poured out the promised gift of the Holy Spirit upon the Roman, now Christian household.

Whether or not this was a repetition of Pentecost has sometimes been challenged. However, Peter's words before the Jerusalem congregation, in defense of his entering a Gentile home, leave little room for argument, for, said he, "as I began to speak, the Holy Spirit fell on them, *even as on us at the beginning*." [41] He is obviously referring to the Spirit's advent at Pentecost, and not to the reception of the Holy Spirit when Jesus breathed new spiritual life into them on the Resurrection day.

Furthermore, the outpouring of the Spirit in the house of Cornelius is described as "the gift of the Spirit." [42] By this phrase, Luke does not refer to the work of the Holy Spirit in regeneration, but to the Pentecostal baptism in the Spirit for power. That tongues are the evidence of the baptism in/filling with the Holy Spirit is unmistakably clear in this place. In fact, the Hebrew believers who accompanied Peter knew that these Gentiles had received "the gift of the Holy Spirit," "For (*gar* [43] equivalent to 'because') they heard them speak with tongues and magnify God."

VII. *The Ephesian "Pentecost"—Acts 19:1–6*

Almost twenty-five years [44] had elapsed since Pentecost, when Paul met certain disciples of John the Baptist, at Ephesus. Learning that they knew only the baptism of John, which was a baptism of repentance, he expounded the gospel more accurately to them, pointing to Jesus as

---

[41] Acts 11:15. Italics mine H.M.E.

[42] Acts 10:45.

[43] Acts 10:46, *gar*, a conjunction "used to express cause, inference, continuation, or to explain." Arndt, Gingrich, Bauer, *op. cit.*, p. 151.

[44] Phillip Schaff, *History of the Christian Church*, I (New York: Charles Scribner's Sons, 1887), 220, 221.

the fulfillment of John's ministry—and then he re-baptized them. Luke recorded the scene in this fashion: "And Paul said, John baptized with the baptism of repentance, saying unto the people that they should believe on him that should come after him, that is, on Jesus. And when they heard this, they were baptized into the name of the Lord Jesus. And when Paul had laid his hands upon them, the Holy Spirit came on them; and they spake with tongues, and prophesied."

Once again the order of events is so clearly marked as to obviate dispute. One can scarcely improve on the observation, "They were therefore baptized again in a Christian sense, and when Paul laid his hands on them, they received the Holy Spirit in Pentecostal fashion." [45] The evidential nature of the *glossolalia* here is heavily underscored by the comment, that "The speaking with tongues and prophesying was external and indubitable proof that the Holy Spirit had come on these twelve uninformed disciples now fully won to the service of Jesus as Messiah." [46] The unequivocal affirmation, "external and indubitable proof," may not be palatable in some theological and ecclesiastical circles, but it is nonetheless consistent with the norm presented in the Scriptures.[47]

[45] F. F. Bruce, *Commentary on the Book of Acts,* p. 386.

[46] Robertson, *Word Pictures in the New Testament,* III, 313.

[47] The context here is a telling rebuttal of Harold Sala's (*op. cit.,* p. 126) appeal to the participle of coincident action in Acts 19:2—"Did ye receive the Holy Spirit when ye believed." The grammatical argument upon which he rests his case is ambiguous, if not outright contradictory. For example, A. T. Robertson (*A Grammar of the Greek New Testament in the Light of Historical Research,* p. 1113) quoted the observation of Moulton "that when the verb *precedes* the aorist participle it is nearly always the participle of coincident action." Yet less than a dozen lines after this quotation, Dr. Robertson himself noted that it is "a characteristic of Luke's style to use frequently the coincident participle (both aorist and present) *placed after* the principle verb." The decisive factor in this discussion is, however, the context. Paul's question must be interpreted in the light of his own subsequent words and actions, if we are to understand what he really meant. When first

The generic relationship of this Ephesian outpouring of the Holy Spirit with the effusion of the Spirit at Pentecost is revealed in the statement, "the Holy Spirit came on them; and they spake with tongues and prophesied." In a discussion in Chapter VI of this study, the reader's attention has already been directed to an often overlooked detail in the interpretation of Acts 2:4. There the word translated "utterance" (i.e., "they began to speak with other tongues, as the Spirit gave them utterance") is used in the Septuagint, version of the Old Testament, not of ordinary conversation, but of the utterance of prophets. From this fact, we concluded, that while on the day of Pentecost the newly Spirit-baptized disciples spoke supernaturally in tongues (i.e., languages they neither knew nor understood themselves), the representatives of the various language groups who heard and understood them speaking in their dialects, heard not tongues but inspired prophecy in their own languages. They heard the disciples extol prophetically the "magnificence" of God. likewise in Ephesus, these two related aspects of inspired utterance are combined, for "they spake with tongues, and prophesied." [48]

In Ephesus also, the normal pattern of the baptism in the Holy Spirit was repeated. Hearing from Paul that Jesus is

---

he baptized these Ephesian converts in water (certainly evidence of their prior salvation), then laid his hands upon them and the Holy Spirit came upon them with "Pentecostal" manifestations, we have the key to his prior inquiry. To illustrate his meaning more clearly, we could paraphrase his question thus: "Did ye receive the Holy Spirit in 'Pentecostal' fulness subsequent to your conversion;" for when they received the Holy Spirit through the laying on of Paul's hands, *this is precisely the way they did receive Him.*

[48] Meyer, *Critical and Exegetical Handbook to the Acts* of the Apostles, p. 367. Meyer's comment is wrong e.g., "These two must according to the technical mode of reference to them in the apostolic church attested by I Cor. xii-xiv, be *distinguished,* and not treated as equivalent, with van Hengel, who finds here merely in general an expression of the inspired praising aloud of God in Christ."

the fulfillment of John's ministry, they believed and received Christian baptism from him. Certainly their regeneration was a prior condition to their baptism in water. Then after their water baptism, their baptism in the Spirit followed—mediated by the laying on of Paul's hands. The point to be emphasized here is that *Paul did not lay his hands on John's disciples to receive the Holy Spirt until after they had received Jesus Christ as Saviour.* He laid his hands upon them only after he was assured that they had become truly Christian. Consistent with the normative pattern of this Biblical experience, when they received the Spirit of the living God in charismatic fulness, they manifested His over-flowing presence by speaking with other tongues.

CHAPTER XIII

They All Spoke With Tongues

The Jews, the Samaritans, the Romans, the persecuting Pharisee, the Ethiopian proselyte, the disciples of John the Baptist—out of all men everywhere until the end of the age, "whosoever shall call upon the name of the Lord shall be saved." And when saved, receive as a birthright, the promised "baptism in the Holy Spirit." For the promised "gift of the Holy Spirit" is to all that are afar off, *even* as many as the Lord our God shall call unto him." And whether stated, or implied, it is a fair conclusion from the Biblical evidence, that tongues are the "external and indubitable proof" of the baptism in/filling with the Holy Spirit.

In the author's opinion, a baptism in the Spirit without the charismatic evidence is not a Biblical datum. It is a theological improvisation dictated by sub-apostolic experience to extenuate the impotence of the Church's life and ministry in the face of secularism, humanism, and atheistic materialism. So it is that other "evidences" of the Spirit-empowered life have been advanced. Perhaps most noteworthy of these is the assertion that Love is the evidence of the baptism in the Holy Spirit. But this is not scriptural. Love is evidence of conversion and the "new birth," for, "We know that we have passed out of death into life, because we love the brethren." [1] Thus Love is not the evidence of the baptism in the Holy Spirit; it is a presupposition of this baptism.

It is likewise often urged, on the basis of I Cor. 12:11—"but all these worketh the one and the same Spirit, dividing to each one severally even as he will"—that the manifestation of any of the "gifts" listed in this context is the evidence that one has been baptized in/filled with the Spirit. The fallacy in this reasoning is its tacit either/or premise, i.e., *either* prophecy, *or* gifts of healing, *or* discernings of spirits, etc., *instead of* tongues. But the disciples healed the sick,[2] spoke prophetically,[3] cast out demons,[4] all before Pentecost. In fact all these supernatural manifestations of the Holy Spirit can be paralleled either in the Old or the New Testaments before Pentecost. They were not then evidence of the baptism in the Holy Spirit. The initial evidence appeared with the first instance of the baptism in the Spirit at Pentecost, and then it was speaking in other tongues as the Spirit gave them utterance.

What this argument fails to take into account is that Paul here presupposes their prior baptism in the Spirit. These charisms of the Holy Spirit are evidence that the Corinthians had already been filled with the Spirit in a Pentecostal manner, with the evidence of tongues implied. These gifts are not presented as a substitute for the initial evidence of the baptism in the Spirit. Rather they are a consequence of that spiritual baptism. It bears repeating here that of all the Spirit's supernatural gifts, *tongues appeared first* in order at Pentecost. *The other gifts followed subsequently.* There is no convincing evidence that this divine order has ever been changed. It was in the context of a

[1] 1 John 3:14.
[2] Matt. 10:8.
[3] Matt. 16:16,17.
[4] Luke 10:17ff.

tongues-speaking church at Corinth that these charisms of
God's Spirit proliferated. It is a matter of record, that when
tongues-speech disappeared from the life and experience of
the Church, the other charisms of the Spirit began to dis-
appear also. Account for this as one will, the fact remains,
that theologians do not rationalize away miracles within the
context of a personal charismatic experience. Men substitute speculation for empirical evidence when they no longer
experience miracles.

In the same vein, the Apostle's words, "do all speak with
tongues?" are often generalized out of their context in the
interest of "proving" that one can be Spirit-filled without
speaking in tongues. A casual reading of the series of rhetorical questions Paul propounded in I Cor. 12:29, 30 implies
a negative answer, and so lends apparent credence to this
assumption. When, however, they are related to their context, this support vanishes. From chapter eleven through
chapter fourteen of this epistle, the apostle Paul discussed
the conduct of the public worship service in the church at
Corinth. The real point of his question then is this: "Do
all speak with tongues?" "Where?" In the public worship
service. (Otherwise, the injunction to interpret tongues, and
discern prophecy loses its point.) The implied answer to his
question is, No! Paul himself cited the "unlearned" (*idiōtai,*
"him that is without gifts," i.e., one who has not received
the baptism in the Spirit) as an example. Paul freely admitted that he could, and did speak in tongues more than all
of them, but he preferred to reserve it for his private devotions. The praying in tongues to which Paul thus alluded [5]
is for private edification. It is prayer and praise addressed to
God, and it is this devotional use of tongues that is an abiding evidence of the Spirit's fulness. The "gift" of tongues,
with its indispensable companion "gift" of interpretation,

[5] I Cor. 14:18.

is a public manifestation for the edification of the whole church. Through it, God speaks to man by way of "revelation, knowledge, prophesying, or teaching." [6]

A Spirit-baptized believer may pray in tongues as he consciously yields himself to the Holy Spirit in worship. He cannot, therefore, speak in tongues as the oracle of God unless the Holy Spirit so chooses to manifest Himself. Paul seems to imply as much when he warned the Corinthians, that "If therefore the whole church be assembled together *and all speak* (i.e., *pray*) *with tongues. . . .,*" [7] they risked the accusation of madness. If "all" could not pray in tongues as the Apostle implied in I Cor. 14:18 & 23, then his argument has no point.

Anticipating a possible objection, let it be noted that the third class condition here cannot be dismissed as a wholly hypothetical case. It is no more hypothetical than the same third class condition in I Cor. 14:14, where Paul wrote: "If I pray in tongues, my spirit prays. . . ." And the fact that he was thus substantiating his point out of his own experience is conclusively show by his affirmation in 14:18: "I thank God I do speak in tongues more than you all."

On the day of Pentecost, they "all" spoke with tongues when they were filled with the Holy Spirit. In Caesarea "the Holy Spirit fell on *all* them that heard the word," and Peter and his companions "heard them speak with tongues and magnify God." A quarter of a century later, Paul met twelve men, disciples of John the Baptist, at Ephesus. After he had baptized them in water, symbolic of their "new birth," he laid his hands upon them and *all* twelve spoke with tongues. In Corinth Paul implies strongly that "all," that is to say, all who had been filled with the Spirit, could speak ("pray") in tongues.

[6] I Cor. 14:6.
[7] I Cor. 14:23. Italics mine H.M.E.

Thus explicitly, as well as implicitly, the evidence of Scripture indicates that "all" spoke with tongues as the initial evidence of their baptism in/filling with the Holy Spirit. To argue from the experience of Philip's Samaritan converts, or from the recorded experience of Paul in Damascus that all did not then, therefore—and this is the point of the objection—need not speak in tongues now, is to argue from silence. Granted that the same objection may be urged against the use of these scriptures to support the thesis that all did (and still do) speak with tongues. However, there is an important difference that gives to the latter view the balance of probability. By a process of analogical reasoning from the experience of the disciples in Jerusalem, Caesarea, and Ephesus (where clearly *all* did speak with tongues when they were baptized in the Holy Spirit), it may be consistently urged that this is the normative pattern throughout the New Testament period.

CHAPTER XIV

"Now Concerning Spiritual Gifts"

(I Cor. 12:1)

For conciseness and comprehensiveness, one can hardly improve upon the definition of spiritual gifts as "free, supernatural gifts perfecting human knowledge, speech, service, and administrative ability, not for personal advantage, but for the good of the Church." [1]

Beginning with I Cor. 11:2, and continuing through I Cor. 14:40, the apostle Paul addressed himself to three matters of practical concern relating to the public worship and decorum of the Corinthian assembly. These are in order (1) the question of the woman's veil, (2) the regulation of abuses in the observance of the Lord's Supper, and (3) "the operation of *the Spirit of God* in the Church, wherein lies the very mystery of its life." [2]

In chapter twelve, the Apostle acquaints his readers with the functions of spiritual gifts in the worship, witness, and ordering of the Church. These operations of the Spirit are introduced by the title *pneumatikōn*, "spirituals," e.g., "Now concerning *spirituals*, brethren." [3]

[1] *The New Testament of Our Lord and Saviour Jesus Christ*, A Revision of the Challoner-Rheims Version, ed. by Catholic Scholars (Paterson: St. Anthony's Guild Press, c. 1941. Footnote p. 471.

[2] Knowling, *op. cit.*, II, 884.

[3] I Cor. 12:1. Italics mine. H.M.E.

The first thing that catches the attention of the student of the Greek New Testament, is the absence of the word "gifts" in the Greek text, a fact the translators of the English text have noted by italicising the word in their translations. The word "spiritual" is an adjective without an expressed object, so the translators supplied an object from the context (i.e., verses 4, 13 etc.), which, in their judgment, most nearly represented the author's thought. As we shall see in the ensuing discussion, the translators' choice is a complicated one. Whether their choice of the word "gifts" is definitive enough to encompass all that the Apostle intended is open to question.

Consulting Paul's words in verses four to seven does suggest the need for broadening one's understanding of the content of the *pneumatikōn* beyond the somewhat restricted implications of the word "gifts." For example, he characterized these supernatural activities of the Holy Spirit thus: "Now there are diversities of gifts (*charismatōn*), but the same Spirit. And there are diversities of ministrations (*diakoniōn*), and the same Lord. And there are diversities of workings (*energēmatōn*), but the same God, who worketh all things in all. But to each one is given the manifestation of the Spirit to profit withal." These three, "gifts," "ministrations," and "workings," are all designated collectively as "manifestations" of the Spirit. They may, therefore, represent three distinct categories of the "spirituals" (*pneumatikōn*). In which case, "gifts" is much too restricted an object for the adjective *pneumatikōn*. On the other hand, G. G. Findlay may be right in saying, that "These are not separate classes of *pneumatika*, but varied designations of the *pneumatika* collectively—a trinity of blessing associating its possessors in turn with *the Spirit, the Lord,* and *God,* the fountain of all." [4]

[4] Findlay, *op. cit.,* II, 887.

However, from a practical standpoint, the emphasis upon "gifts" as "possessions" of the individual has had an adverse effect upon the witness and service of many Spirit-filled Christians. Preoccupation with one's particular "gift" has shifted attention from the Holy Spirit's sovereign prerogative in manifesting spontaneously any and all of His "gifts," "ministrations," or "workings" through any and every yielded believer.

In any event, it would probably be more accurate to use Paul's collective designation, "spiritual manifestations." However, the word "gifts" is too firmly entrenched in the literature, and in vernacular usage to effect a change here without risk of considerable ambiguity. Thus, to avoid needless confusion, the word "gifts" will be retained with the understanding that it comprehends all that the word "manifestations" connotes.

Having alerted the reader to the fact that the translators' role is frequently complicated by ambiguities, we need scarcely apologize for introducing him to a more difficult aspect of the translation yet to be resolved. Succinctly stated, the word "spirituals" (*pneumatikōn*), may be either masculine or neuter in gender. If it is taken as masculine in gender, then the subject under discussion is "spiritual persons." Suggested translations have been advanced such as, "concerning the inspired," [5] and "concerning the men of the Spirit," [6] more specifically "speakers in tongues." [7]

Several considerations support this view. (1) In the larger context, the Apostle dealt with "the mutual relations and behaviour of its members within the society." [8] He sought first to regulate women's conduct in the public services in

---

[5] Hilgenfeld, quoted by Meyer, *Critical and Exegetical Hand-Book to the Epistles to the Corinthians*, p. 275.

[6] Ewald, quoted by Meyer, *loc. cit.*

[7] Meyer, *loc. cit.*, in a comment on Ewald.

[8] Findlay, *op. cit.*, II, 870.

the wearing of the veil,[9] and keeping silent in the assembly.[10] Then he addressed those libertines who were drunken at the Lord's table.[11] Consequently, his remarks to the *pneumatikōn* may be construed, consistently with the context, as directed toward the conduct of charismatically endowed persons in the public assembly. This is unequivocally the whole point of Paul's instructions in chapters eleven through fourteen.

(2) It is noteworthy that "in the immediate context the references are all to persons." [12] The repeated use of the pronoun "you" in verses one through three, along with the pointed reference to the "man speaking in the Spirit of God," illustrates this assertion. Then too, in verse seven the "manifestation of the Spirit" is given to *each one*. Again in verse eleven, the Spirit "divides *to each one* severally." These are not abstract references to "gifts" *per se,* but the emphasis is upon the individual endowed with the gifts of the Spirit. It is, therefore, quite "possible that what the Corinthians had asked about was the position of a *spiritual person* and his testing." [13]

(3) Paul's whole counsel in chapters twelve through fourteen is directed, not to an exposition of the nature of the "gifts" in themselves, but to the regulation of the conduct of the charismatically endowed individuals in the public assembly at Corinth. His is preëminently a practical concern.

In I Cor. 14:37, the Apostle addressed himself to certain charismatically endowed individuals in these words: "If any

[9] I Cor. 11:2-16.
[10] I Cor. 14:33b-36.
[11] I Cor. 12:1ff.
[12] R. St John Parry, *The First Epistle of Paul the Apostle to the Corinthians, The Cambridge Bible for Schools and Colleges,* (ed. by R. St John Parry; Cambridge: University Press, 1916), p. 127.
[13] *Ibid.*

man thinketh himself to be a prophet, or spiritual. . . ."
Here *pneumatikos*, "spiritual," does unquestionably refer
to certain individuals, but to what kind of individuals? It
is possible that *pneumatikos* here is simply a general reference to one "gifted with the Spirit," [14] as Moffatt translated
it. On the contrary, the antecedent "prophet" suggests that
the "spiritual *one*" is also a specific designation for another
category of charismatically endowed persons, as is the
prophet. A. T. Robertson's remark on this verse—"The
prophet or *the one with the gift of tongues*. . . ." [15]—reveals
that this distinguished exegete regarded *pneumatikos* in this
verse as equivalent to a "tongues-speaker." And if this is its
meaning in this place, why not then the same meaning in
12:1ff?

There is a considerable body of evidence, therefore, supporting the interpretation that *pneumatikōn* in 12:1 is to be
understood as masculine in gender. If this be so, the resultant translation would be: "Now concerning spiritual persons." Furthermore, if it be accepted that the sense of
pneumatikos in 14:37 is "one endowed with the gift of
tongues," a further refinement in the translation is possible, i.e., "Now concerning speakers in tongues, brethren. . . ." We shall come around to this possibility later in
a discussion of the phrase "speaking in the Spirit."

On the other hand, other commentators—supported by
the English versions—translate the passage as though *pneumatikōn* were neuter in gender. There is support for this
view also in the context, for unquestionably the *pneumatika*

[14] James Moffatt, *The First Epistle of Paul to the Corinthians*, *The Moffatt New Testament Commentary*, (ed. by James Moffatt; New York: Harper and Brothers, n.d.), p. 230.
[15] Robertson, *Word Pictures in the New Testament*, IV, 185. Italics
mine H.M.E.
Meyer, op. cit., p. 334 dissents from this view, but lists Billroth, David
Schulz, Bauer, Wieseler as interpreting *pneumatikos* as equivalent to *Glossēi
lalōn*.

in 14:1 is neuter, and refers specifically to the charisms of prophesying and tongues. Perhaps, though, we miss the full intent of the passage by approching it with the preconceived notion that the question demands an either/or answer. The right answer may be both/and. It may be that the suggestion of St John Parry is closer to the truth. Perhaps "the ambiguity is due to the fact that the Corinthians used the word in the narrow sense [i.e., of tongues-speakers], and S. Paul . . . so uses it that the wider sense becomes dominant." [16] The context does suggest that Paul used the word in a dual sense, e.g., *pneumatika* of the "gifts" in themselves, and *pneumatikos,* of the "gifted person" (i.e., the speaker in tongues, 14:37). If the ambiguity in the sense of *pneumatikōn,* "spirituals," in 12:1 be resolved by this suggestion, the possible interpretation is: "Now concerning supernatural endowments of the Spirit. brethren. . . ." We shall not crystallize a decision between these alternatives at this point. The discussion of the phrase, "speaking in the Spirit of God," will cast additional light on the subject.

[16] R. St John Parry, *op. cit.,* p. 127.

CHAPTER XV

"Speaking in the Spirit of God"

(I Cor. 12:3; 14:2; 14:14)

Paul's next words likewise have a strong bearing on the discussion of "spirituals." It is begging the question to assume that what follows departs from his announced subject of *pneumatikōn*. In developing this theme, he next appealed directly to a contrast in their own experience, for "Ye know," wrote the Apostle, "that when ye were Gentiles ye were led away unto those dumb idols, howsoever ye might be led. Wherefore I make known unto you, that no man speaking in the Spirit of God saith, Jesus is anathema; and no man can say, Jesus is Lord, but in the Holy Spirit." Note the contrast: "when ye were Gentiles ye were led away [1] unto those dumb idols," but "Now I want you to understand, as Christians." [2] Thus past bondage to dumb idols is contrasted with present experience with an articulate Holy Spirit.

The phrase, "speaking in the Spirit of God," is significant, and requires closer inspection. The use of the dative case with the preposition "in" (*en pneumati theou lalōn,*

---

[1] Robertson & Plummer, *op. cit.*, p. 260. "Here only is apagein found in the N.T., except in the Synoptics and Acts; and there the common meaning is lead away by *force,* rather than by seductive guile, to trials, prison, or imprisonment . . . ."

[2] N.T.M.E.

"speaking in the Spirit of God") is a common idiom. Depending on the context, the preposition "in (*en*) may be used either of sphere or instrumentality." [3] However, "active influence rather than surrounding element seems to be implied here." [4] This is the view adopted by the translators of the *New English Bible* which reads, "speaking under the influence of the Spirit of God."

What then is meant by the phrase, "speaking in the Spirit of God"? The suggestion that the expressions, *"Jesus is anathema, Jesus is Lord* are battle-cries of the spirits of error and of truth contending at Corinth,"· points in the same direction as Chrysostom's view. Writing against the background of an identical pagan culture, he noted, that their idols "though dumb themselves, yet had their oracles, and prophets, and soothsayers, who professed to have *spiritual gifts,* such as the Pythia at Delphia; but do not be deceived," he warned, "their *gifts* may easily be distinguished from ours." [6]

Profoundly important though this suggestion is, we must postpone further consideration of Chrysostom's "contrasting Christian inspiration with the frenzy of the Dionysiac and other mysteries." [7] As we shall endeavor to demonstrate in our reconstruction of certain religious influences in the environment of the early Church, the influence of the mystery cults, in Gnostic guise, does affect one's understanding of the *pneumatikōn,* "spirituals."

The specific question that now presses for an answer is this: "What relationship does "speaking in the Spirit" sus-

---

[3] Robertson, *Word Pictures in the New Testament,* IV, 167. Cf., the same author's statement "that all the N.T. examples of *en* can be explained from the point of view of the locative." The speaking is located in the Spirit. *A Grammar of the Greek New Testament . . . ."* p. 590.

[4] Robertson & Plummer, *op. cit.,* p. 261.

[5] Findlay, *op. cit.,* II, 886.

[6] Wordsworth, *op. cit.,* II, 126.

[7] Robertson & Plummer, *op. cit.,* p. 260.

tain to the subject under discussion in the context, viz.,
"spirituals" (*pneumatikōn*)?

Paradoxically, broadening the examination of the context helps to narrow the possible interpretations. In I Cor.
12:4–11, Paul listed nine of the supernatural manifestations
of the Holy Spirit. These are, "the word of wisdom," "the
word of knowledge," "faith," "gifts of healings," "workings
of miracles," "prophecy," "discerning of spirits," "tongues,"
and "interpretation of tongues."

Again in chapter fourteen, he specifically identified two
of these—i.e., "prophesying" and "tongues"—as *pneumatika*
or "spirituals." Moffatt translated I Cor. 14:2 thus: "For he
who speaks in a 'tongue' addresses God, not men; no one
understands him; for he is talking of divine secrets *in the
Spirit*." [8] Note that *Spirit* is capitalized in this version, in-
dicating that the translator understood that the Holy Spirit
is meant. The *Revised Sandard Version* supports this interpretation, for it reads, "but he utters mysteries *in the Spirit*." [9] Characteristically, the *New English Bible*, seeking a
more idiomatic rendering, paraphrased it thus: "When a
man uses the language of ecstasy . . . he is no doubt inspired." This represents a considerable body of scholarly
opinion which concurs in the judgment that the phrase, "in
the Spirit" refers here to a supernatural manifestation of
the Holy Spirit, namely "tongues-speech."

On the other hand, there are other versions that do not
capitalize "spirit" in 14:2, thereby implying that the "spirit"
spoken of is the speaker's own spirit, as distinct from the
Holy Spirit.

Among commentators who accept this view, support for
it is adduced from I Cor. 14:14: "For if I pray in a tongue,
my spirit prayeth, but my understanding is unfruitful." It

[8] *Op. cit.,* p. 206. Italics mine H.M.E.
[9] Italics mine H.M.E.

is important to notice precisely what Paul said in this place. He is not here contrasting the human spirit with the Holy Spirit, much less implying any antagonism between them, as has been suggested by some commentators. Rather, he contrasted the spirit (*pneuma*) with the understanding (*nous*). The contrast is between the rational and the supra-rational (certainly not the irrational). The perceptive comment of Henry Alford underscores this when he says, "his spirit is the organ of the Holy Spirit." [10] The translators of the *New English Bible* avoided the wooden literalness of a word for word translation, choosing instead to convey the sense of the passage by rendering it thus: If I use such language in my prayer, *the Spirit in me prays,*[11] but my intellect lies fallow."

It is a fair conclusion, that whether the word Spirit is capitalized or not, the meaning is essentially the same. In both I Cor. 14:2 and 14:14, the Holy Spirit is the Author of the speaking. They spake "as the Spirit Himself gives utterance." Significantly, in both these verses "speaking in the Spirit" is equivalent to saying "speaking in tongues."

The correspondence between speaking "in the Spirit" in 14:2,14 and speaking "in the Spirit" in 12:3 is striking, to say the least. In the light of this discussion, it is a reasonable conclusion to deduce from the evidence that Paul's reference to "speaking *in the Spirit* of God" in 12:3 *is also an allusion to speaking in tongues.*

Reverting for a moment to the discussion on the gender of *pneumatikōn* in 12:1, it is reasonable to conclude—especially in the light of St John Parry's suggestion—that the "spirituals" (*pneumatikōn*) are individuals in whom the "gift" (*pneumatika*) of tongues was being manifested.

One naturally wonders why the Apostle should introduce

[10] Alford, *op. cit.*, II, 590.
[11] Italics mine H.M.E.

his discussion of spiritual manifestations by the assurance that "no man speaking in the Spirit of God, saith Jesus is anathema." The tone is one of reassurance, as though it were a reply to a troubled questioner. As a matter of fact, it is probably a reply by Paul to a question sent to him by the Corinthians. This is suggested by the formula with which he introduced the subject. The same formula occurs first in 7:1: "Now concerning the things whereof ye wrote." From the content of chapter seven, it is clear that one of the things about which they had inquired was the question of celibacy versus marriage. Each subsequent use of this formula serves to introduce a subject about which they had raised questions. In 8:1 he wrote: "Now concerning things sacrificed to idols." As already noted, 12:1 opens with the words: "Now concerning spirituals." Finally, the offering for the church at Jerusalem is broached: "Now concerning the collection for the saints" (16:1).

It is because of these queries from the Corinthians to Paul, that so much is known about the internal affairs of the church there. The frankness of their questions, and the equal candor with which he answered them, has often made this assembly of heroic Christians the butt of unwarranted slanders. All too often they have been stigmatized as the most immature and carnal of all the churches which Paul founded. Certainly, it is a more charitable and balanced judgment that says: "All the problems of a modern city church come to the front in Corinth." [12] Nor are the gifts of the Spirit which were in operation there—more specifically the charism of tongues—evidence of the immaturity of these primitive "saints." [13]

On the contrary, it is because the Holy Spirit operated so powerfully in their midst that their sins were exposed.

[12] Robertson, *Word Pictures in the New Testament*, IV, 69.
[13] I Cor. 1:2.

It is not the manifestations of the Spirit's gifts that constitutes evidence of their immaturity. It was their very human propensity for disagreements leading to schism that revealed their spiritual immaturity.[14]

The application is, or ought to be, self-evident. In the present divided state of the Church, let him who is above reproach hurl his verbal brickbats at the Corinthian believers. The very same "Corinthian" sins go unexposed and unreproved in today's churches for the very reason that the Holy Spirit is not working charismatically in their midst. It would be difficult to mask sin in the presence of the Spirit's manifestations in "wisdom," "knowledge," "discerning of spirits," "prophecy," "tongues," and "interpretation of tongues."

Though it is clear that the Corinthians wrote to Paul for instructions concerning "spirituals," the situation that prompted their query is open to speculation. Perhaps there is a suggestion in the Apostle's words of reassurance. Were they troubled by misgivings, aggravated by taunts from adversaries of the Holy Spirit's manifestations, lest they unwittingly blaspheme the Lord in tongues-speech? Were there, as Chrysostom suggests, counterfeit manifestations that raised a question about the validity of the genuine? A paraphrase may help to draw out Paul's meaning more clearly. "I want to reassure you that no Spirit-filled Christian, speaking in the supernatural utterances of the Spirit of God, will ever blaspheme Jesus." Is such a reconstruction far-fetched? Not when one reads some of the equally harsh and opinionated criticisms of "tongues-speaking" in the present charismatic revival, especially by the anti-charismatic advocates within the churches.

[14] I Cor. 3:1ff.

CHAPTER XVI

Natural Talents, or Supernatural Manifestations?

A further word of explanation is needed to clarify some of the common misunderstandings surrounding the character of these *pneumatika,* "spiritual gifts." These charisms are "supernatural" manifestations of the Holy Spirit. They are not "natural" talents. They are supernatural inasmuch as the operation of any and all of them is contingent upon the Divine initiative. Miracle working, except it be a manifestation of Divine initiative and power, is mere chicanery, the word of wisdom is simply human perspicacity, the word of knowledge is but the product of human intellectual effort. This distinction must be kept in the foreground of our discussion if we are to understand the nature of these supernatural manifestations of God's Spirit.

Stated negatively, tongues are not to be confused with a natural facility for mastering foreign languages. The "gift of tongues" is not a short cut to the mastery of a foreign language. "As the Spirit gives utterance" indicates that the vocabulary, syntax, and thought content expressed in "tongues-speech" are in the mind of the Holy Spirit, and not in the mind of the individual speaking. Neither is the manifestation of interpretation of tongues a native ability to translate foreign languages. Much less is prophesying a

natural talent for preaching the Gospel in a persuasive manner. It is not a manifestation of mere human fluency of
speech. It is rather an "intuitive" knowledge of the divine
counsels supernaturally revealed and spontaneously uttered
for the "edification, and exhortation, and consolation" [1] of
the assembled worshipers.

The supernatural nature of these gifts is verified by at
least three lines of reasoning. One, the Holy Spirit is directly referred to nine times in I Cor. 12:1–11 in relation
to His manifestations: e.g., (1) "in the Spirit of God," vs. 3;
(2) "in the Holy Spirit," vs. 3; (3) "the same Spirit," vs. 4;
(4) "the manifestation of the Spirit," vs. 7; (5) "through the
Spirit," vs. 8; (6) "the same Spirit," vs. 8; (7) "in the same
Spirit," vs. 9; (8) "in the one Spirit," vs. 9; (9) "the one and
the same Spirit." vs. 11.

Two, a glance at the context in chapters 12–14 reaffirms
the Spirit's authorship of these charismatic enablements. In
this context, the gifts of the Spirit are discussed in relation
to (1) the unity of Christ's Body, the Church, chapter 12—
observe the parallelism between one Spirit, many gifts, and
one Body, many members; (2) the preëminence of Love,
ch. 13; and (3) the use of the gifts of the Spirit in Christian
worship, especially tongues and prophesying, ch. 14. In this
context, the supernatural nature of these manifestations is
reiterated in the definition appended to one of these charisms, viz., "faith." It is not saving faith, but wonder-work-
ing faith "so as to remove mountains." [2]

Three, the supernatural nature of these gifts is emphasized by the use of the adjective *pneumatika*, "spiritual
gifts." [3]

A recognition of the supernatural origin of these gifts is

---

[1] I Cor. 14:3.
[2] I Cor. 13:2.
[3] I Cor. 14:1. Consult the Supplement for Paul's use of *pneumatikos*.

necessary for a proper understanding of their true nature and function. Of all these spiritual manifestations, tongues is the most frequently misunderstood, and misrepresented. The commonplace assumption that Biblical *glossolalia* is the result of pathological emotional states simply ignores the fact that they are a supernatural manifestation of the Holy Spirit. To ascribe them to the abnormal workings of a damaged psyche is to impugn the veracity of the Biblical records, to say nothing of the integrity of multiplied thousands of tongues-speaking Christians whose emotional health is equal, if not superior, to that of their critics. Perhaps even worse than that, it is closer to blasphemy than to heresy to thus project the neuroses of a neurotic age into the Deity. It is an unwarranted assumption to say that the tongues at Corinth are "the gift of men, who rapt in an ecstasy and no longer quite master of their own reason and consciousness, pour forth their glowing spiritual emotions in strange utterances, rugged, dark, disconnected, quite unfitted to instruct or to influence the minds of others." [4] Were this true, then the self-control counseled by Paul— "if there be no interpreter, let him keep silence in the church; and let him speak to himself, and to God" [5]—would be impossible. On the contrary, the tongues-speaker is in complete control of all his faculties at all times. His "understanding is unfruitful" [6] because he does not understand the words he utters in the Spirit, not because he has lost control of himself. The Holy Spirit never violates the integrity of one's personality. He exercises no coercion save the coercion of Love: "If ye love me," said Jesus, "ye will keep my commandments." [7] The fallacy in the interpretation quoted above is its uncritical correlation of the "gifts"

[4] Thayer, *op. cit.*, p. 188.
[5] I. Cor. 14:28.
[6] I Cor. 14:14.
[7] John 14:15.

of the Holy Spirit with the psychic phenomena encountered in pagan religions, or in spiritism, the inspiration of which is demonic.

Always and everywhere, the Bible distinguishes between the activity of the Holy Spirit and the activity of demonic spirits. The attempt to link Biblical *glossolalia* with the cataleptic trance states of mediums, or other pagan devotees of demonic spirits, reflects unfavorably upon Paul's spiritual discernment. It implies that he could not distinguish one from the other. Certainly Paul's counsels to regulate the Spirit's gifts of tongues and prophecy at Corinth indicates that he did not regard them as spurious. Paul never "regulated" demonic manifestations, he exorcised the "spirits" behind them.[8] Yet the attempt to correlate Biblical tongues with the psychic counterfeits is repeatedly made. The following is another such example: "There is no doubt about the thing referred to namely the broken speech of persons in religious ecstasy. The phenomenon, as found in Hellenistic religion, is described especially by E. Rhode . . . and Reitzenstein."[9] Behind this glib assumption is the erroneous a priori that superficial correlation proves mutual causation.

The tongues at Pentecost were recognizable dialects, or languages. They were not the incoherent ravings of men in a trance state. Neither were they akin to the maudlin mouthings of intoxicated men. When the "wise-acres" of that day tried to shrug it off as such, Peter was at pains to rebut their haughty rationalization, saying, "these are not drunken, as ye suppose."

On the day of Pentecost, they spoke dialects known to many of their auditors "as the Spirit gave them utterance." Luke ascribed these utterances to the direct agency of the

[8] Acts 16:16ff.
[9] Arnd, Gingrich, Bauer, *op. cit.*, p. 161.

Holy Spirit. In Corinth, they spoke "families of languages (*genē glōssōn*)" as a manifestation of the Holy Spirit. In both cases, the Holy Spirit is the one with whom the languages originated. If there was any difference in the nature or expression of the respective utterances, this difference originated with the Holy Spirit, not with the person uttering the language.

Paul further identified the languages at Corinth as the "tongues (languages) of men and of angels." [10] They were the vehicle for expressing the praise and worship of men, who in full possession of all their faculties, had discovered that there are levels of communication with God that transcend the finite limitations of the merely rational. They are not, therefore, sub-rational, they are supra-rational.

There is, furthermore, continuity in Biblical *glossolalia*. There is no difference in kind in the various references to this phenomenon in Scripture. "The gift of tongues," wrote A. T. Robertson, in commenting on the Pentecostal manifestation, "came also on the house of Cornelius at Caesarea (Acts 10:44–47), the disciples of John at Ephesus (Acts 19:6), the disciples at Corinth (I Cor. 14:1–33). It is possible that the gift appeared also at Samaria (Acts 8:18) . . . *The experience is identical in all four instances* and they are . . . for adoration and wonder and worship." [11] Henry Alford affirmed with equal candor that the tongues are "one and the same throughout." [12]

---

[10] I Cor. 13:1.

[11] Robertson, *Word Pictures in the New Testament*, III, 22. Italics mine H.M.E.

[12] Henry Alford, *The Greek Testament*, 5th ed., vol. II (Cambridge: Deighton, Bell and Co., 1865), 15, 122.

Acts 2:4: "How is this *heterais glōssais lalein* related to the *glōssēi lalein* afterward spoken of by St. Paul? I answer that they are *one and the same thing*. *Glōssēi lalein* is to speak in a language, as above explained, *glōssais* (*heterais*, or *kainais*, Mark 16:17) *lalein*, to speak in languages under the same circumstances."

In our own day, there is an increasing number of testimonies by Christians who have spoken known languages "in the Spirit." On one occasion the present author was participating in a healing service in a church on the West Coast of the United States. As he prayed in tongues, an Armenian Baptist woman listened to his "tongue," and identified it as prayer in Russian. Again while praying with a small group for the healing of a missionary who speaks Spanish fluently, the missionary identified his "tongue" as a Spanish dialect. The vocabulary was clearly identified, but the inflexions were strange to her. On another occasion, while praying for the healing of the little daughter of a Japanese Buddhist woman, he spoke a "tongue" she later identified to mutual friends as Japanese. Still more recently, in a ministry service in his own church, an Armenian man, for whom he prayed, identified two foreign languages spoken in prayer. The one was a dialect spoken by the Indian colonial troops of the British Empire which he had heard as a young man in the seaport cities of the Orient. The second language he described as Kurdish, a language he himself speaks. Most recently of all, in fact just a few weeks ago, the phenomenon repeated again. While praying with a young man, acquainted with both Spanish and Portuguese, the writer prayed in a language identified by the young man as Portuguese. When asked what was said, he replied: "You told God my need in high Portugese." Needless to say all of these languages are unknown to the writer, and consequently were spoken "as the Spirit Himself gave utterance."

The same author identified the last sentence of a song

Acts 10:45: "The *lalein glōssais* here is identified with the *lalein heterais glōssais* of ch. 2:4, by the assertion of ch. xi. 15—and this again with the *elaloun glōssais* of xix. 6:—so that the gift was one and the same throughout."

sung "in the Spirit" as Biblical Greek, although the man singing knows no Greek. A Norwegian woman received the baptism in the Holy Spirit at a service in the present writer's church. The next day she prayed in tongues in the presence of some Italian friends who identified the "tongue" she was speaking as Italian, a language with which she is not conversant. In charismatic services in the author's church, other languages have been identified on several occasions. It is also significant to note that each participant in these services prays in a distinctive and clearly recognizable tongue. Vocabulary, inflexions, intonations are all distinctive, and clearly distinguishable. Such experiences lead the present writer not only to affirm Dr. Robertson's words—"The experience is identical in all four instances" referred to in Scripture—but to add—The experience is identical with the Biblical prototype whenever Spirit-filled Christians pray in tongues "as the Spirit gives them utterance."

CHAPTER XVII

"Last, Therefore Least"

(I Cor. 12:10, 28)

"But desire earnestly the greater gifts." With this exhortation, Paul summarized his discussion of the diversity of the "spiritual gifts" (*pneumatika*). It is commonly assumed that these gifts are listed by him in the order of their relative importance. Consequently, those mentioned first must be the most important, while those that are least are placed last. Based upon this premise, the conclusion is accepted, without critical examination, that "tongues are the least of the Holy Spirit's manifestations, because they are mentioned last."

This line of reasoning proceeds syllogistically in somewhat the following manner. Major premise, the gifts of the Spirit are always listed in the order of their relative importance. Minor premise, tongues are mentioned last. Conclusion, tongues are last in the list, therefore, they are the least important.

There are deceptive pitfalls in the use of logic that quickly expose the fallacies in *a priori* assumptions which are dictated by polemics rather than by rational considerations. The truth of the syllogism does not rest in the consistency of its deductions, but in the validity of the premises from which it reasons. It may be formally correct but substantially wrong. If either the major or the minor premise is factually wrong, its conclusions will, of necessity be wrong, no matter how cogent its logic may seem. Consequently, the conclusion drawn in the syllogism above can only be true if its premises are true. This can only be determined by a critical evaluation of the evidence.

In I Cor. 12:28, Paul does list tongues last, and only above interpretation of tongues in I Cor. 12:10. On the basis of this evidence, we can say, at least for the time being, that the minor premise is substantially correct. However, this alone cannot justify the conclusion that tongues are the least of the Spirit's operations. The entire assumption really hinges on the validity of the major premise.

This raises the question, does the apostle Paul list the gifts of the Holy Spirit in the order of their importance? To answer this, it will be necessary to determine whether or not such a value judgment is either stated by Paul, or implied by a comparison of the various enumerations of the gifts in his writings. To the first, it can be answered categorically that he does not make such a statement. In fact, it will be shown later that some of his express statements point in the opposite direction. In answer to the second, his scattered enumerations of the gifts of the Spirit are arranged schematically in the following seven lists. This arrangement is adopted to facilitate analysis. It is self-evident that if there is consistency in the order of the various listings, this in itself will suggest such a value judgment.

I Corinthians 12:8–10

1. "word of wisdom"
   (logos sophias)
2. "word of knowledge"
   (logos gnōseōs)
3. "faith"
   (pistis)

4. "gifts of healings"
   (charismata iamatōn)
5. "workings of miracles"
   (energēmata dunameōn)
6. "prophecy"
   (prophēteia)

7. "discerning of spirits"
   (*diakriseis pneumatōn*)

8. "kinds of tongues"
   (*genē glōssōn*)

I Corinthians 12:28

1. "apostles"
   (*apostoloi*)
2. "prophets"
   (*prophētai*)
3. "teachers"
   (*didaskaloi*)
4. "miracles"
   (*dunameis*)

5. "gifts of healings"
   (*charismata iamatōn*)
6. "helps"
   (*antilēmpseis*)[1]
7. "governments"
   (*kubernēseis*)[2]
8. "kinds of tongues"
   (*genē glōssōn*)

I Corinthians 12:29–30

1. "apostles"
   (*apostoloi*)
2. "prophets"
   (*prophētai*)
3. "teachers"
   (*didaskaloi*)
4. "miracles"
   (*dunameis*)

5. "gifts of healings"
   (*charismatōn iamatōn*)
6. "tongues"
   (*glōssais*)
7. "interpretation"
   (*diermēneuein*)

I Corinthians 13:1, 2

1. "tongues"
   (*glōssais*)
2. "prophecy"
   (*prophēteian*)

3. "knowledge"
   (*gnōsin*)
4. "faith"
   (*pistin*)

---

[1] Robertson, *Word Pictures in the New Testament,* IV, 174. "Probably refers to the work of the deacons . . . ." Robertson & Plummer, *International Critical Commentary,* p. 281, "the work of the diaconate, both male and female."

[2] Robertson, *Word Pictures in the New Testament,* IV, 174. "Probably Paul has in mind bishops (*episcopoi*) or elders (*presbuteroi*)."

Robertson & Plummer, *op. cit.,* 281. "This probably refers to those who superintend the externals of organization, *hoi proistamenoi* (Rom. xii.8; I Thess. v. 12)."

I Corinthians 13:8

1. "prophecies"
   (*prophēteiai*)
2. "tongues"
   (*glōssai*)

3. "knowledge"
   (*gnōsis*)

Ephesians 4:11

1. "apostles"
   (*apostoloi*)
2. "prophets"
   (*prophētai*)
3. "evangelists"
   (*euaggelistai*)

4. "pastors"
   (*poimenes*)
5. "teachers"
   (*didaskaloi*)

Romans 12:6–8

1. "prophecy"
   (*prophēteia*)
2. "ministry" [3]
   (*diakonia*)
3. "teaching"
   (*didaskalia*)

4. "exhorting"
   (*paraklēsis*)
5. "giving"
   (*metadidonai*)
6. "ruling" [4]
   (*proistasthai*)

"Last, therefore least," can only be valid as an interpretative principle, if it can be proven to be applicable to each subsequent situation. If there is consistency in the listing

---

[3] Thayer, *op. cit.*, p. 138, *diakonia*, 4, "The office of deacon in the primitive church . . . Rom. xii 7." Arndt, Gingrich, Bauer, *op. cit.*, p. 183, *diakonia*, 5, "of the office of a deacon, Rom. 12:7."

[4] Robertson, *Word Studies in the New Testament*, IV, 36. "Literally, those who stand in front of you, your leaders in the Lord, the presbyters or bishops and deacons." Probably not the deacons here since they are singled out for mention in vs. 7, i.e., *diakonia*. See above footnote. Robertson & Plummer equate *proistasthai*, "ruling," with *kubernēseis*, "governments"—bishops.

of the gifts of the Spirit, it will argue for the truth of such a presumed "rule of last mention." On the other hand, if the various lists of spiritual gifts are not consistent in their order, it will serve to discredit the assumption that the lesser gifts are mentioned last. If such a rule of interpretation be applied only in special cases to support *a priori* prejudices against tongues, then it is not a valid exegetical rule. It is simply special pleading, and may be dismissed as such without the formality of an apology.

Even a cursory reading of the schematic arrangement of these seven lists reveals a number of omissions, transpositions, and substitutions in Paul's tablulation of these gifts of the Spirit. A comparison of the initial list in I Cor. 12:8–10 with the second list in 12:28 shows several substitutions in the latter. The "word of wisdom," "the word of knowledge," and "faith" are dropped from the first three places, and "apostles," "prophets," and "teachers" are substituted. There are obvious correspondences between the latter and the roster of gifts in Eph. 4:11, e.g., "and he [Christ Jesus] gave some to be apostles; and some, prophets; and some, evangelists; and some, pastors and teachers."

Important, too, is the fact that Paul in I Cor. 12:29 combined charismatic manifestations of the Holy Spirit with the ministry gifts of Christ. These ministry and administrative gifts, called *dōrea* in Greek, i.e., "the gift of Christ," [5] are included under the *charismata* in I Cor. 12:28, 29 as the larger, more general category of God's supernatural "gifts of grace." [6] Nonetheless, there is a valid distinction between them that must neither be blurred nor lost. The *charismata*

---

[5] Eph. 4:7, *dōrea* is used in a collective sense here, and particularized as *domata* in 4:7b, a quotation from Ps. 68:18.

[6] Thayer, *op. cit.*, *charisma*, p. 667.

are "the operation(s) which manifests the Spirit."⁷ The *dōrea* are ministries and offices in the Church. The former are miraculous enablements for the Church's worship and witness. The latter are ministries designed by our Lord "for the perfecting of the saints . . . unto the measure of the stature of the fulness of Christ."⁸ The *charismata* are "distributions *to each one severally*," by the Spirit for the edification of the whole assembly of believers. The *dōrea* are Christ's gifts *of chosen individuals* as officers and administrators of the Church. In the *charismata* the stress is upon the gift itself as a manifestation of the Holy Spirit. In the *dōrea* the emphasis is upon the persons who exercise these gift-ministries.⁹ In a word, the *charismata* are manifestations, the *dōrea* are persons. Their common denominator is the fact that both are "gift(s) of grace, favor(s) which one receives without any merit of their own."¹⁰

Referring again to the first two lists, one notes that "miracles" and "gifts of healings" have been transposed. In addition, "prophecy" and "discerning of spirits" are omitted from the second compilation of gifts in favor of "helps" and "governments." If one accepts the view that "helps" refers to the work of the deacons, and "governments" is an allusion to the ministry of bishops, or elders, then their transposition argues forcefully against the proposition that the gifts are tabulated in order of importance. The office of deacon, or "almoner," is hardly greater than the office of the bishop, or elder. Let it be further noted in passing, that

---

⁷ Robertson & Plummer, *op. cit.,* p. 264. "In *he phanerosis . . . tou Pneumatos,* the genitive is probably objective, 'the operation which manifests the Spirit, rather than subjective,' 'the manifestation which the Spirit produces.' There are many such doubtful genitives; Moul.—Win. p. 232."

⁸ Eph. 4:12,13.

⁹ Salmond, *op. cit.,* III, 339.

¹⁰ Thayer, *op. cit.,* charisma, p. 667.

the "interpretation of tongues" is also omitted in the second catalogue of gifts.

The third list of gifts in I Cor. 12:29,30 follows the arrangement of the second for the first five gifts, e.g., "apostles," "prophets," "teachers," "miracles," and "gifts of healings." Four that are included in the second are omitted in the third, viz., "faith," "discerning of spirits," "helps," and "governments."

The fourth catalogue of the Spirit's gifts in I Cor. 13:1, 2 places "tongues" first, even before "prophecy" and "knowledge," with "faith" put in last place. Then the Apostle *transposed* this order in 13:8 with "prophecies" *first,* "tongues" *second,* and "knowledge" *last.* If the supposititious "rule of last mention" were valid, we would have to argue that "knowledge" was least in 13:8.

In Rom. 12:6–8, the order of spiritual gifts also deviates from the lists found in I Cor. 12–14. The office of the "deacon" (*diakonia,* "ministry") is placed second, following "prophecy," but preceding both "teaching" and "ruling," i.e., before the office of the "bishop," or "elder." "Exhorting" is listed as a separate manifestation in Rom. 12:8, but in I Cor. 14:3, it is described as a function of "prophesying." The roster in Rom. 12:6–8 adds a spiritual gift not listed before, namely, "giving."

Thus a compilation and comparison of spiritual gifts listed by Paul shows no consistency in order, or arrangement, with the notable exception of the ministry gifts, or *dōrea.*[11] The various transpositions, omissions, and substitutions in the listing of the *charismata* suggests a random recital, rather than a discernible pattern. In the face of this evidence, it is doubtful, indeed, that there is a "rule of last mention" operative in these lists of spiritual gifts. If it were,

[11] Eph. 4:11; I Cor. 12:28; I Cor. 12:29,30.

then "faith" would be least, because last in 13:2, "knowledge" would be least because last in 13:8, while the function
of the "deacon" would take precedence over the bishop or
elder.

CHAPTER XVIII

"Desire Earnestly the Greater Gifts"

(I Cor. 12:31)

From the foregoing analysis of Paul's listing of the gifts of the Holy Spirit, it is clear that he implied no value judgment upon the intrinsic worth of the various gifts by their placement in the several lists. There is one noteworthy exception to this general principle which we will examine later in this chapter.

First, however, several additional observations concerning the fictitious "rule of last mention" deserve attention. Such an arbitrary interpretive principle not only defies consistent application to the various inventories of spiritual gifts, it cannot be applied consistently elsewhere in the same context. For example, Paul wrote in 13:13, "But now abideth faith, hope, love, these three. . . ." If the "rule of last mention" were valid, then "love" would be the least of these spiritual virtues, simply because it is mentioned last. This is obviously untrue, inasmuch as Paul expressly said that, "the greatest of these is love." Perhaps one might be tempted to assume from this that the reverse is true, namely, that the least important is mentioned first, and the most important placed last for emphasis. As a matter of fact, this is precisely what some commentators have attempted to do, as we shall now see.

It is unfortunate, not to add, confusing, that competent scholars have involved themselves in painful contradictions by tacitly accepting either a fictitious "rule of last mention," or its mirror image, "a rule of first mention." In what is clearly a polemic against the charismatic gifts of the "Irving-ites," one scholar wrote of tongues in I Cor. 12:10: "Hence Paul placed this gift lowest of all. It created wonder, but did little real good." [1] Nor is this a mere passing comment, for the same author repeated this "last, therefore, least" judgment in a comment on tongues in 12:28, saying pointedly, "last again." [2] However, when confronted with tongues *in first place* in I Cor. 13:1, straightway he reversed himself, saying, "Mentioned first because really least." [3] Clearly it strains all logical consistency to affirm that tongues are *least because mentioned last,* then in the next breath to declare that tongues are *really least because mentioned first.* It is a tortured logic that affirms as true mutually contradictory propositions. Can it be that "yes" is "no"? "right" is "wrong"? "truth" is "falsehood"?—and the case for "tongues" has no chance of an impartial hearing?

Even more devious is the rationalization of tongues in I Cor. 13:1 by two other commentators. In their own words: "The Apostle takes the lowest of these spiritual gifts first, because the Corinthians specially needed to be set right about them, and also because the least valuable of the special gifts made the strongest contrast to the excellence of love. . . . *There is a climax in the succession glōssai* ['tongues'], *prophēteia* ['prophecy'], *pistis,* ['faith'], *psōmisō* ['to give away all one's property bit by bit'], *kai paradō* ['and if I give up, i.e., my body to be burned'].'' [4]

This is a reversal of the "rule of last mention" to accomo-

---

[1] Robertson, *Word Pictures in the New Testament,* IV, 179.
[2] *Ibid.,* p. 174.
[3] *Ibid.,* p. 179.
[4] Robertson & Plummer, *op. cit.,* p. 288.

date the facts to prior biases. Apparently prejudice and consistency are incompatible. Tongues are to be condemned out of hand regardless of the reasons, or lack of facts, adduced. Attention must be focused upon a glaring two-fold fallacy in this quotation.

First of all, the above list omits "knowledge" (*gnōsin*), which comes between "prophecy" and "faith" in the text of I Cor. 13:2. This omission is significant. In I Cor. 12:8,9 these gifts are listed as "knowledge," "faith," "prophecy," "tongues." An inverted order, therefore, should read "tongues," "prophecy," "faith," "knowledge." Such an inverted order would be necessary in any "climax in succession." Now notice that *"knowledge" precedes "faith"* in 13:2. If the order were inverted, the opposite should be true, *"faith" should precede "knowledge."* It is obvious then that there is no inversion in 13:2 in the order of "knowledge" and "faith." They occupy the same relative positions they do in the original list in 12:8,9. The only way, therefore, that a "climax in succession" in the order of the gifts in 13:1–3 can be maintained, is by omitting "knowledge." But this smacks of apologetics, rather than exegesis. Furthermore, it cannot be argued that "all knowledge" in 13:2 is merely an expansion of the idea of "prophecy," for "knowledge" and "prophecy" are treated as separate and distinct charisms in the context.

In the second place, such a "climax in succession" is contradicted by the transposition of the order of these same gifts in 13:8, e.g., "prophecy," "tongues," "knowledge," rather than "tongues," "prophecy," "knowledge" as in 13:1f. The whole idea of a "climax in succession" from least to greatest strikes us as simply an arbitrary fiction.

These attempts to depreciate tongues as a spiritual gift are based upon arbitrary assumptions. They represent deductions from prejudice rather inductions from facts. If such 'invincible" prejudices are accepted in lieu of evidence from facts, then tongues would be the least of the spiritual gifts no matter where they appeared in the various lists of the *charismata*. In effect, such prejudice is simply saying, "My mind is made up, do not confuse me with the facts."

Overlooked heretofore is an explicit parallelism in Pauline thought that sets the whole matter in Biblical perspective. In I Cor. 12:18 he wrote: "God hath set the members . . . in the body," and added in 12:28, "God hath set some in the church, first apostles, etc." As God has set the members in the body (i.e., the Church), so also He has set the gifts and ministries of the Holy Spirit in the Church. And as there are no inferior members in the body, so also there are no inferior gifts in the body. One member may be subordinate to another for the sake of the functioning of the body. The subordinate members are not, therefore, inferior. Jesus, in the days of His flesh, became subordinate to the Father. He is not, therefore, inferior. The wife is subordinate to the husband. She is not, in consequence of that, inferior. So also, the subordination of one gift to another does not, by virtue of that fact, imply inferiority.

Remembering that Paul included the ministry gifts (*dōrea*, Eph. 4:7,11) with the *charismata* in I Cor. 12:28–30 as the larger category, we are now in possession of a clue to the identity of the "greater gifts." The use of the word "*dōrea*" to characterize the ministry gifts suggests their importance, for this word "is reserved for the highest and best gift." [5] In addition, in 12:28 Paul explicitly tabulated these ministry gifts in numerical order. This is the one exception to the Apostle's random order in cataloguing spiritual gifts.

[5] William Sanday & Arthur Headlam, *A Critical and Exegetical Commentary on the Epistle to the Romans, The International Critical Commentary*, ed., by E. A. Briggs, S. R. Driver, & Alfred Plummer, 13th ed.; New York: Charles Scribner's Sons, 1911, p. 140.

It intimates that when he said, *"first* apostles, *secondly* prophets, *thirdly* teachers," he was expressing a value judgment upon this specific category of gifts. The apostles are, therefore, "possessors of the most important spiritual gift I Cor. 12:28f." [6]

It is this expressed enumeration of these particular gifts that sets them off from the rest of the *charismata* as the most important. Consequently, when Paul exhorted his readers to "desire earnestly the greater gifts," it is both logical and consistent with the context, to interpret these "greater gifts" as the ones he has himself set off from the others by an arithmetical enumeration, e.g., "first . . . , second . . . , third. . . ." We conclude then that the "greater gifts" are "apostles," "prophets," and "teachers" in that order. Anticipating an objection at this point, let it be understood for now, that Love is not one of the gifts of the Holy Spirit. Discussion of this must, however, be postponed until chapter twenty.

[6] Arndt, Gingrich, Bauer, *op cit., apostolos,* 3 p. 99.

CHAPTER XIX

Prophets and Prophecying

A consideration of the first and third of these ministry gifts, namely, apostles and teachers, need not detain us. However, a further clarification of the second, "prophets," is a practical necessity. The distinction between "prophecy" as a manifestation of the Spirit, and "prophecy" as a ministry gift of Christ to His Church needs to be clearly drawn. Their interrelations are such that some have assumed that they are one and the same. Nor is this assumption entirely amiss when they are considered solely as a revelatory function of the Holy Spirit. But in their scope and applications, there are important distinctions that must be taken into account.

The office of the prophet is a specific order of ministry in the apostolic church. The importance of the office is reflected in the high priority given to it in Pauline thought, and in "the frequency with which they are referred to (Acts xi.28; xv.32; I Cor. xiv., etc.) and the prominent position they had in the primitive church." [1]

From the Biblical record certain definitive aspects of their ministry and influence can be gleaned. As in the case of the prophet Agabus—who journeyed from Jerusalem to Antioch prophesying a coming famine,[2] then later traveled from Judaea to Caesarea, and in an acted parable predicted Paul's

[2] Acts 11:27ff.
[1] Salmond, *op. cit.*, III, 299.

impending imprisonment at Jerusalem [3]—the prophets were frequently itinerants. They spoke with the authority of the revelations they bore. At Antioch, Agabus "signified by the Spirit" the coming famine.[4] In Caesarea, the prophetic declamation was enforced by a "Thus saith the Holy Spirit." [5] However, their oracles were not delivered in an ecstatic, or trance state, for "the spirits of the prophets are subject to the prophets." [6] In the worship services of the churches, their utterances were to be self-regulated, speaking "by two or three," and were subject to the discipline and discernment of the rest of the prophets.[7]

At Antioch, it was through them that the Holy Spirit called Barnabas and Saul into missionary service, and "the imposition of hands upon Paul and Barnabas—whether for a special mission or to a distinct order it matters not—was at the dictation of prophets." [8] The prophets also played a part in the calling [9] and ordination of elders.[10] It is in this sense that the words of Paul addressed to Timothy are to be understood, i.e., "according to the prophecies which led the way to thee." [11] The prophecies referred to "are utterances of the prophets, such as Silas (and not excluding Paul himself) who were with St. Paul when the ordination of Timothy became possible; utterances which pointed out the young man as a person suitable for the ministry, *led the way to him*." [12]

---

[3] Acts 21:10.
[4] Acts 11:28.
[5] Acts 21:11.
[6] I Cor. 14:32.
[7] I Cor. 14:29.
[8] Newport J. D. White, *The First and Second Epistles to Timothy, The Expositor's Greek Testament*, IV (Grand Rapids: Wm. B. Eerdmans, n.d.), 100.
[9] I Tim. 1:18.
[10] I Tim. 4:14.
[11] I Tim. 1:18.
[12] White, *op. cit.*, IV, 100.

Furthermore, the offices of prophet and teacher are noted separately in each instance. Though both gifts might be exercised alternatively by the same person, they are nonetheless regarded as separate and distinct, as for example in Antioch where prophets and teachers were ministering together when the Holy Spirit called Barnabas and Saul to missionary service. This distinction is further maintained when Paul and Barnabas returned from the first Jerusalem church conference, convened to settle the legalistic questions raised by the Judaizers. They were accompanied by two prophets, Judas and Silas, who "being themselves also prophets, exhorted the brethren with many words, and confirmed them." [13] "The prophetic character of the speakers would," in the opinion of J. Rawson Lumby, "give to their words the force of revelation," [14] thus making the terms of the Jerusalem settlement more palatable to both Jewish and Gentile believers in Antioch. After their departure, the continuing ministry of teaching was carried on by Paul and Barnabas.[15]

The comments of S. D. Salmond provide a fitting summary of the facts: "The prophets were preachers or exhorters, to whom revelations of spiritual truth were imparted, and who spoke in the Spirit . . . but not in ecstacy or as one in a trance. . . . Further, he was usually, if not always, itinerant. This order of prophets continued to have a place in the Church for a considerable period." [16] They are mentioned frequently in the Didache, while Eusebius preserves

[13] Acts 15:32.
[14] *The Acts of the Apostles, Cambridge Bible for Schools and Colleges* (Cambridge: University Press, 1934), p. 199.
[15] Acts 15:35.
[16] *Op cit.,* III, 330. "The statements made regarding them in the early non-canonical literature (*The Teaching of the Twelve, Clem. Alex. Strom.,* the *Shepherd of Hermas,* etc.) show how they continued to exist and work beyond the Apostolic Age . . . ." *Ibid.,* p. 300.

the names of two of them at Philadelphia, Quadratus and Ammia respectively.[17]

In a more general sense, the gift of "prophesying" was not limited to a separate office. The prophetic promise of Joel, quoted by Peter on the day of Pentecost, is this; "your sons and daughters shall prophesy," and "my servants . . . and my handmaidens . . . shall prophesy." [18] Paul's comment to the Corinthian church echoes this prophetic promise—"ye all can prophesy one by one." [19] True, some commentators would limit the "all" here to the order of the prophets. But the apostle Paul's exhortation—to "desire earnestly spiritual gifts, but rather that ye may prophesy," [20] —suggests that this gift was within the reach of the whole assembly and not just the order of recognized prophets. All might aspire to "prophesy" in the worship services of the Church, not all could be "prophets" in the technical sense of the term.

This larger connotation of prophecy is reflected in the experience of the Ephesian converts of Paul, who "spake with tongues *and prophesied*," [21] after the Holy Spirit came upon them through the imposition of the Apostle's hands. That tongues and prophecy were uttered spontaneously by those baptized in, that is to say, filled with the Holy Spirit, has already been discussed at length. It should suffice here simply to remind the reader that on the day of Pentecost, the tongues-speech of the Christians is described by a word used only of prophetic utterance in the Septuagint. The manifestation of tongues-prophecy will be expounded later in an examination of I Cor. 14:6. Suffice it to point out

17 *Ibid.*, p. 330.
18 Acts 2:17, 18.
19 I Cor. 14:31.
20 I Cor. 14:1.
21 Acts 19:6. Italics mine H.M.E.

here that prophesying was apparently not restricted to those who were regarded as prophets. Nor ought this to seem strange, for the Community of the New Covenant is a prophetic community. When the Holy Spirit so moved them severally, or collectively, the Divine afflatus would enable all to prophesy in "unpremeditated apocalyptic utterances in the Christian meetings." [22]

The four virgin daughters of Philip, the evangelist-deacon, who prophesied [23] presents a special problem. Their experience has given countenance to the view that "With N[ew] T[estament] prophets we have also N[ew] T[estament] prophetesses." [24] Three considerations militate against this view.

One, Paul explicitly forbade women to teach or to have authority over a man.[25] It seems fair to conclude that his reference is to the ministry of "teacher," which carried with it the authority and responsibility for authoritative pronouncements on doctrine. By parity of reasoning, the same prohibition would extend to all the ministry gifts including that of the prophet. A. T. Robertson remarked: "At any rate there was no order of women prophets or official ministers." [26]

Two, aside from the problematical example of Philip's daughters, there is no instance of New Testament prophetesses. The prophetess, Anna, daughter of Phanuel, who greeted the presentation of the child Jesus in the Temple with prophetic insight, was an Old Testament prophetess.[27] The only other instance in the New Testament, in which the title prophetess is ascribed to a woman, is Jezebel, whose

[22] Robertson, *Word Pictures in the New Testament*, VI, 270.
[23] Acts 21:9.
[24] Salmond, *op. cit.*, III, 329.
[25] I Tim. 2:12.
[26] Robertson, *Word Pictures in the New Testament*, III, 363.
[27] Luke 2:36.

claims are qualified by the clause, "who calleth herself a prophetess." [28] The description of her activities makes it clear that she was a false-prophetess.

Three, it is said of the daughters of Philip that they prophesied, but in the same context, Agabus is called a prophet. Although nothing is said directly about the content of their prophesying, the text does contain a hint. In each Christian assembly where Paul stopped on his journey to Jerusalem, their fellowship and worship were punctuated by recurrent revelations of the tribulation that awaited him at Jerusalem. The Apostle confided this to the elders of the church at Ephesus during their hurried meeting at Miletus, the seaport of Ephesus, saying, "that the Holy Spirit testifieth unto me in every city, saying that bonds and afflictions abide me." [29] The "disciples" at Tyre, where Paul tarried for seven days, reiterated the warning "through the Spirit." [30] Agabus came down from Judaea to Caesarea, and, perhaps in Philip's house, predicted Paul's imprisonment at Jerusalem. The prophetic burden of Philip's daughters was, perhaps, one more link in the recurring cycle of revelations of the apostle Paul's impending tribulation. Through a critical reconstruction of the text, Spitta arrived at this same conclusion, noting, that "they prophesied with tears over the fate of Paul." [31] It need not, therefore, be assumed that they occupied the office of prophet, which, as we have suggested, was forbidden to women. Their experience falls within the provision made for women to exercise the gifts of the Spirit in the church worship services, including "praying and prophesying." [32]

That it was customary for men and women to participate

[28] Rev. 2:20.
[29] Acts 20:23.
[30] Acts 21:4.
[31] Quoted by Knowling, *op. cit.*, II, 445, 446.
[32] I Cor. 11:5.

jointly in the corporate worship in prayer and prophesying, is so stated in the first Corinthian epistle of Paul: "Every man praying or prophesying, having his head covered, dishonoreth his head. But every woman praying or prophesying with her head unveiled dishonoreth her head." [33] Note that the woman is not forbidden to pray and to prophesy in the worship service, but she is to have her head veiled as "a sign of authority." [34]

Paul does not forbid women to exercise the gifts of the Spirit in the worship of the local assembly, and this has a bearing upon his injunction, "let women keep silence in the churches." [35] He is not, as some have contended, forbidding women to speak in tongues in the congregational services. From the context, he seems rather to prohibit undisciplined discussion that would interrupt the service, for, counseled Paul, "if they would learn anything, let them ask their own husbands at home." [36] In the opinion of James Moffatt, "Paul objected strongly to a practice, evidently popular at Corinth, of matrons taking part in the discussion or interpretation of what had been said by some prophet or teacher during the service." [37]

In conclusion, it is in this dual sense that prophesying is presented in the New Testament: one, as a charismatic manifestation of the Holy Spirit open to every Christian; and two, as the specific function of the prophetic office.

[33] *Ibid.*
[34] I Cor. 11:10.
[35] I Cor. 14:34.
[36] I Cor. 14:35.
[37] Moffatt, *op. cit.,* p. 232.

CHAPTER XX

"The Greatest of These Is Love"

(I Cor. 13:13)

Contrary to popular misconception. Love is not one of the "greater gifts" Paul exhorted his readers to desire. Strictly speaking, it is not one of the *charismata* at all. Love is, rather, a "fruit of the Spirit." [1] That this is neither a new nor novel view of the facts is attested by the comment of Hermann Olshausen: "Chapter xiii clearly shows that love is no Charisma, it is contrasted with all the other gifts." [2] Now in the natural order, fruit is evidence of life. So also in the supernatural order, "fruit" is evidence of supernatural life, that is, of the "new birth," and every Spirit-begotten Christian may bear the "fruit of the Spirit" by virtue of his spiritual rebirth. On the other hand, the "gifts" of the Spirit are evidence of the baptism in the Holy Spirit.

Love is much more than a gift of the Spirit, for the gifts of God are Love's bestowals. This fact is at the heart of the Gospel: "For *God so loved* the world, that *he gave* his only begotten Son, that whosoever believeth on him should not perish, but have eternal life." [3] Thus "eternal life" is a gift

[1] Gal. 5:22.
[2] *Biblical Commentary on the New Testament,* 1st American ed., trans. by A. C. Kendrick, IV (New York: Sheldon & Company, 1860), 345.
[3] John 3:16. Italics mine H.M.E.

of God's redemptive Love. But His Love is antecedent to all of His gifts, while His gifts are the manifestation of His Love. In point of fact, there can be no gifts without a Giver, and Love is the initiative in all the Divine gifts.

Though one speak with tongues, prophesy, have knowledge of the divine purposes, manifest supernatural faith, and even suffer martydom, it is useless and worthless without Love. Paul is saying, in effect, that to manifest the gifts of the Spirit without Love, is to separate the gift from the Divine Giver, for *Love is what God is in Himself. His gifts are what He does* supernaturally in and through His Church. Love is ontological, the gifts are functional. Reluctant though some theologians may be to recognize metaphysical attributes in the Deity, Love is such an ontological distinction. In the profound simplicity of John's affirmation, "God is Love." [4] A word of caution at this point is in order. We cannot invert this declaration and say, that Love is God. Truly "love is an attribute of God," [5] but God is greater than the sum of His attributes, and no one attribute encompasses all that God is.

Christians "come to share in the very being of God" [6] through regeneration, for in these words "Peter is referring to the new birth. . . ." [7] And the Divine nature, or "being," manifests itself in us in the "fruit of the Spirit," the highest expression of which is Love. It cannot be emphasized too strongly, that God's Love, which "has flooded our inmost heart through the Holy Spirit," [8] is the highest expression of the "Divine nature" of which Christians "become partak-

---

[4] John 4:8, 16.
[5] J.D. Jones, quoted by Robertson, *Word Pictures in the New Testament*, IV, 180.
[6] II Peter 1:4 N.E.B.
[7] Robertson, *Word Pictures in the New Testament*, VI, 150.
[8] Rom. 5:5 N.E.B.

ers" through the "new birth"—for "the greatest of these is Love."

Paul does not draw a contrast between Love and gifts (i.e., tongues, prophecy, knowledge, faith, etc.). The former is an expression of His nature, the latter are supernatural manifestations of His personality. Put another way, Love is an attribute of the Divine Essence, the gifts are predicates of Divine Personality, whereby God reveals His identity and purposes. Love initiates the gifts; the gifts reveal the Love-source from whence they come. The reader will miss the point of Paul's panegyric on Love in I Cor. 13, if he regards it as an either/or option between Love and gifts. *Love does not exclude the* operation of the Spirit's gifts. It is, instead, the source and dynamic whereby they are made effectual.

Paul qualified his exhortation to "desire earnestly the greater gifts" by adding: "And moreover a most excellent way (than simply desiring even the 'greater gifts') show I unto you." [9] He then developed this theme, the "most excellent way," in a series of negative propositions.[10] These propositions are stated in a series of third class conditions—"a supposable case." [11] They read as follows: "If I speak with the tongues of men and of angels, but have not love . . . and if I have the gift of prophecy . . .; and if [12] I know all mysteries and all knowledge; and if I have all faith . . . but have not love . . . And if I bestow all my goods to feed the poor and if I give my body to be burned, but have not love. . . ."

It should be noted that the conditions set forth in these clauses are not merely fictitious assumptions for the sake of illustration. For instance, the condition as stated does not

[9] I Cor. 12:31.
[10] I Cor. 13:1-3.
[11] Robertson, *Word Pictures in the New Testament*, IV, 176.
[12] *kai ean* or *kan* is understood before *eidō*.

simply imply a doubt that the Apostle spoke in tongues. He said categorically: "I thank God, I speak with tongues more than you all." [13] Nor is his statement—"If I have the gift of prophecy"—meant to imply that he did not prophesy, for Paul was a prophet. He did, furthermore, evidence supernatural faith. His life was one of constant self-denial for the sake of others. His physical safety was continually in jeopardy—it is "the concurrent testimony of ecclesiastical antiquity, that he was beheaded at Rome. . . ." [14] Rather, the force of the hypothesis rests in the dependent clause *(apodasis)*, "but have not love." He implied that it is possible to do all these things without the motivation of Love, but the consequences are fruitless and barren. If speech in tongues be not energized by Love, one is "become sounding brass or a clanging cymbal." The exercise of the other gifts of prophecy, knowledge, or faith without Love is to be nothing. Acts of benevolence, even the supreme sacrifice of martyrdom, "profiteth nothing," unless it be motivated by Love.

Neither does this exhaust the application of this principle, for, although Paul enumerated only five spiritual charisms, what he said of these applies equally to all the Holy Spirit's operations and influences. For example, without Love, the apostles are dictators,[15] the elders and deacons are merely busybodies and the teacher pedants.

The exposition of these gifts in their relation to Love prompted a short digression by Paul on the characteristics of Love. In a moving encomium on Love, he penned its noblest exposition found anywhere else in Scripture, or in any literature. With almost Laconian brevity, he set forth

---

[13] I Cor. 14:18.

[14] *Dr. Wm. Smith's Dictionary of the Bible*, rev. & ed., by H. B. Hackett & Ezra Abbott, III (Boston: Houghton, Mifflin and Company, 1896), 239b.

[15] I am indebted to my friend and colleague, the Rev. Wm. Wilson, for this trenchant observation.

the nature of Love,[16] the immutability of Love,[17] and the primacy of Love over every gracement of the Spirit of God.[18] Thus he concluded: "But now abideth faith, hope, love, these three: and the greatest of these is love."

The words, "But now abideth," are *logical* not *temporal* in significance.[19] The importance of this needs to be underscored. Paul does not mean, that *"for the present* Faith and Hope 'abide' with Love, but Love alone 'abides' forever." [20] It is not a contrast "between love which is imperishable and faith and hope which are perishable, but between ephemeral gifts and enduring graces." [21] He pointedly contrasted the "these three" of 13:13 with the "other three" of verse 8,[22] i.e., faith, hope, love over against prophecies, tongues, knowledge. Concerning the former, "Paul puts the three on the same footing in respect of enduringness . . . pointedly adding Faith and Hope to share and support the 'abiding' of Love; 'love *is greater* among these' not more lasting." [23] Even in the eternal state "into which the *charismata* will not continue, Christians will not cease to believe, to hope, to love." [24] It is the permanence of saving faith in the ages to come (i.e., "their abiding trust in the atonement which took place through the death of Christ"), that "keeps the glorified in *continued possession* of salvation." [25]

Turning again to the negative propositions with which Paul began the development of his theme, "the most excel-

[16] I Cor. 13:3-7.
[17] I Cor. 13:8-12.
[18] I Cor. 13:13.
[19] *nuni de menei.* Findlay, *op. cit.,* II, 901. Cf., also Robertson & Plummer, *op. cit.,* p. 300. "The *nuni* is not temporal but logical. . . ."
[20] Findlay, *op. cit.,* II, 901.
[21] Meyer, *Critical and Exegitical Hand-Book to the Corinthians,* note by T. W. Chambers, Amer. ed., p. 311.
[22] Findlay, *op. cit.,* II, 901.
[23] *Ibid.*
[24] Meyer, *op. cit.,* p. 309.
[25] *Ibid.,* p. 308.

lent way," his argument may be illustrated in another way. Instead of stating these conditions negatively, they may be stated affirmatively, and the opposite conclusion drawn from them. For example, "If I speak with the tongues of men and of angels, *and I have love also,"* what then should I conclude? Stated another way, if one combines the gifts of the Holy Spirit with the Love of the Spirit, what then is the result? Unquestionably the consequences are the opposite of those drawn when the hypothesis is stated negatively. Tongues *coupled with Love* are both meaningful and edifying. Prophecy, knowledge and faith *united with Love* contribute substance and reality to Christian character. Benevolence and martyrdom *initiated by Love* bear eternal fruit in Christian experience and witness. Therefore, the combining of Love with the gifts of the Holy Spirit is the "most excellent way" expounded by Paul. Love without gifts is not the choice the Apostle offers to us. This is a false disjunctive. It is rather Love *plus* the gifts of the Spirit. There can be no reasonable doubt of this, for Paul the apostle says as much in his summation of this theme, e.g., "Follow the way of Love, while you set your heart on the gifts of the Spirit." [26]

The all to glib assertion that tongues are a mark of spiritual immaturity which Paul here counseled the Corinthians to discard in favor of Love, is not even remotely suggested in the text. Were this assumption applied with logical consistency to the whole passage, then prophecy, knowledge, faith, acts of charity, and martyrdom must too be discarded in favor of Love. *If Love excludes tongues, consistency demands that it exclude all the others.* Even the most adamant antagonists of *glossolalia* dare not advocate such a drastic purge of the text—or of Christian experience for that matter. As a matter of fact, to strip Love of all its individualized

[26] I Cor. 14:1, N.T.M.E.

manifestations—prophecy, tongues, knowledge, faith, benevolence, sacrifice, etc.—would be to relegate this metaphysical attribute of God to the limbo of the inscrutable and
the incommunicable. How then could the Church experience or express Divine Love? Consequently, the apostle
Paul taught that the gifts of the Holy Spirit are never an
end in themselves. They must be used to articulate the Love
of God.

Since Paul wrote of these gifts in the same terms, to dismiss one is to dismiss all—to retain some is to retain all.
Unequivocally, he declared, that "If one speaks in tongues
without Love, he is an empty echo. And if he has prophecy,
knowledge, and faith without Love, he is nothing. Even if
one voluntarily endures martyrdom for his faith, but is devoid of Love, it is of no profit to him." The unity of thought
here is inescapable. Therefore, to dismiss tongues with the
epithet "spiritual immaturity," etc. is to stoop to the demogoguery of the shibboleth. To stigmatize one charism of the
Spirit of God above all others, in so cavalier a fashion, cannot be dignified as exposition. It is polemics, pure and
simple.

There is no scriptural justification for saying that tongues
were dividing the Corinthian church. As a matter of record,
it was not tongues, it was teachers that introduced division
into the assembly at Corinth. "For," wrote Paul to the
Corinthians, "it hath been signified unto me concerning
you, my brethren, by them that are of the household of
Chloe, that each one of you saith, I am of Paul; and I of
Apollos; and I of Cephas; and I of Christ. Is Christ divided?
was Paul crucified for you? or were ye baptized into the
name of Paul?" [27]

True to human nature, a parallel situation is developing
in the contemporary charismatic renewal of the churches.

[27] I Cor. 1:11-13.

Glossolalia per se is not nearly so divisive as the dogmatic pronouncements of sundry teachers on the subject. It is denial of, or disobedience to, "the commandment of the Lord," [28] that is intrinsically divisive. The ecclesiastical censures of bishops, synods, conventions, or commissions are unambiguous repudiation of the apostolic decree, "and forbid not to speak with tongues." [29] Actually, the full import of this prohibition is even stronger than this translation conveys, as we shall see in the proper place.

Ecclesiastical coercion of charismatic Christians is even more subversive of the unity of the Church, than the manifestations of the gifts of the Holy Spirit ever could be. As already pointed out by the great Apostle himself, it is in the ordered operation of the gifts of God's Spirit, as interpersonal ministries, that the unity of the Body of Christ (the Church) is ideally manifested.[30] All the manifestations of the Spirit are given for "the common good." [31] They are to be sought for "the edifying of the church," [32] for the ultimate goal of all of God's gifts is that we may "all attain to the unity of the faith." [33] Ecumenicity without Life, union without unity, creed without Christ are semantic perversions. Life, unity, Christ Himself can be made evident only by the sovereign operations of the Holy Spirit.

[28] I Cor. 14:37.
[29] I Cor. 14:39.
[30] I Cor. 12:12ff.
[31] I Cor. 12:7 R.S.V.
[32] I Cor. 14:12.
[33] Eph. 4:13.

CHAPTER XXI

The Apostle Paul's Attitude Toward Tongues

(I Cor. 14:1,5,6,12,14,18,39)

To speak in tongues, or not to speak in tongues? Where did the apostle Paul stand in relation to this vexed question? That the utterances given by the Holy Spirit are under the volitional control of the speaker is quite clear from his counsels to both tongues-speakers and prophets. The former are to "keep silence in the church," and to "speak to himself and to God," (i.e., "in tongues"), "if there be no interpreter" present in the service.[1] Such an admonition obviously presupposes voluntary control of their speech organs by the one speaking in tongues. This very fact exposes the fallacy of the assertion that tongues "was supposed to represent a divine monologue, bursting through the lips of the *unconscious enthusiast.*" [2]

Nor was the declamation of the prophet an uncontrollable outburst in an ecstatic state. The same counsel applied to the prophets as well as to the speaker in tongues. They are to speak by two or three in succession,[3] but "if a revela-

[1] I Cor. 14:27,28.
[2] Moffatt, *op. cit.*, p. 208. Italics mine H.M.E.
[3] I Cor. 14:29

tion be made to another sitting by, let the first keep silence." [4] Added to this is the unqualified declaration, that "the spirits of the prophets are subject to the prophets." [5]

It is this very rational and voluntary control by the Spirit-filled Christian that distinguishes the *charismata* of the Holy Spirit from the cataleptic states of trance mediums and pagan psychics. The charismatic manifestations of the Holy Spirit involve a reciprocal relationship between the Holy Spirit and the human spirit. The only coercion the Spirit of God uses is the coercion of love. The Spirit-filled Christian is *permeated with,* not *invaded by,* the Divine Spirit. The charismatic manifestations of the Spirit are *voluntary responses,* not *involuntary reactions,* to the Holy Spirit's initiative. Confusion in the expression of the Spirit's gifts results from *lack of discipline, not loss of consciousness.* Such confusion is not inherent in the operation of the gifts themselves, but in the lack of restraint of the individual worshipper.

One of the most unrestrained services the present writer ever attended was a prayer meeting in which every worshipper prayed simultaneously in English, with a considerable display of both noise and emotion. Their expression of intensely revivalistic fervor was non-charismatic in character. Denominationally, the same group is unabashedly anti-tongues.

The point we are making here is this: there is nothing inherently emotional in *glossolalia.* Some display more emotion than others, but in general no more than when speaking their vernacular tongue. The emotional overtones are inherent in the individual speaker's temperament, not in the gifts themselves. The utterance in other tongues is a manifestation of the Holy Spirit's personality. The emo-

---

[4] I Cor 14:30.
[5] I Cor. 14:32.

tional response that may, or may not, accompany it is a manifestation of the speaker's personality.

Did Paul, therefore, depreciate the intrinsic value of tongues because he counseled restraint in their use in the public services of the church? Of course not! As well say that he depreciated the value of prophecy because he counseled discipline in its manifestation. Paul's attitude toward *glossolalia,* as revealed in his actual pronouncements, merits a more sympathetic and objective appraisal than the critics of tongues have so far been willing to concede. We simply urge that Paul be allowed to speak for himself.

I. *I Cor. 14:1, 5—"Now I Would Have You All Speak With Tongues"*

Our appraisal of Paul's attitude toward tongues begins logically with an assessment of the meaning of his exhortation to: "Follow after love; yet desire earnestly spiritual gifts, but rather (*mallon de*) that ye may prophesy." [6] The translation, "but rather (*mallon de*)," by the *King James Version,* followed by the *American Standard Version,* implies an antithesis between speaking in tongues and prophesying. This implied opposition between tongues and prophecy suggests, at face value, a judgment by the Apostle upon the intrinsic inferiority of the former to the latter. Pressed out of context—which is not uncommonly done— some read into it the total exclusion of tongues in favor of prophecy. But is this what Paul really said?

The implied adversative force of the translation, "but rather," merits closer scrutiny. Actually the antithetical force is not an inherent part of the meaning of this phrase, for "*mallon de . . .* introduces an expression or thought that supplements and thereby corrects what has preceded." [7]

[6] I Cor. 14:1.
[7] Arndt, Gingrich, Bauer, *op. cit.,* p. 490.

Note well, that "supplements" cannot legitimately be stretched to mean "excludes." The idiom, *mallon de,* can have the sense of "instead of," *if it follows a negative*—as for example Eph. 4:28: "let him that stole steal no more: *but rather* let him labor, working with his hands the thing that is good. . . ." The *New English Bible* translation of this verse is more to the point: "The thief must give up stealing, and instead *(mallon de)* work hard and honestly with his own hands. . . ." This is precisely the point at issue in the use of this idiom in I Cor. 14:1, 5, where, in neither instance, is *mallon de* used with a negative. The adversative force may, consequently, be ruled out of the interpretation of both of these verses in I Corinthians. The basic comparative force of the adverb [8] comes to the fore then, and this may be expressed more clearly by translating it "to a greater degree."

This point is more clearly illustrated by the use of this same phrase in Rom. 8:34: "It is Christ Jesus that died, yea rather, that was raised from the dead. . . ." Once again, the *New English Bible* rendering of this idiom is more precise: "It is Christ—Christ who died, and more than that *(mallon de)*, was raised from the dead. . . ." Here the clause introduced by *mallon de*—"and *more than that,* was raised from the dead"—is not in opposition to (i.e., does not exclude) the first clause, "It is Christ—Christ who died." *Mallon de* "supplements and thereby corrects" by the addition of a supplementary fact. The fact that Christ was raised from the dead is not set in antithesis to the fact that He had died.

What effect do these grammatical insights have upon one's understanding of I Cor. 14:1 and 5? Applied to the translation of verse one, it may justifiably be translated: "Follow after love; and desire earnestly spiritual gifts, *and more than that,* that ye may prophesy." The *Revised Stan-*

[8] *Mallon* is the comparative of the adverb *mala.*

dard Version says essentially the same thing, e.g., "especially that you may prophesy." The *American Standard Version*, following the *King James Version*, erroneously translates *mallon de* with the adversative force in verse five also: "Now I would have you all speak with tongues, but rather that ye should prophesy. . . ." However, in conformity to the grammatical facts, it may be translated more accurately thus: "Now I would have you all speak with tongues, and more than that, that ye should prophesy. . . ." The *New American Standard Bible* approximates this rendering with the translation, "but even more." All of which leads to the conclusion that Paul did not imply that prophesying excluded tongues, or any other spiritual gift for that matter.

The primacy apparently attributed to prophecy over the other spiritual gifts, specifically tongues, is not, however, an unqualified preëminence. It must be borne in mind that Paul speaks here of prophecy and tongues in a given context, namely, the services of the worshipping community of believers. This in itself imposes certain limitations upon what he said regarding prophecy, or any of the other gifts. The Apostle's concern is a very practical one. Inasmuch as prayer in tongues edifies only the one speaking,[9] therefore, prophecy which ministers "edification, and exhortation, and consolation" to the assembled worshippers is preferred in the church services.[10]

Paul's endorsement of prophecy over tongues is, consequently, provisional, for he wrote, "greater is he that prophesieth than he that speaketh with tongues, *except (ektos ei mē)*[11] he interpret, that the church may receive edifying."[12]

[9] I Cor. 14:4.
[10] 14:3.
[11] Findlay, *op cit.*, II, 903. "*ektos ei mē* is a Pauline pleonasm . . . consisting of *ektos ei* (except if) and *ei mē* (unless) run together." Did Paul use this lengthened form for emphasis?
[12] I Cor. 14:5. Italics mine H.M.E.

Thus the apostle Paul qualified his value judgment on prophecy in two respects.

One, prophecy is greater than tongues in the worship services of the Church, because it is readily intelligible to all. Later in the same chapter, he wrote again: "I thank God, I speak with tongues more than you all: howbeit in the church I had rather speak five words with my understanding. . . ." Knowing experientially the power of tongues for self-edification, he apparently reserved prayer in tongues for his private devotions.

Two, tongues accompanied by interpretation are equal to prophecy, for, "The power to interpret *superadded* to the glossolalia . . . puts the mystic speaker on a level with the prophet: first 'uttering mysteries' . . . and then making them plain to his hearers, he accomplished in two acts what the prophet does in one." [13] The prophet was known "as proclaimer and interpreter of the divine revelations." [14] In this sense, too, the "prophetic" [15] utterance in tongues with interpretation was as much prophecy as the speaking forth of divine mysteries in the vernacular.

Apart from an *a priori* presumption, it is difficult to detect a Pauline prejudice in his words: "Now I would have you all speak with tongues. . . ." [16] The *Revised Standard Version* rendering of this verse is even stronger than the one quoted above: "Now I want you all to speak in tongues. . . ." It is only fair to say that he valued tongues as a charism of the Holy Spirit. The preference expressed for prophecy was dictated by the practical concerns of corporate worship. Prophecy in the language(s) current among them inspired and edified because it was immediately understood. Tongues without interpretation did not do this.

---

[13] Findlay, *op. cit.*, II, 903.
[14] Arndt, Gingrich, Bauer, *op. cit.*, *prophētēs*, p. 730.
[15] Acts 2:4.
[16] I Cor. 14:5.

The value judgment thus expressed is a utilitarian one, not an assessment of intrinsic worth.

II. *I Cor. 14:6—"If I Come Unto You Speaking With Tongues"*

A certain ambiguity veils the interpretation of the next passage to be considered, but it is an ambiguity that must be grappled with, if we would be fair to Paul's attitude toward tongues. The text in question is I Cor. 14:6: "But now, brethren, if I come unto you speaking with tongues, what shall I profit you, unless I speak to you either by way of revelation, or of knowledge, or of prophesying, or of teaching."

To begin, it will be necessary to analyse the sentence structure, and to define the relationship of the parts to the whole. The sentence under scrutiny is a compound one, in which the several clauses "may be either coordinate *(paratatic)* or subordinate *(hypotatic)*." [17] This means that its individual statements (or clauses) may be either "parallel with each other or dependent on one another." [18]

Thus two possibilities are open to the interpreter of this verse. In the first place, he may regard the clauses as coordinate. Then the sense of the passage could be this: "If I come speaking with Tongues, instead of speaking either in the way of revelation, etc." [19] Mark the introduction of the adversative "instead of." This view not only interprets the clauses making up the sentence as independent, but by the translation "instead of" *(ean mē)* introduces a disjunctive element into the translation. Thus this view injects a mutually exclusive contrast between the "tongues-speech" of the first clause and "revelation" etc., (spoken in the vernacular)

[17] Robertson & Davis, *op. cit.*, p. 203.
[18] *Ibid.*
[19] Robertson & Plummer, *op. cit.*, p. 307.

of the second clause. If this interpretation be embraced, then it could be argued that Paul disparaged "tongues-speech" as unprofitable. The corollary is then plain. If the church is to receive revelation, knowledge, prophecy, or teaching, then speaking in tongues must be abandoned in favor of the language(s) spoken in any given congregation. The weakness of this view is that it introduces a false disjunctive into the author's thought.

The second interpretation is to regard the third clause, "unless I speak to you either by way of revelation, etc.," as subordinate to the first clause. Again much hinges upon the significance of the conditional conjunction *(ean mē)* which joins the third clause to the preceding ones. Grammatically, this conditional conjunction indicates that the clause which it introduces is subordinate to the initial clause.[20] As a subordinate clause, it does not introduce a new subject (i.e., "revelation, etc.," spoken in the vernacular), but elaborates some fact, or facts, relating to the subject of the initial clause, namely, "tongues-speech." The translation of the *New English Bible* is in harmony with this view in its translation of this passage, to wit, "unless what I say contains something by way of revelation, etc." The effect of this translation upon the interpretation of the verse may be sharpened by asking, "unless what I say—How?" The answer is obvious, viz., "unless what I say in tongues."

Paul might have phrased it differently, and written, "if I come unto you speaking with tongues, what shall I profit you, unless you understand the revelation, etc., which I have spoken in tongues." The Apostle acknowledged, with thanksgiving, that he exercised the gift of tongues, and he might just as well have been his own interpreter. Instead of

---

[20] Robertson & Davis, *op. cit.*, p. 203. "The hypotactic sentence likewise will either have conjunctions (relative like *hos;* temporal like *hote;* comparative like *hōsper;* causal like *hoti;* final like *hina;* conditional like *ei, ean . . . .*"

generalizing, however, "he specifies the two *kinds* [21] of discourse in which he might give *an interpretation of his speech in tongues,* and says, *If I shall have come to you speaking in tongues, what shall I profit you, if I shall not have spoken to you* (for the sake, namely, of expounding my speech in tongues, ver. 5), either in revelation, etc. . . ." [22]

In this second interpretation, there is no contrast between speaking in tongues and revelation, etc., in the vernacular dialects. Instead, tongues are the vehicle for conveying revelation, knowledge, prophecy, and teaching. For this reason, Paul summarized his instruction in this section, verses 5–13, with the inferential conjunction, "wherefore" *(dio)*; e.g., "Wherefore let him that speaketh in a tongue pray that he may interpret." The conjunction looks back to verse 5, and concludes this section of the Apostle's thought.

In essence, he said that since tongues with interpretation are equivalent to prophecy, therefore, "let him that speaketh in a tongue pray that he may interpret," so that the revelation, knowledge, prophecy or teaching contained in the tongues-speech may be made intelligible to all the worshippers. Speech that is not understood is to the hearer an unintelligible barbarism. This is true of tongues unless they are interpreted. He did not, for that reason, advise the discontinuance of tongues-speech, rather he urged them to pray for the interpretation of such speech.

III. *I Cor. 14:12 (1, 39)—"Desire Earnestly Spiritual Gifts"*

So often the blanket assumption is made that the Christian is not to seek the gifts of the Spirit. It is frequently phrased something like this: "If God wants me to have

---

[21] Meyer, *Critical and Exegetical Hand-Book to the Corinthians,* p. 316. ". . . not *four,* but two charismatic modes of teaching are here *designated* —*prophecy* and *didascalia.* For the former, the condition is *apocalupsis;* for the latter, *gnosis.*"

[22] *Ibid.*

them, He will give them to me." On the surface, this affirmation sounds convincingly pious. Actually, it is merely
platitudinous. There is a rather obvious error in the tacit
assumption that grace operates irresistibly upon the passive,
even indifferent child of God. The ancient Psalmist, for
instance, knew nothing of such pious self-deception when
he sang: "As the hart panteth after the water brooks, So
panteth my soul after thee, O God. My soul thirsteth for
God, for the living God." [23] To this heart cry, the words of
our Saviour Jesus Christ read like the Divine requital of
the Psalmist's ardor: "Blessed are they that hunger and
thirst after righteousness: for they shall be filled." [24] So too,
in the bestowal of the Holy Spirit's gifts, Divine initiative
courts human response. It does not function by arbitrary
decree. Spiritual gifts are not God's decrees, they are His
promises, preconditioned by our response to certain conditions which He has clearly stated. God's gifts and gracements are for those who earnestly desire them, or Paul's
words are meaningless; to wit, "desire earnestly spiritual
gifts," [25] and "desire earnestly to prophesy." [26]

The apostle Paul counseled an active appropriation of
the gifts of the Spirit in I Cor. 14:12. Here he amplified his
exhortation to include the controlling motivation prompt-
ing the desire for the Spirit's manifestations, saying, "since
ye are zealous of spiritual gifts, seek that ye may abound
unto the edifying of the church."

Here too, there is some obscurity in the English translation. As it reads above, the verb, "seek *(zēteite),* has no direct object expressed. The purpose clause [27] which follows—

---

[23] Psalm 42:1,2a.
[24] Matt. 5:5.
[25] I Cor. 14:1.
[26] I Cor. 14:39.
[27] Findlay, *op. cit.,* II, 905. *"hina (perisseuēte)* bears its ordinary sense as
conjunction of purpose."

"that ye may abound"—is not the object of the verb, "seek." As a matter of fact, the verb in this very purpose clause, namely, "that ye may abound (*perisseuēte*), is also without an object expressed. It is, therefore, important for the interpretation of the verse to notice that both verbs find their "object supplied beforehand in the previous clause," [28] i.e., by "what was previously meant by *pneumatōn, spiritual gifts.*" [29] The meaning of the verse may be paraphrased thus: "So also ye, since ye are zealous of spiritual gifts, seek that you may abound in spiritual gifts [30] unto the edifying of the church." Another rendering, that comes closer to reproducing the word order and emphasis of the original reads thus: "for the edifying of the church seek (them, i.e., spiritual gifts) that ye may abound therein." [31]

Paul's endorsement for seeking spiritual gifts is here a general one embracing all of the Spirit's gifts. The *New English Bible,* in what amounts to a paraphrase of this verse, has sharpened the emphasis: "You are, I know, eager for gifts of the Spirit; then aspire above all to excel in those which build up the church." In the next verse "interpretation of tongues" is one of the gifts "which build up the church." Note again the sequence of thought: "So also ye, since ye are zealous of spiritual gifts, seek spiritual gifts that ye may abound therein unto the edifying of the church. Wherefore, let him that speaketh in a tongue pray that he may interpret."

It cannot reasonably be urged then that tongues and interpretation of tongues are excluded by the Apostle from the gifts to be used for the edifying of the Church. The gift that does not edify the Church is tongues *without* interpretation. As already pointed out, tongues plus interpreta-

[28] *Ibid.*
[29] Meyer, *Critical and Exegetical Hand-Book to the Corinthians,* p. 321.
[30] Thayer, *op. cit., perisseuō,* p. 505.
[31] Findlay, *op. cit.,* II, 905.

tion is equivalent to prophecy, and is to be used for the edification of the assembled worshippers. The assumption that Paul counseled abstention from tongues in the Church is inaccurate. As verses 26–28 and 39 show, Paul did not forbid the use of the gift of tongues. He simply sought to regulate its use in the public services of the churches.

IV. *I Cor. 14:14—"I Will Pray With The Spirit"*

The clearest appraisal by the Apostle of the part played by tongues in his own experience is related in I Cor. 14:14– 18: "For if I pray in tongues," wrote Paul, "my spirit prayeth, but my understanding is unfruitful." Having already called attention to this verse, only one relevant fact needs to be underscored here before proceeding, i.e., prayer in tongues is prayer on a supra-rational level of personality. Therefore, when he continued, "I will pray with the spirit," he referred to prayer in tongues. By the same token, when he said, "and I will pray with the understanding also," he referred to prayer in the vernacular. In the light of 14:13, Henry Alford explained that by the words, "I will pray with the understanding also," the Apostle meant, "I will interpret my prayer (i.e., in tongues) for the benefit of myself and the church." [32] This is a possible interpretation, however, anyone who prays in tongues is aware that while praying, one may switch from tongues to their own language, and back again into tongues. Amplifying this thought, Paul continued: "I will sing with the spirit," that is to say, "in tongues," and "I will sing with the understanding also." Following Alford's suggestion, this may be a reference to an interpretation of the song previously sung in tongues. Singing in tongues with an accompanying "sung" interpre-

[32] *Op. cit.*, II. 594. Interpretation was not indispensable to the edification of the one praying in tongues. Such prayer, whether understood or not, edified the one so praying. I Cor. 14:4. "He that speaketh in a tongue edifieth himself." Cf. also 14:28.

tation is encountered more or less frequently in the present charismatic revival, and the edifying power of this mode of worship must be experienced to be appreciated.

He continued his autobiographical comments thus: "Else if thou bless (i.e., 'God' [35]) with the spirit," that is in tongues, "how shall he that filleth the place of the unlearned say the Amen at thy giving of thanks." By the "unlearned," the Apostle alluded to "the one destitute of the gift of tongues," [34] or to "a kind of proselyte or catechumen." [35] Hence, "prayer with the understanding," i.e., in the vernacular languages, was necessary for the sake of these catechumens. Certainly, no censure for such charismatic prayer is even hinted at in what follows. On the contrary, Paul pointedly said, "For thou verily givest thanks well," and he unquestionably meant by that prayers of thanksgiving in tongues.

While prayer in tongues without an accompanying interpretation is inadequate for the mutual edification the corporate worship should provide, this cannot be construed to mean that tongues are intrinsically inferior to the other gifts of the Spirit. Such disparagement of this gift cannot be legitimately deduced from Paul's statements in this (or, for that matter, any other) context. After all, "speaking with other tongues, as the Holy Spirit gives utterance," is a manifestation of the Spirit's supernatural personality. One wonders at the presumption that would arrogate to itself the right to make such value judgments upon the workings of God's own Spirit. In the final analysis, only God Himself can pass such judgments upon His workings. It is to be hoped that such a reminder would serve as a deterrent upon some of the extravagant, even slanderous jibes modern crit-

---

[33] Findlay, *op. cit.*, II, p. 907.
[34] Thayer, *op. cit., idiōtēs*, p. 297.
[35] Arndt, Gingrich, Bauer, *op. cit., idiōtēs*, p. 371.

ics of the charismatic renewal of the Church level at "speaking with other tongues." Far more wholesome is Paul's expressed attitude—and this brings us to the heart of the matter.

V. *I Cor. 14:18, 19—"I Thank God, I Speak With Tongues More Than You All"*

Perhaps no other verse in these three chapters of I Corinthians has been the subject of more tortured exegesis than 14:18, 19. Apart from invincible prejudice, it is incomprehensible how Paul's words can be so misconstrued as to assert that he depreciated on the one hand what he praised on the other. But let him speak for himself: "I thank God, I speak with tongues more than you all." Obviously, as the sequel indicates, tongues played a large part in his private devotions, and the great Apostle speaks with reverence and gratitude of this manifestation of the Holy Spirit in his own experience. Only an intransigent bias against tongues could twist his words here in an effort to evade their plain import.

It is a strange exegetical conceit that would warp these words to read: "I thank God, I speak more languages than you all," meaning thereby, learned languages, not charismatic utterances. This "translation" is grammatically wrong, because it misconstrues the word "more" *(mallon)* as an adjective modifying the noun "tongues." It is not an adjective, it is a comparative adverb modifying the verb, "speak." The clause is correctly translated, "I speak in tongues more than you all." [36]

Though the above mistranslation of the passage has been widely disseminated recently, its roots apparently go back into Patristic History. It is said, that "Jerome in Notes, re-

---

[36] Arndt, Gingrich, Bauer, *op. cit., mallon,* p. 490. "I (can) speak in tongues more than you all."

fers the *mallon to the other Apostles,* as though Paul exulted in being a better linguist than any of the twelve." [37] This is text out of context exposition, for Paul is addressing the Corinthian church, not the other Apostles. The comparison is drawn between the charismatic experience of Paul, and the charismatic experience of the Corinthians, and not between himself and the rest of the Apostles. Robertson and Plummer single out this very interpretation for rebuttal, saying, "Here we have strong evidence that Tongues are not foreign languages [i.e., learned languages]. He does not say that he speaks 'in more tongues.' " [38]

Such an arbitrary explanation of the text as the above does not deserve the name of exegesis, nor would it merit serious consideration, if it were not that it is finding some currency among certain groups in the Church today.

Most of the derogatory comments about tongues sooner or later appeal to Paul's words in verse 19, and are more a matter of emphasis than of exegesis. This verse is often pressed beyond measure in an attempt to make it nullify what the Apostle had already said in a positive vein about tongues in the preceding verse. For this reason, we must deal with the question raised by verse 19.

After the doxology for tongues in verse 18, to what extent, and in what direction did he modify this by saying, "howbeit in the church I had rather speak five words with my understanding, that I might instruct others also, than ten thousand words in a tongue"?

Was he taking back with his left hand what he had previously proffered with his right? Is this *ipso facto* evidence

---

[37] Findlay, *op. cit.,* II, 908. "The Vulgate, omitting *mallon,* reads *omnium vestrum lingua loguor,* making Paul thank God that he could speak in every tongue used at Corinth." The Confraternity version of the Challoner-Rheims version follows the Vulgate here: "I speak with all your languages."
[38] Robertson & Plummer, *op. cit.,* p. 314.

that Paul did not really value tongues, but was deftly ac-
comodating himself to the situation in Corinth, in hopes of
remedying presumed abuses? The assumption does not
really do justice to the context, nor to Paul's integrity either.
For example, in the pattern of primitive Christian worship
outlined in 14:26–33, provision is made for every manifestation of the Holy Spirit. Here the Apostle wrote: "When
ye come together, each one hath a psalm, hath a teaching,
hath a revelation, hath a tongue, hath an interpretation."
From this representative sampling, it may rightly be concluded that he anticipated that every gift of the Holy Spirit
would be in evidence during the corporate worship services
of the church. He simply counseled the ordering of these
manifestations, that would be most beneficial to all concerned, namely, "Let all things be done unto edifying."

Everyone baptized in, i.e., filled with the Spirit, may pray
in tongues—abiding evidence of the Spirit's fulness. But not
every one will be prompted by the Holy Spirit to speak in
tongues with an accompanying interpretation in the corporate worship of the church, "by way of revelation, or of
knowledge, or of prophesying, or of teaching." When Paul
said, "I had rather speak five words with my understanding,
that I might instruct others . . .," he was simply imple-
menting his own advice to "desire earnestly the greater
gifts"—of which, he said, the third in order of importance
was the gift of "teacher." Without deprecating tongues, he
was setting this gift (*charisma*) of the Holy Spirit in its
proper relation to the greater gift (*dōrea*) of Christ, namely,
that of teacher.

In summary then, the evidence indicates that Paul did
not depreciate tongues as a lesser charism. Used in private
devotions, he thanked God for the full measure of the gift
in his own life, for therewith he edified himself. The edification thus received was manifested in the efficacy of his

service for our Lord and Saviour, Jesus Christ. In the use of tongues in public worship, he counseled restraint for the sake of the uninitiated or the catechumens, and that all the other gifts might receive equal emphasis. Coupled with interpretation, though it will edify the Church. Without interpretation it edifies only the one so worshipping. As will be pointed out subsequently, Paul also counseled restraint for the sake of the "unbeliever" who attended the services. It cannot justly be deduced, therefore, that Paul simply "honed an ax" in these chapters against the gift of tongues. Even when there is no interpretation, he counseled the one praying in tongues not to stop entirely, but to continue to pray in tongues silently, speaking "to himself, and to God."

If more Christians would act upon the Apostle's advice, the churches would yet come to life. If most of the worshippers at any given worship service would pray "ten thousand words in a tongue" before they went to church, they would need only five words in the vernacular from the preacher to get the job done. Hyperbole? Perhaps! But there is considerably more than a grain of truth in it. If the modern Christian went to church services having first "edified themselves in tongues," [39] the average service would have more the tone of a jubilee than a requiem. No matter how aesthetically embellished "divine worship" may be (and this is said with full appreciation for the value of liturgical worship) without the spontaneous life of the Divine Spirit made manifest, the ceremonies of religious worship are scarcely more than the shroud for man's spiritual aspirations. No matter how artfully the liturgies of worship may be elaborated, without the charismatic life of the Spirit of God to animate them, worship deteriorates into a wake. Devoid of

[39] I am indebted to a colleague, the Rev. David du Plessis for the above observation.

the Spirit's supernatural manifestations, the cathedral is a crypt, while contrariwise, the catacombs, envigorated by the Holy Spirit's ebullient life, become the cradle of the Church's conquests.

If the Church today covets Apostolic results, let is begin with an Apostolic experience—"I thank God, I speak with tongues more than you all. . . ."

CHAPTER XXII

Whence the Party-Strife at Corinth?

(I Cor. : 11ff)

"Tongues are least," declaim the critics, yet Paul devoted more space, in the Corinthian context, to this discussion of tongues than to the discussion of love. Was this a paradox, or a polemic on his part? Was it because, as so many have assumed, he was doing some "knuckle rapping" over a "childish" absorption with tongues by immature Corinthian believers? Was it an overindulgence in tongues-speech that he sought to correct? Or was Paul confronted with a diametrically opposite situation in Corinth? It will be the task of these final chapters to supply an answer.

The Corinthian church was a divided church. The apostle Paul castigated this party spirit as carnal and immature.[1] He pleaded with them to cease and to desist from this flagrant disunity, or else he would come and deal personally with the partisan instigators. He warned: "Some are arrogant, as though I were not coming to you. But I will come to you soon, if the Lord wills, and I will find out not the talk of these arrogant people but their power. For the kingdom of God does not consist in talk but in power. What do you wish? Shall I come to you with a rod, or with love in a

---

[1] I Cor. 3:1ff.

spirit of gentleness?" [2] It is this very schismatic spirit in Corinth that underscores the Apostle's discussion of the Body,
the Church,[3]—a unity ideally evidenced in the Body-minis-
try supplied by the gifts of the Spirit of the Lord. It is likely
that he again addressed himself to this very party-spirit
when he exhorted them, "in wicked disposition [4] to be as
babes." [5] That is to say, "be a child as far as wickedness is
concerned." [6] To which Paul added, "but in mind *(phresin)*
be men." The subtle nuance between "mind" *(phresin)*
here, and "understanding" *(nous* in verse 14, is suggestive.

The *nous* is "the reflective consciousness," [7] the intellect
or reason. *Phresin* means *"the heart,"* [8] as the seat of the
passions,[9] thence, "the *heart* or *mind,* as the seat of the mental faculties, perception, thought." [10] Thus it relates "mind"
(phresin) more to the emotional nature than to the intellectual faculty. Can we not sharpen Paul's meaning here by
translating, "Brethren, be not childish in *heart,* but in
wicked disposition be childlike, and in heart be mature."

In the light of the party-strife that blighted the Corinthian church, the impression grows on one that Paul, in the
choice of *phresin* juxtaposed to *nous* here, was taking notice
again of the passions that clouded sober judgment among
the Corinthians. He was pleading for emotional maturity,
and a gentle disposition among them, not for intellectual
attainment *per se.* As a matter of record, some among them

---

[2] I Cor. 4:18-21 R.S.V.

[3] I. Cor. 12:12ff.

[4] Thayer, *op. cit., kakia,* p. 320.

[5] I Cor. 14:20.

[6] Arndt, Gingrich, Bauer, *op. cit., kakia,* p. 397.

[7] Hermann Cremer, *Biblico-Theological Lexicon of New Testament Greek,* p. 456.

[8] Thayer, *op. cit., phrēn,* p. 658. "Septuagint several times in Prov. for *leb* [heart]."

[9] Liddell & Scott, *op. cit., phrēn,* p. 1692.

[10] *Ibid.*

already prided themselves upon an intellectualized "wisdom" abjured by Paul who spoke, "not in persuasive words of wisdom, but in demonstration of the Spirit and power." [11] Unquestionably this was a *charismatic* "demonstration of the Spirit and power" to which he was to refer again in his epistle to the Romans 15:18, 19, to wit: "For I will not dare to speak of any things save those which Christ wrought through me, for the obedience of the Gentiles, by word and deed, *in the power of signs and wonders, in the power of the Holy Spirit;* so that from Jerusalem, and round about even unto Illyricum, I have fully preached the gospel of Christ." [12] In a nut shell, violent partisan passions must not corrupt the manifestations of the Holy Spirit's gifts.

Inasmuch as this party-strife in the Corinthian church must have effected its whole life, two questions press for an answer. First, what was the nature of these warring factions? Second, what effect did these parties have on the manifestations of the Spirit's gifts?

There are numerous suggested answers to the first question, however, Archibald Robertson and Alfred Plummer were close to the truth when they suggested that: "The 'parties' at Corinth, therefore, are the local results of streams of influence which show themselves at work elsewhere in the N. T. We may distinguish them respectively as St. Paul and his Gospel, Hellenistic intellectualism (Apollos), conciliatory conservatism, or 'the Gospel of the circumcision' (Kephas), and 'zealots for the law,' hostile to the Apostleship of St. Paul. These last were the exclusive party." [13]

The Pauline and Petrine "parties" are sufficiently clear

---

[11] I Cor. 2:4.
[12] Italics mine, H.M.E.
[13] *Op. cit.*, p. 12.

from other scriptures, and need not be elaborated upon here. However, the enigmatic figure of Apollos, along with the party that took his name, and the elusive "Christ" party, demand further investigation.

What little is known Biblically of Apollos is contained in a few scattered references. From Acts 18:24–19:1, we learn that he was a Jew of Alexandria, instructed in the Scriptures, eloquent in speech, knowing the baptism (consequently the doctrine) of John the Baptist, and, after being instructed by Priscilla and Aquilla, he left Ephesus for Corinth. Furthermore, in I Cor. 1:12; 3:5,6,22; and 4:6, his name is linked with one of the sectarian parties in Corinth. Next, in I Cor. 16:12, it is recorded that he refused Paul's importunity to return to Corinth. The final reference to him is found in Paul's instructions to Titus to assist Zenas, the lawyer, and Apollos in their preparations for a journey.

Little enough to go on, to be sure, but in addition to the suggestion that his name was linked with those espousing a Hellenistic intellectualism, there are several other provocative implications at hand. As an Alexandrian Jew, he probably was imbued with the syncretistic philosophy of Philo, who undertook to reinterpret the Old Testament in terms of Greek philosophical speculations.

Apollos would, therefore, be representative of Diaspora Judaism, which to a considerable extent had adopted Greek culture. Their Bible was the Greek translation of the Hebrew, known as the Septuagint. They not only adopted Greek names, but used the Greek language even in their worship. Their communal organizations were influenced to some extent by Hellenistic prototypes. Fired by an intense missionary zeal, they ardently sought to convert their pagan neighbors, for, "The Jews of the Diaspora were possessed with the conviction that they were destined to realize the prophetic word, 'I have set thee for a light of the nations.' " [14] Apollos' instruction in the Scriptures would be that of Diaspora Judaism, rather than that of normative Palestinian Judaism.

A parallel to such an influence by Alexandrian theology through Apollos is anticipated in the reconstruction of the Colossian heresy by W. J. Conybeare and J. S. Howson, who wrote of it as follows: "The most probable view, therefore, seems to be, that some Alexandrian Jew had appeared at Colossae, professing a belief in Christianity, and imbued with the Greek 'philosophy' of the school of Philo, but combining with it the Rabbinical theosophy and angelology which afterwards were embodied in the Kabbala, and an extravagant asceticism, which also afterwards distinguished several sects of the Gnostics." [15] The parallels with the situation at Corinth will be drawn out a little further on.

There is a tendency today to relate most, if not all of these influences to the Essenes. Unquestionably the *Dead Sea Scrolls* reveal parallel developments, but is it perhaps too enthusiastic a judgment that would ascribe their origin to the Essene hermeneutic. It would seem rather that such parallel developments reflect mutual borrowings from, and interaction with, the religious and cultural currents of the Hellenistic world.

In addition to the synopsis of the theological influences of Alexandrian theology already given, there was a strong Messianic emphasis in Apollos' preaching—"he spake and taught accurately the things concerning Jesus" [16]—which derived from the teaching of John the Baptist. As one

[14] George H. Box, "The Historical and Religious Background of the Early Christian Movement," *The Abingdon Bible Commentary*, ed. by Frederick Carl Eiselen, Edwin Lewis, and David G. Downey, (New York: Abingdon-Cokesbury Press, 1929), p. 847.

[15] W. J. Conybeare and J. S. Howson, *The Life and Epistles of St. Paul*, II (New York: Charles Scribners and Co., 1869), 383.

[16] Acts 18:25.

"knowing only the baptism of John," he had imbibed the strong Messianic expectations of the Forerunner. As a disciple of John, he would undoubtedly reflect, to a greater or lesser degree, the emphases of his ministry, and, "it is generally recognized that John forms the most important channel through which eschatological and soteriological ideas and practices passed from Essene or proto-Gnostic sources into Christianity." [17]

Apollos' rhetorical polish was an added touch of Greek culture, and contrasts sharply with the avowed simplicity of Paul's own preaching at Corinth; concerning which he wrote: "And I, brethren, when I came unto you, came not with excellency of speech or of wisdom, proclaiming to you the testimony of God. For I determined not to know anything among you, save Jesus Christ, and him crucified." [18]

How far the influence of Alexandrian theology and proto-Gnostic elements influenced his ministry after he had been instructed by Priscilla and Aquila is a moot question. It is reasonable to assume, and the first Corinthian epistle of Paul bears out the assumption, that he did not divest himself of these influences entirely, for his contact with Priscilla and Aquila suggests an intellectual reorientation, rather than the radical change that conversion would imply. Indeed it is stated expressly by Luke, that they "expounded unto him the way of God more accurately." [19] These influences, though sublimated, may well have exerted an effect, either directly or indirectly, upon the party-strife in Corinth.

The party whose watchword was, "I am of Christ," is even more difficult to classify than the former. Worthy of

[17] William Foxwell Albright, *From Stone Age to Christianity*, 2nd ed., (Garden City: Doubleday Anchor Books, Doubleday & Company, Inc., 1957), p. 377.

[18] I Cor. 2:1,2.

[19] Acts 18:26.

consideration is the suggestion of James Moffatt, that "The cry, therefore, seems to voice a party which may be identified . . . with some ultra-spiritual devotees or *high-flying gnostics who made a mystical Christ, no human* leader, the centre of religion." [20] Thus the cry, "I am of Christ," may well denote early Christological speculations which characterized later Gnostic teachings.

Some thirty years after Paul wrote the Corinthian epistles, the Docetic and Cerinthian Gnostics championed clearly defined views of the person of Christ. The former "dened the actual humanity of Christ," while "the Cerinthian Gnostics distinguished between the man Jesus and the *aeon* Christ that came on him at his baptism and left him on the Cross." [21] In the second and third century Valentinian Gnostic system, the *aeons* which made up the *plēroma,* or fulness of the Godhead, numbered thirty.[22]

The Gnostic systems all shared a dualism in which spirit was conceived as good, and matter as evil. The Incarnation was, therefore, an impossibility, because the Divine Essence could not come into direct contact with matter. The *aeons* were a hierarchy of "being" that mediated the contact of the "spiritual" with the "material." For the "Christian" Gnostics this posed a fundamental problem in Christology. Indeed, for them, the Incarnation of the Christ was in appearance only. This became known as Docetic Gnosticism, from the Greek word meaning "to seem." Cerinthus added the view that Jesus and Christ were not one and the same being. According to him, Jesus was "a mere man, at the

---

[20] Moffatt, *op. cit.,* p. 10. Italics mine, H.M.E.

[21] Robertson, *Word Pictures in the New Testament,* VI, 200.

[22] William R. Nelson, *The Interpretation of the Revelation of John in Valentinian Gnosis and the Evangelium Veritatis,* an unpublished manuscript study tracing the philosophical, mythological, and magical expansions of this system of Gnostic thought, especially in relation to the Apocalypse of John, circa, 1961.

time of his baptism the celestial Christ descended—'he came by water' . . . —and used him as a medium for his revelations; although the words were Christ's the voice was that of Jesus, so no one could really hear Christ speak, while he certainly could not be seen or touched. . . . When Christ concluded his message, he left Jesus and the latter was crucified, an event that had no religious significance, as Christ was not involved; 'he did not come by blood,' according to Cerinthus." [23]

Paul's words in I Cor. 12:3 may well point in the direction of some such heresy, e.g., "no man can say, 'Jesus is Lord' except under the influence of the Holy Spirit." [24] The fact that "the Gnostics would not call Jesus 'Lord,' " [25] suggests that Paul's words represented a convenient rule of thumb for distinguishing Spirit-filled Christians from such proto-Gnostics as the "Christ" party at Corinth.

It was fashionable for earlier commentators to date Gnosticism as a late heresy, equating it with its developed forms as found in the second and third centuries. In fact, Godet's conjecture that the "Christ" party at Corinth "were Gnostics before Gnosticism," was considered "an anachronism" by Findlay.[26] However other scholars recognize that Gnosticism was a "type of religious thought widespread in the world into which Christianity came." [27] Nor have more recent studies altered fundamentally this viewpoint. From his examination of the *Evangelium Veritatis* by Valentinus, William Nelson concluded, that "This authentic Gnostic source has given us a clearer picture of the great current

---

[23] Burton Scott Easton, "The Epistle of John," *The Abingdon Commentary,* p. 1350.

[24] *New English Bible.*

[25] James Alex. Robertson, "Philippians," *The Abingdon Commentary,* p. 1239.

[26] Findlay, *op. cit.,* II, 765.

[27] C. H. Dodd, "Colossians," *The Abingdon Commentary,* p. 1250.

of spiritual life with which Christianity came into contact in its earliest years as it grew towards a World Church." [28]

As a religious system, Gnosticism was an eclectic blend of Greek intellectualism and mystical elements derived from the Oriental mystery cults. C. G. Dodd characterized it as "a mixture, or syncretism, of Greek and Oriental religions, supported by a kind of philosophy or pseudo-philosophy borrowing largely from Platonism and Stoicism." [29] As such, the name "is vague, as it describes a method rather than a result, and covers all sorts of systems. Gnostics might be ascetic and puritanical to the last degree, or they might be debased libertines who quite literally gloried in their shame. They might be men of high mental attainments— some of the second-century Gnostics were able speculative thinkers—or they might be intellectually beneath contempt." [30]

The very name Gnosticism, from the Greek meaning "to know," implies the possession of a superior wisdom, which is hidden from others." [31] In the theosophical speculations which characterized it, a distinction was introduced between esoteric and exoteric doctrines. For the vulgar, blind faith was sufficient, "while knowledge is the exclusive possession" [32] of the Gnostic initiate.

Historically, the question of proto-Gnostic and Judaeo-Gnostic sources is an elusive one. This is in large measure due to the fact that its documentary remains come largely from the second century, and later. There are, however, scattered, though nonetheless authentic, evidences of its greater antiquity.

[28] *Loc. cit.*
[29] *Op. cit.,* p. 1250.
[30] Easton, *op. cit.,* p. 1350.
[31] J. B. Lightfoot, *Saint Paul's Epistles to the Colossians and to Philemon,* (London: Macmillan and Co., 1892), p. 75.
[32] *Ibid.*

Scarcely had the Church reached beyond the boundaries of Jerusalem and Judaea, when it was confronted with Gnosticism in a developed form. In Samaria, Philip, the evangelist-deacon, came into contact with Simon the sorcerer,[33] who, according to Irenaeus and Hippolytus, was "the earliest Gnostic known" [34] to them. In this regard, the claim that Simon Magus was "the father of Gnosticism," [35] must be modified. In a specific sense, this contains a measure of truth, for Simon Magus is credited with "the first known Gnostic system." [36] However, in a general sense, this claim is misleading, for, in the words of W. F. Albright, "there is now direct evidence that some of the central ideas of the Gnostic system go back into the ancient Orient." [37] The most then that can be claimed for Simon is that he codified and systematized ideas already current in the intellectual ferment of his day.

The place of magic in Gnosticism is provocative of further study. Suffice it to point out here, that Simon is described as a sorcerer, while one, Marcus a magician, is known to have been a follower of Valentinus a century or more later.[38] Is it coincidence, or, as is more likely, did the theosophical speculations of Gnosticism provide a fertile soil in which magic throve?

In the apocryphal Wisdom of Solomon, the author sets God in contrast with matter in an essentially Gnostic manner, and treats the body as the soul's prison which exists before birth, and after death. This would imply that in the

[33] Acts 8:9ff.
[34] Albright, *op. cit.*, p. 370.
[35] Jean Danielou, *The Dead Sea Scrolls and Primitive Christianity*, A Mentor Omega Book (New York: The New American Library, c. 1958), p. 94.
[36] Albright, *op. cit.*, p. 371.
[37] *Ibid.*, p. 370.
[38] Nelson, *loc. cit.*

first century B.C., a Jewish Gnosis had begun to crystallize.[39]
Certainly, the material for such was at hand by the middle
of the first century A.D., when Simon Magus is reputed to
have formulated such a system. Though a younger contemporary of Philo in Alexandria, there is no evidence that he
drew directly from the latter. Rather, each seems to have
been influenced by "a common proto-Gnostic background." [40] In addition to Simon, the Talmud names a
Johanan ben Zakkai, also a contemporary of the apostle
Paul, as the "earliest Jewish scholar with Gnostic tendencies." [41]

The polemic against Gnosticism is quite pronounced in
some of Paul's epistles. The epistle to the Colossians, written some eight or ten years after I Corinthians, reflects these
influences to such a degree that A. T. Robertson wrote:
"One cannot understand Colossians without some knowledge of Gnosticism." [42] The heretics in Colossae introduced
the worship of angels, suggestive of the *aeons* that mediated
between matter and spirit in Gnostic speculations. Coupled
with this was a form of asceticism, and a *gnosis* derogatory
of Jesus Christ. They added rigid observances of Jewish fes-
tivals and Sabbaths suggestive of a Judaic Gnosticism. All
these elements were apparently "combined by some of the
early Gnostics." [43]

In the Pastoral Epistles, the "fables and endless genealo-
gies," [44] the "profane and old wives' fables," [45] and the
"Jewish fables," [46] "were probably fanciful myths concern-

---

[39] Albright, *op. cit.*, p. 370.
[40] *Ibid.*, p. 371
[41] *Ibid.*, footnote, p. 37.
[42] *Word Pictures in the New Testament*, IV, 472.
[43] Conybeare & Howson, *op. cit.*, II, 383.
[44] I Tim. 1:4.
[45] I Tim. 4:7.
[46] Titus 1:14.

ing the origin and emanation of spiritual beings," [47] which the Gnostics of the second century systematized into hierarchies of intermediate beings, or *aeons,* between "the Absolute God and evil matter." [48] In the Kabbala, a collection of Jewish traditional theology, in which Jewish superstition and Gentile speculation blended, there are "many fabulous statements concerning such emanations." [49]

We conclude from this that though most of the literary remains of Gnosticism date from the second century, and later, it had a much more ancient origin. Its influence appears in the history of the Church as early as Philip's encounter with Simon, the sorcerer, at the outset of the Church's world-wide missionary endeavors. A recognition of this fact helps to explain much that otherwise may be obscure in Paul's counsels to the Corinthian church.

The challenge of this subtle, alien religious force was intensified as Christianity reached out to the Diaspora, and thence into the pagan world. The evidence suggests a determined effort to infiltrate the new Christian communities, and to subvert them into Gnosticism. It was not until near the end of the first century that an orthodox apologetic began to crystallize a separation between the two. However, in the Corinthian context to which Paul wrote, orthodoxy and Gnostic heterodoxy existed side by side in the form of rival parties within the church.

[47] Conybeare & Howson, *op. cit.,* I, 451.
[48] C. T. Wood, *The Life Letters, and Religion of St. Paul,* 2nd ed., (Edinburgh: T. & T. Clark, 1932), p. 367.
[49] Conybeare & Howson, *op. cit.,* I, 451.

CHAPTER XXIII

Gnostic Influences at Corinth

Evidences of the confrontation between Christian orthodoxy and Gnosticism in the Corinthian church are not lacking in Paul's first Corinthian epistle.

I. *I Cor. 2:6ff—"We Speak Wisdom . . ."*

Paul's discussion of "wisdom in 2:6 may well be a refutation of incipient Gnostic tendencies there, e.g., "We speak wisdom, however, among them that are full grown (*en tois teleiois*): yet a wisdom not of this world. . . ." The very phraseology suggests, as Robertson and Plummer have pointed out, "an allusion to the technical language of mystical initiation," [1] common among the Gnostics. The difference between men in spiritual attainment is recognized by Paul, but in the opinion of C. T. Wood, "it is vital to notice that he does not erect a barrier between the advanced Christian and the babe in Christ (as the Gnostics did, for instance)."[2]

II. *I Cor. 5:1ff—"Immorality Such As Even The Pagans Do Not Tolerate"*

A second illustration may be seen in the enormity of the guilt, over against the almost inexplicable apathy of the

[1] *Op. cit.,* p. 35.
[2] *Op. cit.,* p. 181

church toward the man guilty of incest—"I actually hear reports of sexual immorality among you, immorality such as even pagans do not tolerate: the union of a man with his father's wife." [3] Granted that Corinth, with its thousand prostitutes dedicated to the worship of Aphrodite, the Greek goddess of love, was one of the most licentious cities of the ancient world. Almost every student of the New Testament, sooner or later, discovers, that "the very name to Corinthianize meant immorality." [4] But this is hardly sufficient to explain the Apostle's strong language—"immorality such as even the pagans do not tolerate."

In view of the gravity of the situation, it hardly seems appropriate to understand his words here as exaggeration for the sake of emphasis. After all, genuine conversion involves a "new birth". It does imply a new moral consciousness, and a changed life. It is not only the enormity of the moral delinquency, but even more, the local congregation's attitude of egotistical tolerance that beggars the explanation that prior pagan habits plus the contaminating moral climate of Corinth are sufficient to explain the situation. Rather, this moral turpitude, dominating a powerful segment of the Corinthian assembly, may well reflect the licentious attitude of an influential Gnostic element there.

As already noted, some of these advocated a rigid asceticism, while others reacted against ascetic practices, and went "to the opposite extreme of unrestrained licentiousness." [5] Both reactions were the result of a false conception of matter as intrinsically evil. Only a moral depravity as extreme as that practiced by some Gnostics is sufficient to explain the church's "pride" in such degrading immorality. Such unnatural vice cannot be explained as an immature regression

[3] I Cor 5:1ff. *New English Bible.*
[4] Robertson, *Word Pictures in the New Testament*, III, 294.
[5] Lightfoot, *Saint Paul's Epistles to the Colossians and to Philemon*, p. 78.

to pre-Christian habits. Paul's words indicate that it was abnormally debased, even for the dissolute society of Corinth. Judged in the light of the Biblical ethic, it is intolerable. There can be no compromise between revealed morality and a social ethic based on the lowest common denominator of self-gratification. Without the philosophical and religious speculations of some such system as Gnosticism provided, the tension with revealed morality would have condemned it out of hand in the Corinthian assembly.

III. *I Cor. 7—Celibacy vs. Marriage*

A double moral standard is implied also in the discussion of celibacy versus marriage in I Cor. 7. Here a rigid asceticism, such as that advocated by certain Gnostics, would place a premium upon celibacy over marriage as the ideal spiritual state. If this seems like having one's cake, and eating it too—i.e., condoning incest on the one hand, and celibacy on the other—it must be underscored, that these extremes were advocated by rival schools of thought among the Gnostics themselves.

In such a world view as theirs, in which matter was believed to be intrinsically evil, it assumed some importance to know how to keep one's higher spiritual nature unsullied by escaping the hurtful influences of contact with matter.[6] It is understandable then that celibacy would commend itself to some as reducing some of the grosser defilement of matter. In this aspect, at least, man's sensual nature would be subdued, "and the spirit thus set free, would be sublimated, and rise to its proper level." [7]

Opposed to such celibate views would be the attitude of Old Testament value judgments on the desirability of marriage, represented by the followers of Peter and Paul, him-

---

6 *Ibid.*, p. 77.
7 *Ibid.*

self. It needs to be remembered here, that Paul, in his first epistle to Timothy, branded the "forbidding to marry," as one of "the doctrines of demons." [8] The resultant friction between the proponents of these two opposed points of view on so sensitive a subject would contribute to the fragmentation of the Corinthian church. The celibate "ideal" has always been alien to normative Judiac tradition. Essene asceticism is not typical of normative Judaism, or at least of that type of Old Testament piety that triumphed in Judaism. The genius of Essene monasticism in Messianic and Apocalyptic, not unlike the underlying assumptions in Paul's solution to the question of celibacy versus marriage at Corinth. The resolution of this conflict he propounded in the following words: "I think that in view of the impending distress it is well for a person to remain as he is. Are you bound to a wife? Do not seek to be free. Are you free from a wife? Do not seek marriage. But if you marry, you do not sin, and if a girl marries she does not sin. Yet those who marry will have worldly trouble, and I would spare you that. I mean, brethren, the appointed time has grown very short. . . ." [9]

This tension between traditional Jewish views of marriage and the celibate state has not changed even today. In Herbert Weiner's penetrating chronicle of religious encounters in contemporary Israel, Father Jochanan, a Catholic priest, commented on the difficuly he found in explaining the celibate idea to contemporary Israelies. In discussions in the kibbutzim, he was repeatedly asked how he could reconcile celibacy with his faith in the Torah, whose first commandment is "to be fruitful and multiply." [10]

[8] I Tim. 4:1-3.
[9] I Cor. 7:26-29.
[10] *The Wild Goats of Ein Gedi* (Meridan Books; New York: The World Publishing Company, Philadelphia: The Jewish Publishing Society of America, c. 1961, pp. 88, 89.

IV. *I Cor. 8–10–"Concerning Things Sacrificed To Idols"*

Radically conflicting viewpoints come to the fore again in Paul's discussion of the eating of meats sacrificed to idols.[11] It was the militant antagonism of the legalists in the Church that forced the church at Antioch to appeal to the apostles and elders at Jerusalem to resolve the question, to wit, "Must Gentile converts to Christianity assume the yoke of the ceremonial law of Judaism as a prerequisite?" Their answer was a memorandum initiated by James, and endorsed by the Jerusalem council, which read in part: "For it seemed good to the Holy Spirit, and to us, to lay upon you no greater burden than these necessary things: that ye abstain from things sacrificed to idols, and from blood, and from things strangled, and from fornication. . . ."[12]

At Corinth the question of eating "things sacrificed to idols," precipitated a conflict between Epicurean hedonism, in the guise of Gnostic libertinism, and Judiac scrupulousness. Paul placed his answer on the highest level of love when he concluded: "All things are lawful; but not all things are expedient. All things are lawful; but not all things edify. Let no man seek his own, but each his neighbor's good."[13] Nor was Corinth the only place where the same influences produced tensions over the same question. In Colossae, the ascetic tendencies of Gnosticism gained the upper hand. There the apostle Paul was obliged, according to A. T. Robertson, to "condemn the ascetic practices of the Gnostics."[14] Categorically, he wrote: "Let no man therefore judge you in meat, or in drink, or in respect of a feast day or a new moon or a sabbath day."[15] These ascetic

---

[11] I Cor. 8-10.
[12] Acts 15:28.
[13] I Cor. 10:23.
[14] *Word Pictures in the New Testament*, IV, 578.
[15] Col. 2:16.

proscriptions, Paul characterized as "the precepts and doctrines of men." [16] On the other hand, the libertine influence triumphed later in Thyatira where, "Jezebel, who calleth herself a prophetess . . . teacheth and seduceth my servants to commit fornication, and to eat things sacrificed to idols." [17]

The nature of the group at Corinth to whom Paul addressed his remarks about eating meat sacrificed to idols is suggested in his opening words: "Knowledge (*gnosis*) puffeth up, but love edifieth." [18] Notice that it is a certain type of *gnosis* that he thus rebuked as the source of pride. It was this same *gnosis* that caused them to treat with pride, rather than censure, the man guilty of incest.

V. *I Cor. 15—"How Say Some Among You There Is No Resurrection"*

Finally, the discussion of the resurrection [19] becomes clearer when seen against the backdrop of Gnostic speculation. It is in this direction that Paul's word's point: "Now if Christ is preached that he hath been raised from the dead, how say some among you that there is no resurrection of the dead?" [20] In the view of James Moffatt, those who challenged the doctrine of the resurrection "were not skeptics or Christians of a Sadducean temper . . . they were mystical enthusiasts of the Greek type who could not see anything relevant to spiritual Christianity in any doctrines which drew upon Jewish belief about bodily resurrection after death as needful to immortal life." [21] This description can be crystallized in one word, Gnosticism. This assumption is supported by

[16] Col. 2:22.
[17] Rev. 2:20.
[18] I Cor. 8:1.
[19] I Cor. 15:12.
[20] I Cor. 15:12.
[21] *Op. cit.,* p. 240.

Paul's extended description of the resurrection body, which begins as an explicit rebuttal to a heretical assertion: "But some one will say, How are the dead raised? and with what manner of body do they come?" [22] It is difficult to side-step the conclusion that the heretics addressed here were Gnostics, who typically would not "assign a body to the exalted Christ or to glorified believers." [23]

The foregoing evidence, admittedly incomplete, is nonetheless adequate enough to indicate quite clearly that the Apollos party, and the Christ party at Corinth represented Gnostic influences and speculations. The Apollos party probably reflected the two streams of Gnostic influence coming through Apollos; i.e., first, as an adept in Philonian (Alexandrian) philosophy, and second, as a disciple of John the Baptist, with his Essene influences. The Christ party is more elusive, but it may well have embodied more pronouncedly Gentile influences from Greek philosophy and Oriental theosophy. The convergent streams of Gnostic influence go far to explain the contradictory extremes of licentiousness and asceticism found in Paul's epistles to Corinth, and elsewhere.

True, the advocate of any thesis is apt to yield to a common human weakness, and to overstate his position for the sake of emphasis. This we have tried to avoid, relying upon the force of the evidence itself to remove this premise of Gnostic influences in the Corinthian church from the sphere of an educated guess, and to give to it a high degree of probability.

[22] I Cor. 15:35ff.
[23] James Alex. Robertson, "Philippians," *The Abingdon Commentary*, p. 1239.

CHAPTER XXIV

"Forbid Not to Speak With Tongues"

(I Cor. 14:39)

At last the end of an arduous, but nevertheless, rewarding task is in sight. The way is now clear to apply the insights gleaned from our preceding study to our second question which we propounded in chapter twenty-two: "What effect did the various parties at Corinth have upon the manifestations of the gifts of the Holy Spirit—especially 'tongues' and 'prophesying'?" The crux of the matter is to be found in a verse whose real significance has either been denied, or veiled in ambiguity.

The conclusion to Paul's discussion of the *charismata* is summarized in two brief injunctions: "wherefore, my brethren, desire earnestly to prophesy, and forbid not to speak with tongues." [1] Unfortunately, the English translation does not adequately reproduce the force of the idiom in the original language. There the word "forbid" is a present imperative with the negative *mē,* "not," preceding it. The import of this idiom is *prohibitive.* It is not *concessive,* as is so often tacitly assumed. To illustrate—the Apostle did not say, "desire earnestly to prophesy as the greater gift, and if, by reason of your childish infatuation with *glossolalia,* you must speak in tongues, then you may indulge yourselves a little." Quite the contrary, for the present im-

[1] I Cor. 14:39.

perative in a prohibition does not support such an assumption.

It is important to note, that *"A prohibition in the present imperative demands that action then in progress be stopped."* [2] For example the *American Standard Version* rendering of Matt. 7:1 is, "Judge not, that ye be not judged." But this translation does not do justice to the real import of the idiom, which could be more accurately translated, "Stop judging, lest you be judged." Another illustration is Rev. 5:4, 5: "And I wept much, because no one was found worthy to open the book . . . and one of the elders saith unto me, Weep not." More precisely rendered, it means, "I was weeping . . . he said to me, Stop weeping."

Therefore, to do full justice to the idiom, I Cor. 14:39 should be translated: "Stop forbidding to speak with tongues." [3] The "action then in progress," that Paul bade them to stop, was not excessive tongues-speech. On the contrary, it was the *forbidding* to speak in tongues that he admonished them to stop. The apostle Paul, therefore, addressed his attention to a practice then current in the Corinthian assembly, namely, the prohibiting of speech in other tongues. He was not generalizing a future contingency, i.e., "if anyone should speak in tongues, do not stop him." The implication is plain, that there was an influential party at Corinth which sought to forbid speaking in tongues, and Paul enjoined the continuance of this practice. His words may be paraphrased thus: "Stop your current practice of forbidding the speaking in tongues."

This immediately prompts the question: "Whence did

---

[2] Dana & Mantey, *op. cit.*, p. 301. Italics mine, H.M.E.

[3] The objection of Robertson & Plummer, *op cit.*, p. 328, to this rendering is not well taken. The passages in I Tim. 4:14 and 5:22, which they cited against it, may be cited with equal appropriateness in favor of this translation. In the final analysis, the implication remains, that their rebuttal rests, not so much upon exegetical considerations, as upon a theological bias against tongues.

this practice of forbidding tongues-speech originate?" The answer lies ready at hand in the party strife that fragmented the Corinthian church on so many other issues. James Moffatt defined the issue clearly when he wrote: "Some sober-minded Christians in the local church, as at Thessalonica, evidently were shocked; *they desired to check the habit* (xiv. 39)." [4] Lest the allusion to Thessalonica be overlooked, let the reader take note, that Corinth was not the only church disturbed by the activities of an anti-charismatic faction. In Corinth it was forbidding "tongues-speech," while at Thessalonica it was "despising prophesying,"—a fact to be commented on subsequently.

In the light of the historical and religious context, the question posed by Dr. Moffatt needs to be sharpened a little more. We agree that someone at Corinth was trying to stop tongues-speech, but did this result from the scruples of some "sober-minded Christians?" Or, was it a more fundamental clash in viewpoint between factions already identified at Corinth? It is our view, that the latter alternative is more consistent with the historical and religious context to which the Corinthian epistles were addressed.

Such an anti-charismatic influence would hardly come from the avowed followers of Peter, for he had been present at Pentecost, and his subsequent charismatic ministry is clearly spelled out in the book of the Acts. Nor is it reasonable to thus indict the Pauline party, for Paul magnified the richness of his own charismatic endowments. The alternative then is either the party of Apollos, or the Christ party—or a coalition of both. And as already argued, both of these represented Gnostic influences.

Is it possible that the anti-charismatic agitation originated with them? Quite probably. Why? Here the nature of Gnosticism furnishes a further clue. It was not simply a

[4] *Op. cit.,* p. 211. Italics mine, H.M.E.

rational, speculative system of philosophy. Its religious expressions were frequently orgiastic. Even its boasted esoteric knowledge (*gnōsis*) *"derived in part from ecstatic experiences."* [5]

As already observed, Paul's opening remarks on the Holy Spirit's charismatic manifestations [6] may contain more than a hint here of a contrast between the genuine gifts of the Spirit, and counterfeit charisms of an essentially demonic nature. "The air was full of the mystery cults like the Eleusinian mysteries, Mithraism, the vogue of Isis, what not," wrote A. T. Robertson, and the mystery cults in Gnostic guise do affect our understanding of the religious context of the *charismata*. We repeat here our findings in chapter fifteen; to wit, "the influence of the mystery cults, in Gnostic guise, does affect one's understanding of the *pneumatikōn*" in the primitive Church. Chrysostom warned that their idols "though dumb themselves, yet had their oracles, and prophets, and soothsayers, who professed to have *spiritual gifts,* such as the Pythia at Delphi; but do not be deceived, their gifts may easily be distinguished from ours." [7]

The rendering of the *New English Bible* makes such a contrast explicit: "You know how, in the days when you were still pagan, you would be seized by some power which drove you to those dumb heathen gods." [8] Paul was saying in effect, that "Those of you who were brought up as pagans are familiar with the frenzied cries of the cults. You know the religious impulses that once swept you into seances where devotees had their experiences of divine (?) [demonic] possession." [9]

---

5 Easton, *op cit.*, p. 1350. Italics mine, H.M.E.
6 I Cor. 12:1-3.
7 Wordsworth, *op. cit.*, II, 126.
8 I Cor. 12:2.
9 Moffatt, *op. cit.*, p. 178.

The implications for our understanding of the manifestations of the gifts of the Holy Spirit deserve to be probed more deeply in the light of these facts. Was the charismatic ebullience of the Holy Spirit offensive to "some sober-minded Christians," as Moffatt suggested? Or were counterfeit "ecstatics" alarmed at the threat of exposure by the spontaneous vitality of the Spirit's charismatic manifestations? Did Paul suggest this when he wrote: "But if all prophesy, and there come in one unbelieving or unlearned, he is reproved by all, he is judged by all; *the secrets of his heart are made manifest;* and so he will fall down on his face and worship God, declaring that God is among you indeed." [10]

Obviously, this is not prophesying that ministers "edification, and exhortation, and consolation" [11] to the Christian brotherhood. Rather this is prophesying that exposes the deceit and duplicity of the heart, as, for instance, in the case of Ananias and his wife Sapphira.[12] With this aspect of prophesying at work in Corinth, and also in Thessalonica, the consequences may have been just as drastic for the dissemblers in these churches as they were for Ananias and Sapphira, who paid with their lives for lying to the Holy Spirit.

Furthermore, this punitive aspect of prophecy is hinted at in Paul's sentence passed, *in absentia,* upon the man in the Corinthian assembly who was guilty of incest: e.g., "I verily, being absent in the body but present in spirit, have already as though I were present judged him that hath so wrought this thing, in the name of our Lord Jesus, ye being gathered together, and my spirit, with the power of our Lord Jesus, to deliver such a one unto Satan for the de-

[10] I Cor. 14:24, 25. Italics mine, H.M.E.
[11] I Cor. 14:3.
[12] Acts 5:1ff.

struction of the flesh, that the spirit may be saved in the day of the Lord Jesus." [13]

Before the reconstruction we have offered tentatively here is peremptorily brushed aside, it would be well to remind ourselves that the anti-charismatic spirit exposed itself outside the Corinthian assembly. As already noted, the apostle Paul wrote to the Thessalonians: "'Stop quenching the Spirit; stop despising prophesyings." [14] Only an arbitrary re-definition of "prophesying" could deny that the Apostle here meant the same charismatic manifestation of prophesying to which he referred in his Corinthian epistle.

The very words, "despising," [15] and "forbidding," [16] indicate something of the intensity of the opposition to the Holy Spirit's gifts of "prophesying" and "tongues." In Thessalonica "prophesying" was under fire, and in Corinth "tongues"—which with "interpretation of tongues" is equivalent to "prophecy"—was under the ban. Surely, there is some significance to the fact that opposition crystallized against gifts that are, in part, revelatory.

Within the context of this anti-charismatic spirit, Paul's words, "desire earnestly spiritual gifts." [17]—and the "spiritual gifts" (*pneumatika*) singled out for discussion in I Cor. 14 are primarily "prophesying" and "tongues"—set these gifts in a new perspective in the Corinthian church. It should be obvious, that the admonition to the Corinthians, "desire earnestly to prophecy," is the affirmative counterpart of his prohibition addressed to the Thessalonians, "stop despising prophesyings." Both say essentially the same thing.

[13] I Cor. 5:3-5.
[14] I Thess. 5:19,20. The idiom is the same as in I Cor. 14:39, a present imperative in a prohibition. It means, "Stop an action already in progress."
[15] I Thess. 5:18.
[16] I Cor. 14:39.
[17] I Cor. 14:1.

In both instances, Paul reversed the judgment of the anti-charismatic party.

There is another possible reconstruction of events in Corinth that fits the facts. It is not beyond the realm of possibility that the "sober-minded Christians," postulated by Dr. Moffatt, with or without the cooperation of Gnostic elements of more speculative bent of mind, may have initiated the prohibition of tongues in the worship of the assembly. Alarmed at the patently unspiritual excesses of Gnostic "ecstatics", and not being able to cope with such counterfeit manifestations, they may have consented to the radical expedient of forbidding all "spiritual" manifestations. The expedient may have represented a counsel of despair which Paul sought to counter by reinstating tongues and prophesying to their proper place in the worship of the church where "each one hath a psalm, hath a teaching, hath a revelation, hath a tongue, hath an interpretation." [18]

There are those today who also advocate "throwing the baby out with the bath water," but this was not Paul's solution. He defined the bona fide operations of the Holy Spirit, especially with regard to tongues and prophesying. Then he hedged each with certain safeguards. Tongues were to be manifested in the public worship when accompanied by the companion gift of interpretation. Prophesying was subject to the discernment of the order of prophets. In every case, self control is the dominant note, for "the spirits of the prophets are subject to the prophets." [19] Contemporary descriptions take note of the fact that such self control was totally lacking in the orgiastic ecstacies of the mystery cults. Hence, these safeguards would protect the church by distinguishing the counterfeit from the genuine manifestations of the Holy Spirit.

[18] I Cor. 14:26ff.
[19] I Cor. 14:32.

CHAPTER XXV

"Men Unlearned or Unbelieving"

(I Cor. 14:23)

The identification of the Apollos' party and the Christ'
party at Corinth with Gnosticism sheds light upon Paul's
quotation from the prophet Isaiah in I Cor. 14:21: "In the
law it is written, By men of strange tongues and by the lips
of strangers will I speak unto this people; and not even thus
will they hear me, saith the Lord." Was this quotation of
Isaiah 28:11 simply a loose verbal application, in rabbinical
style, of two otherwise unrelated scriptures? Or is there an
inner connection, the statement of a general principle valid
in both contexts?

In Isaiah, the prophet addressed Jerusalem and her
scoffing rulers as "this people." The unintelligible tongues
of foreign invaders were to be a sign of Divine judgment
upon them. Paul declared that the "tongues" in Corinth
were a sign to the unbelievers (*apistoi*) there. In both instances, the common denominator was the "sign" value of
the tongues used. What connection is there then between
the "sign" of tongues to "this people" in Isaiah, and the
"sign" of tongues to the "unbelievers" in Corinth? But perhaps we ought to ask first, who were these unbelievers" in
the church at Corinth? Were they, as Moffatt claimed, "outsiders at Corinth [who] did not belong to the Lord's

people"?[1] Or were they "unbelievers" who had attached themselves to the church there, and masqueraded as Christians? A survey of the use of "unbeliever" (*apistos*) in the Pauline epistles suggests some provocative answers.

"Out of sixteen occurences of the world *apistos* in the Pauline Epistles, fourteen are found in the Ep(istles) to the Corinthians," according to J. H. Barnard.[2] Often the Apostle designated the heathen by it. However, in several instances, he used *apistos* of false teachers. For example, "Be not unequally yoked with unbelievers,"[3] may be a contrast with the heathen, or it may be a reference to the false teachers who "bring you into bondage."[4] In Titus 1:15, the reference "to them that are defiled and unbelieving," is a descriptive comment on those who teach "Jewish fables, and commandments of men." As already suggested, these were probably false teachers of Judaeo-Gnostic persuasion.

The use of *apistos* in II Cor. 4:4 could be another example of this restricted usage. True, it may simply be a general reference to the heathen—"in their case the god of this age has blinded their unbelieving minds."[5] The antecedent subject of this clause, however, is found in the preceding verse, e.g. "And even if our gospel is veiled, it is veiled in them that perish." The allusion to a "veiled" gospel refers directly to Israel, past, whose "minds were hardened;"[6] and present, "for until this very day at the reading of the old covenant the same veil remaineth."[7] From the context, therefore, it is reasonable to assume that in speaking of "their unbelieving minds," to which his

[1] *Op. cit.*, p. 223.
[2] *The Second Epistle to the Corinthians, The Expositor's Greek Testament*, III, 60.
[3] II Cor. 6:14.
[4] II Cor. 11:22.
[5] Arndt, Gingrich, Bauer, *op. cit., apistos*, p. 85.
[6] II Cor. 3:14.
[7] *Ibid.*

"gospel is veiled," Paul was not making reference to the heathen in general, but to recalcitrant Israel in particular. This can be narrowed even further, for the Apostle has in mind throughout this epistle certain individuals anonymously referred to as "the many, corrupting the word of God," [8] i.e., *false teachers within the church.*

This use of *apistos,* as an epithet for "teachers of error," [9] recurs in the post-Apostolic age in the epistles of Ignatius, bishop of Antioch, I Trallians 10, and I Smyrnaeans 2, 5. Both epistles were probably written in the first decade, or decade and a half, of the second century (circa 107 A.D., or 116 A.D.),[10] the former from Smyrna, the latter from Troas, while Ignatius was on his journey to Rome where he suffered martyrdom. In the shorter version of the letter to the Trallians, he wrote: "But if, as some that are without God, that is, the *unbelieving,* say, that He only seemed to suffer. . . ." [11] The Docetic Gnosticism Ignatius was rebutting here is made even more explicit in the longer version of his letter: "But if, as some that are without God, that is, the *unbelieving,* say, He became man in appearance [only], that He did not in reality take unto Him a body, that He died in appearance [merely], and did not indeed suffer. . . ." [12]

Again in his epistle to the Smyrnaeans, his allusion to Gnostic teaching is equally obvious in this statement: "And He suffered truly, even as also He truly raised up himself, not, as certain *unbelievers* maintain, that He only seemed to suffer, *as they themselves only seem to be* [*Christians*]." [13]

[8] II Cor. 3:17.
[9] Arndt, Gingrich, Bauer, *op. cit., apistos,* p. 85.
[10] *Ante-Nicene Christian Library, The Apostolic Fathers,* ed. by Alexander Roberts & James Donaldson, I (Edinburgh: T. & T. Clark, 1876), pp. 143, 144.
[11] *Ibid.,* p. 201.
[12] *Ibid.*
[13] *Ibid.,* p. 241.

He mentioned again those who were "not confessing that He was [truly] possessed of a body," saying, "Yea, far be it from me to make any mention of them, until they repent and return to (a true belief in) Christ's passion, which is our resurrection." [14] Note the equation here of "unbelievers" (*apistoi*) with false teachers (Gnostics) who yet professed to be Christians.

How deep his alarm was at the influence of these insidious Gnostic teachers may be judged from his description of these "false teachers" as, "beasts in the shape of men, whom you must not receive, but, if it be possible, not even to meet with; only you must pray to God for them, if by any means they may be brought to repentance, which, however, will be very difficult." [15] Ignatius' concern for the repentance of these false teachers echoes Paul's burden in a similar situation at Corinth; "and I should mourn for many of them that have sinned heretofore, and repented not of the uncleanness and fornication and lasciviousness which they committed." [16]

We must pause at this point to clarify our methodology. It is not our purpose to read back these post-Apostolic uses of the word *apistos* for "false teachers" into the Biblical usage, but rather, to point out that this is an extension of a usage already found in Paul's epistles. Ignatius is indebted to Paul, not Paul to Ignatius.

In the interpretation of the "unbelievers" at Corinth, there are now two possibilities. One, the usual view that they were heathen who, for one reason or another, entered the Christian services. It is not, however, clear that the outsider was casually admitted to these Christian assemblies, as is customarily assumed by expositors. True, they might be

14 *Ibid.*, p. 245. Italics mine, H.M.E.
15 *Ibid.*, pp. 243, 244
16 II Cor. 12:21.

admitted to them, as they were to the synagogue. On the other hand, since the Eucharist was part of every service, and, in addition, their worship services were conducted in private homes, outsiders were not likely to be admitted indiscriminately.[17] In verse 23 the "unbeliever" is linked with the "unlearned" (*idiōtai,* "him that is without gifts")[18] as having access to the Christian assembly. The very terminology, "unlearned," suggests rather the vocabulary of Gnostic initiation.

If the phrase, "thy giving of thanks," in verse 16 is a reference to the Lord's Supper[19]—and the corporate "Amen" referred to there "was a prominent feature of the Eucharist"[20]—it shows that the "unlearned" were present at the Communion Service, as well as the *apistoi,* or "unbelievers". The custom of excluding the catechumen—if this be what is meant by *idiōtai*—from the observance of the Lord's Table was apparently a later development. However, the exclusion of the heathen from this the celebration of the central mystery of the Christian faith, is a foregone conclusion. The view that the "unbelievers" at Corinth were casual outsiders is not convincing.

Alternatively, the abuses which Paul rebuked at the Love-Feasts and the Lord's Table in Corinth reflect the libertine tendencies associated with certain Gnostic influences already seen at work in the Corinthian church. This introduces a consideration of the second possibility, viz., that these "unbelievers" were adherents of the Gnostic parties there, who, being outwardly identified with the church, had access to its worship services. In the light of Paul's use of *apistoi* as a designation for "false teachers" of Gnostic persuasion, this identification is quite reasonable.

[17] Robertson & Plummer, *op. cit.,* p. 318.
[18] A.S.V., R.S.V., footnote to I Cor. 14:16.
[19] Wordsworth, *op cit.,* II, 133.
[20] Parry *op. cit.,* pp. 152,153.

Furthermore, the reaction of the *idiōtai* ("novices"), and the *apistoi* ("false teachers"), to tongues is essentially the same as that of the anti-charismatic party, or parties, at Corinth, namely, opposition.

A general observation points in this direction also. In this epistle, Paul dealt with the various aspects of the party strife, and its effect upon the church's life and worship. He was not concerned with the problems affecting the pagan community, except as these affected the experience of the Corinthian church, e.g., meats sacrificed to idols, etc.

This brings us back to the question of the sign value of tongues, and the connection between the "sign" of tongues to "this people" in Isaiah, and to the "unbelievers" and "unlearned" in Corinth.[21]

The clue to this question is to be found in Isaiah's prophecy. In the Old Testament passage, "the prophet in the name of the Lord is threatening drunken priests and prophets of Jerusalem that he will speak to them through the unintelligible language or babble of foreign invaders, though even that punishing experience *will not induce them to obey the Lord.*"[22] Herein lies the point of contact between the prophecy of Isaiah and Paul's application of this prophecy to the situation in Corinth. In Isaiah, the alien tongues were to be a sign that God had spoken through his prophet. *Their response would be a scornful disregard both of the oracle and its "tongues sign."* By analogy, therefore, just as the "tongues" in Isaiah hardened

[21] Paul's allusion to tongues as a sign for "unbelievers" instead of "believers" (14:22) has caused some difficulty among expositors. The solution offered by J. B. Philipps for the felt contradiction in the verse is too radical. He felt himself constrained "from the sense of the next three verses," to regard Paul's words in verse 22 as "either a slip of the pen on the part of Paul, or more probably, a copyist's error." N.T.M.E., footnote to I Cor. 14:22. The "sign" of tongues on the day of Pentecost was likewise to the unsaved multitude, not to the disciples. It was confirmation for all to see and to hear of the Lord's supernatural enablements.

[22] Moffat, *op. cit.,* p. 223. Italics mine, H.M.E.

apostate Israelites in unbelief, *so also the "tongues" in the Corinthian assembly would harden these "unbelievers" and "unlearned" ("novices") in unbelief and disobedience.*

Observe the parallelism: "If . . . all speak with tongues, and there come in men unlearned or unbelieving, will they not say you are mad." This is just what had happened at Pentecost when the newly Spirit-filled believers spoke in tongues, and some of their auditors mocked them saying; "They are filled with new wine." [23] In Isaiah's day "they [would] not hear the Lord," for the "tongues sign" simply hardened them in unbelief. In Jerusalem at Pentecost, perverse Israelites mocked the disciples, accusing them of drunkenness. At Corinth, Paul warned that intractable "unbelievers" would scorn them as "mad." (Did this reflect a judgment already articulated by those opposed to "tongues"? It is easily understood that such otherwise unidentified *apistoi,* who stressed *gnōsis,* or esoteric "knowledge," as the path of spiritual attainment, would thus rail at spiritual manifestations among their less sophisticated "co-religionists.")

In both cases, "this people" of Isaiah's day, and the "unlearned" and "unbelievers" of Corinth, outwardly, at least, were identified with the Covenant Community. They were *in* but not *of* these Communities, hence, they neither understood nor responded to God's charismatic manifestations in the midst of His people.

It ought to be added here that when Paul said, "If therefore the whole church be assembled together and all speak with tongues," he referred to tongues used devotionally. If all pray with tongues, without interpretation, there will be no exposure of sin, consequently no repentance. However, as already pointed out, on the basis of I Cor. 14:6, tongues with interpretation is equivalent to prophecy. Thereby,

[23] Acts. 2:13.

God does communicate "revelation," "knowledge," "prophecy," and "teaching." Even as prophecy in the vernacular may expose "the secrets of the heart," so also tongues with intepretation may accomplish the same end—but not tongues alone.

CHAPTER XXVI

"Let All Things Be Done Unto Edifying"

(I Cor. 14:26)

If "tongues" were intrinsically wrong, Paul would not have included them in his epitome of primitive Christian worship, nor would he have restricted them to two or three utterances with interpretation. He would simply have banned them entirely.

His summary of charismatic worship is presented in I Cor. 14:26: "What is it then, brethren? When ye come together, each one hath a psalm, hath a teaching, hath a revelation, hath a tongue, hath an intepretation. Let all things be done unto edifying." This description gives an insight into *normative* Christian worship in the Apostolic Age. We concur with the judgment of B. B. Warfield who remarked: "There is no reason to believe that the infant congregation at Corinth was singular in this. He [Paul] even makes the transition to the next item of his advice in the significant words, 'as in all the churches of the saints'." [1]

Ephesians 5:18 suggests a rather pointed allusion to charismatic worship in the words, "but be filled with the Spirit, speaking to one another in psalms and hymns and spiritual (i.e., *pneumatikais,* 'supernatural') [2] songs. . . ."

---

[1] *Counterfeit Miracles,* (New York: Charles Scribner's Sons, 1918), p. 5.
[2] Consult the Supplement to Chapter XVI on Paul's use of *pneumatikos.*

Heinrich Meyer saw a correlation between "spiritual songs, i.e., inspired by the Holy Spirit, and Paul's words, "I will sing with the spirit," i.e., "in tongues." [3] Along with the almost identical passage in Colossians 3:16, it bears the stamp of charismatic worship. These evidences of charismatic worship at Corinth, Ephesus, and Colossae tend to confirm the opinion of Warfield, that "We are justified in considering it characteristic of the Apostolic churches that such miraculous gifts should be displayed in them. The exception would be, not a church *with,* but a church *without* such gifts." [4]

If all the gifts of the Holy Spirit are to manifest the Spirit's presence and power for the edification of the whole worshipping community—"for the common good." [5]—the absence of these supernatural enablements of the Spirit is a mute, but nonetheless eloquent, commentary upon the impoverished worship experience of much of contemporary Christianity. Critics of charismatic worship are quick to point to the Apostle's admonition—"But let all things be done decently and in order" [6]—without pausing to realize that the "ordering" Paul counseled applies to the operation of the gifts of the Holy Spirit. Such Apostolic Order can only apply where the gifts of the Spirit of God are in operation. Where there are no gifts of the Spirit manifested, there is nothing to thus "order." Trite, but true, for many a weary preacher "Divine order" conjures up an image of a weary, mildly distraught pastor, late Saturday night, cranking out mimeographed copies of the Order of Worship for the next morning's church service.

Measured by the Biblical norm, our contemporary "gift-

[3] *Critical and Exegetical Hand-Book to the Epistle to the Ephesians,* p. 506.
[4] *Op. cit.,* p. 5. Italics mine, H.M.E.
[5] I Cor. 12:7. R.S.V.
[6] I Cor. 14:40.

less" worship services are out of Divine Order. As a matter of fact, there is little to set in Apostolic order. They are largely the conventionalized memorabilia of the long past charismatic activities of the Holy Spirit. For example, confirmation is a reminiscence of the early days when Spirit-filled men laid their hands on converts, and they too were filled with the Spirit, and spoke with other tongues, guided supernaturally in their utterances by the Spirit of God. The holy "chrism" recalls the ancient healing ministry of the Church, when Spirit-filled elders responded to the call of the sick, and prayed the prayer of faith over them, "having anointed them with oil in the name of the Lord," [7] and they were healed. The spontaneous "unpremeditated apocalyptic utterances" of the prophetic community of believers have been largely stilled. Unlike ancient Israel, the Church no longer "kills the prophets," [8] it simply ignores them. The demoniacs have been psychodynamically "labeled," and remain in their wretched bondage, witness to a Christianity that is charismatically impotent. Not only have some theologians undertaken to write God's epitaph, but others have relegated Devil and demons to the never, never land of pious myth. The revelatory "word of wisdom, and of knowledge" have been traded off for the cultured ratiocinations of the professional ecclesiastic. And to believe in miracles . . .! Much less to testify that one has seen one transpire . . .! How naive! The sophisticated modern Christian is embarrassed by what he deems mythical regressions in the Scriptures. Holy Writ must be de-mythologized to void the intellectual embarrassment of its supposedly unscientific worldview. But like the hunter who sold his gun to purchase bullets, such a Christianity has neither "a bird in the hand," nor "one in the bushes." In compromising the Biblical

[7] James 5:14.
[8] Luke 11:47.

metaphysic, the Church's Sadduceean counselors would make the Gospel relevant to modern society by "escaping the scandal of the Cross;" [9] and by the "wisdom" of their *gnōsis* (not the charismatic "word of wisdom"), would make "the cross of Christ . . . void." [10] But a Christ without a Cross, and a Resurrection is no Christ at all, and a Divine Spirit without supernatural manifestations is robbed of the attributes of personality.

The plea to maintain an open mind to Truth from every and any source is blatant hypocrisy on any man's lips, unless and until, he too is willing to have an open mind to what the Holy Spirit is saying charismatically to the Church today. If Love has a language all its own, so too does Faith—"He that hath an ear, let him hear what the Spirit saith to the churches." [11]

On the day of Pentecost, Peter waited in the upper room with the one hundred and twenty disciples still tarrying in Jerusalem after Christ's ascension. With the rest of Christ's followers there, he too was "filled with the Holy Spirit, and began to speak with other tongues, as the Spirit gave utterance." Having spoken to God in tongues, he turned to the assembled multitudes, and in the midst of a Spirit-filled, charismatically endowed Church, preached the Gospel with supernatural power; and "there were added unto them in that day about three thousand souls." Then this Galilean fisherman, accompanied by John, went up to the Temple "at the hour of prayer." Seeing there a lame man sitting before the gate called "Beautiful," he answered his plea for alms with the unforgettable words: "Silver and gold have I none; but what I have, that give I thee. In the name of Jesus Christ of Nazareth, walk." This same Peter had quailed be-

---

9 Gal. 5:11.
10 I Cor. 1:17.
11 Rev. 3:22.

fore the accusing finger of a serving maid, and denied his Master, not once, but thrice, and that with cursing. Yet summoned before the very Sanhedrin that had condemned Jesus, he amazed them with his boldness and wisdom. And so the record runs. . . .

Baptized in, that is to say, filled with the Spirit, and having spoken to God as the Spirit gave to him supernatural speech "in other tongues," he testified with power to the multitudes, spoke in faith the word of healing to the impotent man, answered with boldness the charges of the authorities. Does not his example say to us, that the Church needs an Apostolic experience to achieve Apostolic results in an Apocalyptic age?

CHAPTER XXVII

"Rivers of Living Water"

(John 7:37–39)

During a momentary lull in the Temple service on the last, or great day of the feast of Tabernacles, A.D. 26 or 29,[1] "Jesus stood and cried, saying, If any man thirst, let him come unto me and drink. He that believeth on me, as the scripture hath said, from within him shall flow rivers of living water. But this spake he of the Spirit, which they that believed on him were to receive: for the Spirit was not yet given; because Jesus was not yet glorified." [2]

On the day of Pentecost, this river of the Spirit, promised by Jesus, began to flow, for so we understand Peter's words: "This Jesus did God raise up . . . and having received of the Father the promise of the Holy Spirit, he hath poured forth this, which ye see and hear." [3]

No merely academic question then this: Does the Pentecostal "river" still flow with the same supernatural manifestations and results?

A brief reconstruction of the occasion on which Jesus uttered His prophecy of the outpouring of the Spirit en-

[1] A. T. Robertson, *A Harmony of the Gospels for the Student of the Life of Christ* (New York: Harper & Brothers, c. 1950), p. 114.
[2] John 7:37-39.
[3] Acts 2:32,33.

hances its dramatic effect. In the midst of the solemn Temple ceremonies [4] two priests mounted the altar, one to pour wine, the other to pour water from the Pool of Siloam into two silver funnels on the west side of the altar. As symbolic of the outpouring of the Holy Spirit, this pouring of the water was the central point of the service. Jesus' words have a special appropriateness combined with this ritual act. The pouring of the water was immediately followed by the singing of the Hallel. Then followed a short pause for the preparation of the festival sacrifices. It was at this moment, according to the view of Alfred Edersheim, that Jesus' voice reverberated through the Temple. Howbeit, "He interrupted not the services, for they had for the moment ceased: He interpreted, and fulfilled them." [5] Jesus thus declared that this liturgical act of pouring out the water drawn from the Pool of Siloam found its fulfillment in Him. The epexegetical commentary of the evangelist, John, explains the meaning of His words more fully. It was symbolic of the Pentecostal effusion of the Holy Spirit that was yet to come.

More specifically, John's explanatory comment, "for the Spirit was not yet given; because Jesus was not yet glorified," is "a clear reference to the great Pentecost." [6] As demonstrated in a previous chapter, His glorification was not his death, but, as Jesus Himself declared, "the glory which I had with thee (i.e., the Father) before the world was." [7] It was from His ascended "glory" that the Son "poured forth" the "river of living water" which He received from His Father. This is known theologically as the

[4] Alfred Edersheim, *The Life and Times of Jesus the Messiah*, II (4th ed., New York: Anson D. F. Randolph and Company, n.d.), 156 ff. In the midst of conflicting views we have chosen to follow Edersheim here.

[5] *Ibid.*, p. 156.

[6] Robertson, *Word Pictures in the New Testament*, V, 132.

[7] John 17:5.

doctrine of the "procession of the Holy Spirit." It is probably more accurate to say: "The Spirit proceeds from the Father *through* or *by* (not 'and') the Son." [8]

As this "river" of the Holy Spirit poured forth, He manifested His person and presence in supernatural charisms, or gifts. The first of these to be manifested was prophetic utterance in "other tongues", i.e., Spirit-given languages of praise and adoration, a supernatural vehicle for lauding the "magnificence" of God. There followed in rapid sequence a whole spiritual repertoire of miraculous manifestations of which "the word of wisdom," "the word of knowledge," "faith," "gifts of healings," "workings of miracles," "prophecy," "discerning of spirits," "tongues," and "interpretation of tongues" is only a partial listing.[9] The book of Acts is, in truth, an inspired chronicle of this spiritual "river" as the Holy Spirit flowed irresistibly and supernaturally in and through the Apostolic Community.

Pentecost was God's river in spate. Succeeding generations have been prone to regard it as a flash flood, lacking in continuity, but this is not the Biblical view. The mighty manifestations of the Holy Spirit continue as an integral part of the Church's life and witness. As such they are to continue until Jesus comes again.

I. *Acts 10:38, 39—"To All That Are Afar Off"*

In response to the guilt-stricken query of those who heard his "Pentecostal" sermon—"Brethren, what shall we do?"— Peter replied: "Repent ye, and be baptized every one of you in the name of Jesus Christ unto the remission of your sins; and ye shall receive the gift of the Holy Spirit. For to you is the promise, and to you children, and to all that are

[8] August Hopkins Strong, *Systematic Theology*, Three Volumes in One, (Philadelphia: The Judson Press, 1907), p. 323.

[9] I Cor. 12:8-10.

afar off, even as many as the Lord our God shall call unto him." [10]

As already shown, the "gift of the Spirit" cannot be confined to the work of the Spirit in regeneration. In the context, Peter interpreted for his auditors the meaning of the Pentecostal phenomena they were witnessing. The phrase refers expressly to the supernatural manifestations of the Holy Spirit "which they were seeing and hearing." The experience of Cornelius and his household, upon whom "was poured out the gift of the Holy Spirit", also confirms the charismatic connotations of this phrase, "the gift of the Spirit." [11]

Peter's allusion to "the promise" in this context can only refer to the baptism in the Holy Spirit promised by Jesus in Acts 1:4. And it is the scope of "the promised" baptism in the Spirit, that refutes the attempt to confine the Pentecostal experience to the apostolic age. "The promise" is first to the assembled multitude of Jews. Then it embraces their descendants, "sons and daughters of verse 17." [12] Finally, "the horizon widens and includes the Gentiles. Those 'afar off' from the Jews were the heathen." [13] "The promise" of Jesus, even "the gift of the Holy Spirit" in Pentecostal fulness and power, is indeed for "all that are afar off, *even* as many as the Lord our God shall call unto him." The universality of "the promise" is abridged only by the prior condition of repentance, and its concomitant saving faith in Jesus Christ as Saviour and Lord. The Lord is still calling. His "promise" is still in effect. The charismatic revival of

---

[10] Acts 2:38,39.

[11] Knowling, *op. cit.*, II, 91. "The word (tēn dōrean) is used specially of the gift of the Holy Ghost by St. Luke four times in Acts vii.20 x.45. xi.17, but by no other Evangelist (cf. however Luke xi.13), cf. Heb. vi.4 (John iv.10)."

[12] Robertson, *Word Pictures in the New Testament*, III, 36.

[13] *Ibid.*

the churches is thoroughly consistent with the Biblical evidence.

II. *I. Cor. 13:8 "Tongues Shall Cease"*

Attempts to refute these facts are repeatedly aired on reputedly exegetical grounds. I. Cor. 13:8 is frequently pressed out of context for this purpose: "Love never faileth; but whether *there be* tongues, they shall cease; whether *there be* knowledge, it shall be done away." It has been argued from this that tongues, as one of the "sign gifts," ceased at the end of the apostolic age. But the argument is erroneous. Here the Greek words for "they shall be done away," (*katar-gēthēsontai,* future passive), and "they shall cease," (*pausontai,* future middle), are used synonymously,[14] There is no exegetical significance in the use of either the passive or the middle voices with these verbs. The lexicons list no current uses of the word *katargēo* in the middle voice. It is consistently used in the passive instead. By the same token, *pauō* is used consistently in the middle voice.[15] The use of these two forms reflects grammatical and stylistic considerations rather than dogmatic concerns. The writer simply used the forms currently used for each word. It cannot, therefore, be deduced from the forms of these verbs that tongues "will stop themselves" at the end of the apostolic age, while prophecy and knowledge will continue indefinitely. Certainly no terminus is fixed by the use of either word. That these three charisms will come to an end is clearly affirmed by the text. *When they will cease can only be deduced from the context.*

While the verse itself does not tell us when these gifts will finally terminate, the context does indicate it, viz.,

---

14 Arndt, Gingrich, Bauer, *op. cit.,* p. 418.

15 *Ibid.,* p. 643. They list only one passive form, the 2nd aorist infinitive *paenai,* in the post-Biblical *Hermas, Vision.* Note that this form is a verbal noun.

"when that which is perfect is come." [16] The temporal clause
here refers to an "indefinite future time." [17] "That which is
perfect," in the opinion of G. G. Findlay, "is brought about
at the *parousia*—it 'comes' with the Lord from heaven." [18]
As a matter of fact, "The Apostle is saying nothing about
the cessation of *charismata* in this life." [19] Paul did say, "that
these charismata generally, as being designed only for the
aeon of the partial, and not in correspondence with the future aeon of the perfect, will cease to exist at the
Parousia." [20] Most comments on the passage are deeply dyed
with the stated, or implied, assumption that there was
something intrinsically wrong with the manifestation of
tongues at Corinth. As a result, some commentators go out
of their way to malign them. It is certainly a more wholesome and scriptural judgment to conclude, as James Moffatt
did, that "Great as is the value even of prophecy, knowledge,
and 'tongues', their function is confined to the brief interval
till the Lord returns." [21]

The words of the apostle Paul in verse 12 are often overlooked or misconstrued in this connection: e.g., "For now
we see in a mirror, darkly; but then face to face: now I

[16] I. Cor. 13:10.

[17] Robertson, *Word Pictures in the New Testament*, IV, 179. "*Hotan
elthei* is second aorist subjunctive with *hotan*, temporal clause for indefinite
future time."

[18] *Op. cit.*, II, p. 900.

[19] Robertson & Plummer, *op. cit.*, p. 297. "We might have expected St.
Paul to put it in this way, yet he does not. He does not say, 'But when we
shall have come to the perfection of the other world,' etc. He is so full of
the thought of the Second Advent, that he represents the perfection as coming to us. '*When* it shall have *come*'; then, but not till then. The Apostle is
saying nothing about the cessation of *charismata* in this life: prophesyings
and knowledge might always be useful. All that he asserts is, that these
things will have no more use when completeness is revealed; and therefore
they are inferior to Love . . . Chrys. points out that it is only the partial
fragmentary knowledge that will be done away."

[20] Heinrich Meyer, *Critical and Exegetical Hand-Book to the Epistles to
the Corinthians*, p. 305.

[21] Moffatt, *op. cit.*, p. 200.

know in part; but then shall I know fully even as also I was fully known." These words scarcely admit of any other conclusion, for "unquestionably the time alluded to is that of *the coming of the Lord . . .* and this applies to *all these,* not to the last (*gnōsis,* (i.e., 'knowledge')) only." [22]

Expediency and/or apologetic intent has led some to define "that which is perfect (*to teleion*)" [23] as the completed canon of Scripture. In support of this view, the charisms of "prophecy" and "knowledge" are restricted in operation to revelatory gifts given for the sole purpose of communicating the New Testament revelation. However, the whole thesis is devastated by the argument *reductio ad absurdum.* A simple paraphrase of Paul's words will serve to illustrate this contention, e.g., "now," wrote Paul, "I know in part; but then, when the canon of the New Testament is completed, *shall I know* fully even as also I was fully known." The absurdity of this is readily apparent. The Apostle was dead, in all probability martyred, *before* the corpus of the New Testament was completed. By way of contrast, he spoke pointedly of himself, and his own expectations when he said *"then shall I know."* He anticipated the time when his own partial knowledge—"seen in a mirror darkly"—would be completed. Certainly, he was looking forward to the coming of the Lord Jesus Christ when he penned these words, when his own fragmentary knowledge, though superior to most, would be completed.

The apostolic age began with miraculous signs and wonders. On the day of Pentecost, "tongues" were followed by all, and more, of the gifts of the Holy Spirit, in I. Cor. 12–14. The plain testimony of Scripture is that these supernatural manifestations of the Holy Spirit were to continue throughout the whole Church age, terminating only at the

[22] Alford, *op. cit.,* p. 587.

[23] Robertson & Davis, op. cit., p. 205. "The articular neuter adjective is often used in the same sense as an abstract . . ."

Second Advent of our Lord Jesus Christ. Herein lies the charismatic continuity between the various accounts of the baptism in the Spirit in the Acts, with their supernatural accompaniments, and the doctrinal portions of I. Cor. 12–14 in which Paul dealt with the continuing operations of these supernatural enduements of God's Spirit in the worship and witness of the Church.

EPILOGUE

"For These Are Not Drunken, As Ye Suppose"

Notwithstanding the mounting evidence that the churches are in the midst of a charismatic awakening, reluctance on the part of many, and outright hostility on the part of others, will not permit them to acknowledge, even to themselves, that churches and individuals are experiencing "Pentecost" anew. This opposition comes from opposite extremes of the theological spectrum.

Our interest in this opposition to the present charismatic renewal of the churches is neither apologetic nor polemic. Were this our concern, we would not trouble to comment upon it. We do feel obligated, however, to take note of such contrary opinions to determine whether or not they offer a live option to the charismatic experience for the Church.

On the one hand, the anti-supernaturalistic "theologian" denies *a priori* supernatural reality. He lives in a one story universe in which matter is ultimate reality, and physical law the sole "revelation" of Truth. His is a closed universe in which empirical science preempts the role of religion, and miracles are, by definition, deemed impossible. Ironically, the anti-supernaturalistic theologian, in his capitulation to the humanistic, rationalistic, materialistic scientism which dominates our culture, destroys his own reason for being. In such a naturalistic context, the theologian is a sociological anomaly.

Theistic supernaturalism is the very ground and possibility of Theology. The negation of this fact denies empirical validity to Theology as a science. This is the most critical point of tension between anti-supernaturalism, as a philosophy of religion, and the charismatic renewal of the Church. The abstractions and hypotheses of "religious" philosophy have no valid categories with which to evaluate charismatic phenomena. The immanental presuppositions of philosophical and scientific anthropology are too circumscribed to grapple with "man created (and through Christ, recreated) in the image of God." Only within the context of a Christological anthropology can the life and experience of the "spiritual (*pneumatikos*) man" be understood.[1]

On the other hand, opposition to the charismatic awakening of the Church comes from the side of Biblical orthodoxy, which uncompromisingly defends the integrity of the Biblical record (and rightly so), but in the same breath denies charismatic continuity in the contemporary Church. Admittedly, Jesus in the days of His flesh, healed the sick, cleansed the leper, and delivered the demoniac. Unquestionably, the apostolic company, baptised in the Holy Spirit at Pentecost, preached the Gospel with signs following—but, in the view of a scholastic orthodoxy, that was another dispensation (or sealed off subdivision of this dispensation) in the Divine economy. The works Jesus wrought in the days of His flesh, He is dispensationally impotent to do now through His incarnation in His Church.

[1] Parenthetically, the semantic disguise of humanism needs to be stripped away in the interests of Truth. Humanism is not humanitarianism. Ideological humanism is in no sense humanitarian in motive or in manifestation. The distinction must be clearly drawn. The philosophical roots of ideological humanism are in pagan philosophy, where "even the tender mercies of the heathen are unspeakable cruelty." It is only in the "revealed" ethic of the Judaeo-Christian faiths that true humanitarianism exists. The motivation of humanism is ego-centric hedonism, not Christo-centric Love. The final end of humanism is not the emancipation of the race, but its condemnation to ultimate bestiality; for it irrevocably seeks to "change the glory of the incorruptible God for the likeness of corruptible man." (Rom. 1:23).

To the anti-supernaturalistic theologian, miracles are myths. They never did happen, do not take place now, and never will occur. To an orthodoxy, bound to the creeds and traditions of men, miracles did happen "once upon a time," in the infancy of the Church. To the former, they were never historical events, while to the latter, they are scarcely more than historical reminiscences. In a concord of expediency, both sides agree that they cannot happen now. By both, contemporary miracles are resisted as a capricious intervention, at odds with their closed world-views. "The Lord working with them, and confirming the word by the signs that followed," is disposed of as *textually* and *empirically* spurious.

As in the days of primitive Christianity, so also today, the hue and cry after the charismatic Christian is still, "These that have turned the world (or the Church) upside down are come hither also." [2] Epithets like, "heretical," "divisive," "stylized primitivizations," "hysteria," "possible vitamin deficiency," "infantilism," "spiritual rowdyism," "of the flesh," "spiritual pride," represent but a sampling of the anti-charismatic polemic. While of all the Holy Spirit's personal manifestations, the most vehement denunciations are precipitated by *glossolalia*.

Echoes of Pentecost! Peter still defends the charismatic community against the calumnies of its detractors, saying, "For these are not drunken, as ye suppose." [3]

The "sound and fury" of polemics, however, do serve to focus attention upon the urgent claims of the Holy Spirit upon the Church in this day. The corporate Body of Christ must listen to what the Holy Spirit is saying charismatically at this time; or be reduced (1) *in its life* to preoccupation with the trivia of a self-serving institutionalism, (2) *in its*

2 Acts 17:6.
3 Acts 2:15.

witness to "the parroting of the polysyllabic banalities of currently fashionable philosophical, psychological, sociological, and political cliches of a pluralistic society, and (3) *in its identity* to the level of one among many competing ethnic religions in a relativistic culture.

An anti-supernaturalistic "theology" has no solution, only theories, for the human predicament, which is basically man's alienation from God. Instead, it acknowledges its redemptive sterility by its unabashed capitulation to the human predicament, and by its frenetic pursuit of "relevance" to the contemporary mood. "It is part of the problem, not of the solution." [4] It is captive by consent to modern society's ego-centric humanism, whose ontological speculations (Buddha fashion) do not rise above the narcissistic contemplation of its own navel. The practical consequence of which is a "situation ethic" that is little more than a rancid hedonism.

On the other hand, a doctrinaire theological orthodoxy is not a serious option. It is essentially a refurbished scholasticism whose concept of metaphysical reality has congealed in abstract definitions and propositions. It is too prone to confound definition with essence. Consequently, miracles are little more than dogmatic presuppositions in a theological memorabilia. Its continuing strategy is largely retrenchment, rather than dynamic involvement. Intimidated by apostasy, it has largely surrendered all hope of revival, charismatic or otherwise. Characteristically, its ethic is a platitudinous legalism. The force it does exert is typically centripetal. It regards with suspicion-of-heresy, the centrifugal forces of the Gospel that would plunge the Church charismatically into redemptive confrontation with sin, self, and Satan. Its strategy is fundamentally "trench warfare"

---

[4] I am indebted to the Rev. Oral Roberts through whose ministry I first "received" this "word of wisdom."

waged from dogmatic bastions. It is, in the nature of the case, almost inevitable that its heaviest theological "hardware" be trained against charismatic Christians.

If the book of the Acts bears witness to normative Christian experience—and it indubitably does—then by every Biblical standard of measurement contemporary Church-life is subnormal. As a consequence, it does not speak meaningfully, much less authoritatively, to our fragmented modern world. Well may a tormented humanity, staggering on the brink of an apocalyptic abyss, cry out to a Church that knows neither health nor wholeness of faith, life, nor fellowship—"Physician! Heal thyself!"

It is precisely at this point that the Holy Spirit, through the present charismatic awakening of the fragmented Christian Community, speaks urgently to the whole Church on the ecumenical, the denominational, the congregational, and the personal levels of a unity of Spirit and of Life. Only out of the plenitude of its own charismatic "fulness" can the modern Church plunge into redemptive confrontation with an alienated world.

It has been said that "everywhere the apostle Paul went, he had a riot or a revival," and ofttimes both. The book of the Acts is a book full of just such revivals. The significant and frequently overlooked fact is that these were charismatic revivals. The Gospel was preached in a context of charismatic signs, tongues, healings, miracles, exorcisms, etc. This is the Biblical pattern of revival. This is the only pattern of revival commensurate with the challenge and opportunities of our day.

In the face of need so staggering, and opportunity so unparalleled, the Body of Christ must either live "the Life, the Truth, the Way,"—or else get out of the way. It must have charismatic revival to justify its survival.

SUPPLEMENT TO CHAPTER XVI

The Use of Pneumatikos in the Pauline Epistles

1. Rom. 1:11—"That I may impart unto you some spiritual gift (charisma . . . *pneumatikon*)."
   a. *Charisma*, "in the technical Pauline sense *charismata* (A.V. *gifts*) denote *extraordinary powers, distinguishing certain Christians and enabling them to serve the church of Christ, the reception of which is due to the power of divine grace operating in their souls by the Holy Spirit.*" [1]
   b. *Charisma*, "extraordinary gifts of the Holy Ghost dwelling and working in individuals (*charisma pneumatikon*, Rom. 1:11). . . ." [2]
2. Rom. 7:14—"For we know that the law is spiritual (*nomos pneumatikos):* but I am carnal, (*sarkinos*, 'consisting of or composed of flesh' [3]."
   a. Cf., "the law comes from God who is Spirit, and it shares His nature: its affinities are Divine, not human." [4]
   b. Note the contrast is between the Divine law and mortal flesh, between the supernatural and the natural.
3. Rom. 15:27—'For if the Gentiles have been made partakers of their spiritual things (*tois pneumatikois*, R.S.V. 'spiritual

---

[1] Thayer, *op. cit.*, charisma, p. 667.
[2] Cremer, *op. cit.*, p. 613.
[3] Thayer, *op. cit.*, sarkinos, p. 667.
[4] James Denney, *St. Paul's Epistles to the Romans, The Expositor's Greek Testament*, II, ed. by W. Robertson Nicoll (Grand Rapids: Wm. B. Eerdmans Publishing Company, n.d.), p. 641.

blessings'; N.E.B. 'spiritual treasures'), they owe it *to them* also to minister unto them in carnal things *(tois sarkikois,* R.S.V. 'material things'; N.E.B. material needs')."

  a. Cf., *'tois pneumatikois* for the benefits· of Christianity (faith, justification, peace, love, hope, etc.) proceed from the Holy Spirit, are *ta tou pneumatos dōra:* . . . *tois sarkikois* for the earthly possessions concern *the material and physical phenomenal* nature of man, which is his bodily form of existence." [5]

  b. *Ta pneumatika,* "the spiritual or heavenly blessings of the gospel, opp. to *ta sarkika* Rom. xv.27;" [6]

  c. Note, the contrast is between the supernatural blessings of the Holy Spirit, and the material needs of man.

4. I Cor. 2:13—"Which things also we speak, not in words which man's wisdom teacheth, but which the Spirit teacheth; combining spiritual things with spiritual words *(pneumatikois, pneumatika)."* (R.S.V. 'interpreting spiritual truths to those who possess the Spirit:" N.E.B. 'interpreting spiritual truth to those who have the Spirit").

  a. Cf., *"pneumatika,* thoughts, opinions, precepts, maxims ascribable to the Holy Spirit working in the soul, I Cor. ii.13." [7]

  b. Cf., "The apostle's intention is rather to set forth, first antithetically and then also thetically, the manner in which believers speak. Their words also are from the Spirit." [8]

  c. Note, the contrast is between the supernaturally inspired utterances of Divine wisdom, and the natural utterance of human wisdom.

5. I Cor. 2:14, 15—"Now the natural man *(psuchikos anthropos)* receiveth not the things of the Spirit of God: for they

---

[5] Heinrich Meyer, *Critical and Exegetical Hand-Book to the Epistle to the Romans,* p 555.

[6] Thayer, *op. cit., pneumatikos,* p. 523.

[7] Thayer, *op. cit., pneumatikos,* 523.

[8] F. W. Grosheide, *Commentary on the First Epistle to the Corinthians, The New International Commentary on the New Testament,* ed. by F. F. Bruce (Grand Rapids: Wm. B. Eerdmans Publishing Company, [1953]), p. 71.

are foolishness unto him; and he cannot know them, because they are spiritually judged (*pneumatikōs,* adv.). But he that is spiritual (*ho pneumatikos,* N.E.B. 'the man gifted with the Spirit') judgeth all things."

a. Cf., "The latter is a person who has nothing more than an ordinary human soul; the former possesses the divine *pneuma,* . . . this enables him to penetrate the divine mysteries." [9]

b. Cf., *pneumatikos* contrasted with *psuchikos,* the latter *"pertaining to the soul or life,* in our literature always denoting the life of the natural world and whatever belongs to it, *in contrast to the supernatural world which is characterized by pneuma."* [10]

c. Cf., adverbially, *pneumatikōs,* "by the aid of the Holy Spirit." [11]

d. Note the contrast between the natural man and the supernaturally endowed man.

6. I Cor. 3:1—"And I, brethren, could not speak unto you as unto spiritual (*pneumatikois*), but as unto carnal (*sarkinois*), as unto babes in Christ." (N.E.B. "I could not speak to you as I should speak to people who have the Spirit. I had to deal with you on the merely natural plane, as infants in Christ.")

a. Cf., *Sarkinois,* "fleshly, belonging to the realm of the flesh in so far as it is weak, sinful and transitory, carnal (in older usage) . . . I Cor. 3:1 (opposed to *pneumatikos*)." [12]

b. The carnal Christian is the one "ruled by the (sinful) flesh," [13] i.e., by the old Adamic nature. In this context *sarkikos* and *sarkinos* are used interchangeably.

c. Note the conflict between the two natures in the Christian, the one spiritual, i.e., born of the Spirit, the other natural. The flesh nature manifested itself in Corinth in

---

[9] Arndt, Gingrich, Bauer, *op. cit., pneumatikos,* p. 685.

[10] *Ibid.,* p. 902. Italics mine in latter portion of quote. H.M.E.

[11] Thayer, *op. cit.,* p. 523.

[12] Arndt, Gingrich, Bauer, *op. cit.,* sarkinos, p. 902.

[13] Grosheide, *op cit.,* p. 78, footnote.

jealousy, strife, and schism, not in the gifts of the Spirit. All these, including tongues, are described as *pneumatikos,* and not as *sarkinon* or *sarkikon.*

7. I Cor. 9:11—"If we sowed unto you spiritual things (*ta pneumatika*), is it a great matter if we shall reap your carnal things (*ta sarkika,* R.S.V. 'your material benefits': N.E.B. 'a material harvest')."

   a. Cf., "the spiritual or heavenly blessings of the gospel, opposed to *ta sarkika* Rom. xv.27 [I Cor. 9:11]." [14]

   b. Cf., "The contrast is one between the heavenly and the earthly, or between the spiritual and the material." [15]

8. I Cor. 10:3, 4—"and did all (the antecedent subject is, 'our fathers,' i.e., Israel) eat the same spiritual food (*pneumatikon brōma*); and did all drink the same spiritual drink (*pneumatikon poma*): for they drank of a spirit-rock (*pneumatikēs petros*) that followed them: and the rock was Christ." (R.S.V. & N.E.B. "supernatural food," "supernatural drink," "supernatural Rock").

   a. Cf., *pneumatikos,* "produced by the sole power of God himself without natural instrumentality, supernatural, *broma, poma, petra* I Cor. x.3, 4." [16]

   b. Note the use of *pneumatikos* here as equivalent to supernatural.

9. I Cor. 12:1—"Now concerning spiritual *gifts* (*tōn pneumatikōn,* N.E.B. 'about gifts of the Spirit')." Cf., Rom. 1:11 above on *charismata.*

10. I Cor. 14:1—"yet desire earnestly spiritual *gifts."*

    a. C.f., *"Ta pneumatika,* spiritual gifts,—of endowments called *charismata* (see *charisma*), I Cor xii.1; xiv.1." [17]

    b. Cf., the comments on Rom. 1:11 for *charisma.*

    c. Note that these spiritual gifts are supernatural not natural endowments.

11. I Cor. 14:37—"If any one thinketh himself to be a prophet, or spiritual (*pneumatikos*). . . ."

14 Thayer, *op. cit., pneumatikos,* p. 523.
15 Grosheide, *op. cit.,* p. 207.
16 Thayer, *op. cit., pneumatikos,* p. 523.
17 *Ibid.,* p. 523.

    a. Cf., "masculine *(ho) pneumatikos possessing the Spirit, the one who possesses the Spirit* (with *prophētēs*) I Cor. 14:37." [18]

    b. Cf., "The prophet or the one with the gift of tongues. . . ." [19]

12. I Cor. 15:44, 46—"it is sown a natural body *(sōma psuchikon,* R.S.V. 'physical body'; N.E.B. 'animal body'), it is raised a spiritual body *(sōma pneumatikon).* If there is a natural body *(sōma psuchikon),* there is also a spiritual *body (pneumatikon)* . . . Howbeit that is not first which is spiritual *(pneumatikon),* but that which is natural *(psuchikon),* then that which is spiritual *(pneumatikon).*"

    a. Cf., *pneumatikos,* "The word occurs also in I Cor. 2, 15; 15, 44.46, in contrast with *psuchikos,* . . . with the sense of *pneuma* as = the divine life principle of the *kainē ktisis* [new creation]." [20]

    b. Cf., "That which belongs to the supernatural order of being is described as *pneumatikos:* accordingly, the resurrection body. . . . I Cor. 15:44a." [21]

    c. Note again the contrast between the supernatural and the natural.

13. Gal. 6:1—"ye who are spiritual *(hoi pneumatikoi)* restore such a one in a spirit of gentleness." (N.E.B. "you who are endowed with the Spirit").

    a. Cf., "*(hoi) pneumatikoi (the) spirit-filled people* . . .; Gal. 6:1." [22]

    b. Cf., "*one who is filled with and governed by the Spirit of God* . . . Gal. 6:1." [23]

14. Eph. 1:3—"Blessed be the God and Father of our Lord Jesus Christ, who hath blessed us with every spiritual blessing *(eulogiai pneumatikēi)* in heavenly *places (en tois epouraniois)* in Christ."

---

[18] Arndt, Gingrich, Bauer, *op. cit., pneumatikos* p. 685.
[19] Robertson, *Word Pictures in the New Testament,* IV, 185.
[20] Cremer, *op. cit.,* p. 532.
[21] Arndt, Gingrich, Bauer, *op. cit., pneumatikos,* p. 685.
[22] *Ibid.*
[23] Thayer, *op. cit., pneumatikos,* p. 523.

    a. Cf., *"emanating from the Divine Spirit,* or *exhibiting its effects and so its character: . . . eulogia,* Eph. 1:3." [24]

    b. Cf. *"en tois epouraniois* must then here be referred as a *local* predication to *eulogiai pneumatikei,* defining broadly and comprehensively the region and sphere where our true home is (Phil iii.20), where our hope is laid up (Col i.5), and whence the blessings of the Spirit, the *dōrea hē epouraniois* (Heb. vi.4), truly come." [25]

    c. Note *pneumatikēi* is used here of supernatural blessings.

15. Eph. 5:18, 19 (Cf., Col. 3:16)—"But be filled with the Spirit; speaking one to another in psalms and hymns and spiritual songs *(ōidais pneumatikais)."*

    a. Cf., *"pneumatikais* is attached to the *ōidais* not merely to differentiate these *ōidai* as religious and not secular, *but to describe them as inspired by the Holy* Ghost." [26]

    b. Cf., "To this last epithet *ōidais pneumatikais* is added, —sc. not merely, 'of religious import,' . . . but in accordance with the last clause of ver. 18, 'such as the Holy Spirit inspired and gave utterance to'." [27]

    c. Cf., "that the Christians, filled by the Spirit *improvised* psalms, is clear from I Cor. xiv, 15, 26." [28] The reference to I Cor. 15:15 alludes to Paul's words, "I will sing with the spirit," = singing in tongues, cf., 14:14. It suggests that Eph. 5:19 and Col. 3:16 refer to charismatic worship just as at Corinth.

16. Eph. 6:12—"Our wrestling . . . is against the spiritual *hosts (pneumatika,* N.E.B. 'superhuman forces'), of wickedness in the heavenly places *(en tois epouraniois)."*

    a. Cf., "the spirit-forces of evil Eph. 6:12." [29]

---

[24] *Ibid.*

[25] Charles J. Ellicott, *A Critical and Grammatical Commentary on St. Paul's Epistle to the Ephesians,* (Andover: Warren F. Draper, 1890), p. 17.

[26] S. D. F. Salmon, *The Epistle to the Ephesians, The Expositor's Greek Testament,* ed. by W. Robertson Nicoll, III (Grand Rapids: Wm. B. Eerdmans, n.d.), 364. Italics mine, H.M.E.

[27] Ellicott, *op cit.,* p. 129.

[28] Heinrich Meyer, *Critical and Exegetical Hand-Book to the Epistle to the Ephesians,* p. 506.

[29] Arndt, Gingrich, Bauer *op. cit., pneumatikos,* p. 685.

b. Note the connotation "supernatural" with *pneumatika* is self evident.

17. Col. 1:9—"that ye may be filled with the knowledge of his will in all spiritual wisdom and understanding (*sophia kai sunesei pneumatikēi*)."

a. Cf., *"sunesis pneumatikēi* understanding given by the Spirit 1:9." [30]

b. Note, it is supernatural (*pneumatikēi*) wisdom and understanding that makes possible the knowledge of God's will.

Conclusion: The use of pneumatikos in the epistles of Paul always bear the connotation "supernatural."

a. The gifts of the Spirit (*charismata pneumatika*) are not natural talents. They are supernatural manifestations of the Holy Spirit.

b. The following opinion must, therefore, be rejected: "St. Paul has in mind the kind of gifts—partly what we should call natural and partly transcending the ordinary workings of nature—described in I Cor. xii-xiv; Rom. xii. 6ff." [31] In Pauline usage *pneumatika* is always supernatural.

[30] *Ibid.*

[31] William Sanday, and Arthur C. Headlam, *A Critical and Exegetical Commentary on the Epistle to the Romans, The International Critical Commentary* (13th ed.; New York: Charles Scribner's Sons, 1911), p. 21.

Bibliography

Bible Versions

Nestle, Erwin and Aland, Kurt (eds.), *Novum Testamentum Graece,* 25th ed., Stuttgart: Würtembergische Bibelamstalt, 1963.

New American Standard Bible, New Testament, Nashville: Broadman Press, [c. The Lockman Foundation, 1963.]

Rahlfs, Alfred (ed.), *Septuaginta,* 4th ed., 2 vols., Stuttgart: Privileg. Würtemburgische Bibelamstalt, 1950.

The Holy Bible, American Standard Version, New York: Thomas Nelson & Sons, 1901.

The New Testament of Our Lord and Saviour Jesus Christ, A revision of the Challoner-Rheims Version, ed. by Catholic scholars, Paterson: St. Anthony's Guild Press, 1941.

The New Testament in Four Versions: King James, Revised Standard, Phillips Modern English, New English Bible, Christianity Today Edition, New York: The Iverson-Ford Associates, 1963.

Weigle, Luther A. (ed.), *The New Testament Octapla,* New York: Thomas Nelson & Sons, 1946.

Lexicons and Grammars

Arndt, F. William and Gingrich, Wilbur F., (trans. of Walter Bauer), *A Greek-English Lexicon of the New Testament and Other Early Christian Literature,* Chicago: The University of Chicago Press, [1957.]

Cremer, Hermann, *Biblico-Theological Lexicon of New Testament Greek,* trans. by D. W. Simon and William Urwick, Edinburgh: T. & T. Clark, 1872.

Crosby, Henry Lamar and Schaeffer, John Nevin, *An Intro-duction to Greek,* New York: Allyn and Bacon, [1928].

Dana, H. E. and Mantey, Julius, *A Manual Grammar of the Greek New Testament,* New York: The Macmillan Company, [1955].

Liddell, Henry George and Scott, Robert, *A Greek-English Lexicon,* 7th ed., New York: Harper & Brothers, 1889.

Robertson, A.T., *A Grammar of the Greek New Testament in The Light of Historical Research,* Nashville: Broadman Press, [1934].

Robertson, A. T. and Davis, W. Hersey, *A New Short Grammar of the Greek New Testament,* New York: Harper & Brothers, [1933].

Thayer, Joseph Henry, *A Greek-English Lexicon of the New Testament,* New York: American Book Company, 1889.

General Works

Abbott, Lyman, *An Illustrated Commentary on the Gospels,* New York: A. S. Barnes & Company, 1906.

Albright, William Foxwell, *From Stone Age To Christianity,* 2nd ed., Garden City: Doubleday Anchor Books, Doubleday & Company, Inc., 1957.

Alford, Henry, *The Greek Testament,* 5th ed., vol. II, Cambridge: Deighton, Bell and Co., 1865.

Bernard, J. H., *The Second Epistle to the Corinthians, The Expositor's Greek Testament,* ed. by W. Robertson Nicoll, vol. III, Grand Rapids: Wm. B. Eerdmans, n.d.

Box, George H., *The Historical and Religious Background of the Early Christian Movement, The Abingdon Bible Commentary,* ed. by Frederick Carl Eiselen, Edwin Lewis, and David G. Downey, Nashville: Abingdon-Cokesbury Press, [1929].

Bruce, Alexander Balmain, *The Synoptic Gospels, The Expositor's Greek Testament,* ed. by W. Robertson Nicoll, vol. I, Grand Rapids: Wm. B. Eerdmans, n.d.

Bruce, F. F. (ed.), *Commentary on the Book of the Acts, The*

New International Commentary on the New Testament, Grand Rapids: Wm. B. Eerdmans, 1964.

Charles, R. H. (ed.), *The Apocrypha and Pseudepigrapha,* vol. I, Oxford: The Clarendon Press, 1963.

Clarke, Adam, *The New Testament of Our Lord and Saviour Jesus Christ,* 2 vols., New York: T. Mason & G. Lane, 1837.

Conybeare, W. J. and Howson, J. S., *The Life and Epistles of St. Paul,* vol. II, New York: Charles Scribner & Co., 1869.

Danielou, Jean, *The Dead Sea Scrolls and Primitive Christianity,* A Mentor Omega Book, New York: The New American Library, [1958].

Denney, James, *St. Paul's Epistle to the Romans, The Expositor's Greek Testament,* ed. by W. Robertson Nicoll, vol. II, Grand Rapids: Wm. B. Eerdmans, n.d.

Dodd, C. H., *Colossians, The Abingdon Bible Commentary,* ed. by Frederick Carl Eiselen, Edwin Lewis, and David G. Downey, Nashville: Abingdon-Cokesbury Press, [1929].

Dods, Marcus, *The Gospel of John, The Expositor's Greek Testament,* ed. by W. Robertson Nicoll, vol. I, Grand Rapids: Wm. B. Eerdmans, n.d.

Easton, Burton Scott, *The Epistles of John, The Abingdon Bible Commentary,* ed. by Frederick Carle Eiselen, Edwin Lewis, and David G. Downey, Nashville: Abingdon-Cokesbury Press, [1929].

Edersheim, Alfred, *The Life and Times of Jesus the Messiah,* vol. II, 4th ed., New York: Anson D. F. Randolph and Company, n.d.

Edwards, Thomas Charles, *A Commentary on the First Epistle to the Corinthians,* 2nd ed., New York: A. C. Strong & Son, 1886.

Ellicott, Charles J., *A Critical and Grammatical Commentary on St. Paul's Epistle to the Ephesians,* Andover: Warren F. Draper, 1890.

Findlay, G. G., *St. Paul's First Epistle to the Corinthians, The Expositor's Greek Testament,* ed. by W. Robertson Nicoll, vol. II, Grand Rapids: Wm. B. Eerdmans, n.d.

Godet, F., *Commentary on the Gospel of St. John,* Clarke's Foreign Theological Library, 4th series, LI, trans. by S. Taylor & M. D. Cusin, vol. III, Edinburgh: T. & T. Clarke, 1900.

————. Commentary on the Gospel of St. Luke, Clark's Foreign Theological Library, 4th series, XLVI, trans. by M. D. Cusin, vol. II, Edinburgh: T. & T. Clarke, 1878.

Grosheide, F. W., *Commentary on the First Epistle to the Corinthians, The New International Commentary on the New Testament,* ed. by F. F. Bruce, Grand Rapids: Wm. B. Eerdmans, 1953.

Hackett, Horatio B., *A Commentary on the Acts of the Apostles, An American Commentary on the New Testament,* ed. by Alvah Hovey, Philadelphia: American Baptist Publication Society, 1882.

Hackett, H. B. and Abbott, Ezra (eds.), *Dr. Wm. Smith's Dictionary of the Bible,* vol. III, Boston: Houghton, Mifflin and Company, 1896.

Howard, Wilbert F., The Gospel According to St. John, "Exegesis", *The Interpreter's Bible,* ed. by George Arthur Buttrick *et. al.,* vol. VIII, Nashville: Abingdon-Cokesbury Press, [1952].

Kendrick, A. C., *Commentary on the Epistle to the Hebrews, An American Commentary on the New Testament,* ed. by Alvah Hovey, Philadelphia: The American Baptist Publication Society, 1889.

Knowling, R. J., *The Acts of the Apostles, The Expositor's Greek Testament,* ed. by W. Robertson Nicoll, vol. II, Grand Rapids: Wm. B. Eerdmans Company, n.d.

Lightfoot, J. B., *Saint Paul's Epistle to the Galatians,* London: Macmillan and Company, 1896.

————. *Saint Paul's Epistles to the Colossians and to Philemon,* London: Macmillan and Company, 1892.

Luce, H. K. (ed.), *The Gospel According to St. Luke, The Cambridge Bible for Schools and Colleges,* Cambridge: The University Press, 1936.

Lumby, J. Rawson, *The Acts of the Apostles, Cambridge Bible for Schools and Colleges,* Cambridge: The University Press, 1934.

Macgregor, G. H. C., *The Gospel of John, The Moffatt New Testament Commentary*, ed. by James Moffatt, New York: Harper & Brothers, n.d.

Meyer, Heinrich A. W., *Critical and Exegetical Hand-Book to the Acts of the Apostles*, trans. from 4th German ed. by Paton J. Gloag, New York: Funk & Wagnalls, 1883.

————. *Critical and Exegetical Hand-Book to the Corinthians*, trans. from 5th German ed. by D. Douglas Bannerman, ed. by William P. Dickson, New York: Funk & Wagnalls, 1884.

————. *Critical and Exegetical Hand-Book to the Epistle Ephesians*, trans. from 4th German ed. by Morris J. Evans, rev. and ed. by William P. Dickson, New York: Funk & Wagnalls, 1884.

————. *Critical and Exegetical Hand-Book to the Epistle to the Romans*, trans. from 5th German ed. by John C. Moore and Edwin Johnson, rev. and ed. by William P. Dickson, New York: Funk & Wagnalls, 1884.

————. *Critical and Exegetical Hand-Book to the Gospel of John*, trans. from 5th German ed. by William Urwick, New York: Funk & Wagnalls, 1884.

Moffatt, James, *The First Epistle of Paul to the Corinthians, The Moffatt New Testament Commentary*, ed. by James Moffatt, New York: Harper & Brothers, n.d.

Montgomery, James, "Hail to the Lord's Anointed," *Christian Worship, A Hymnal*, Philadelphia: Judson Press, 1941.

Morgan, G. Campbell, *The Acts of the Apostles*, New York: Fleming H. Revell, 1924.

Nelson, William R., *The Interpretation of the Revelation of John in Valentinian Gnosis and the Evangelium Veritatis*, an unpublished manuscript study tracing the philosophical, mythological, and magical expansions of the system of Gnostic thought, especially in relation to the Apocalypse of John, circa 1961.

Olshausen, Hermann, *Biblical Commentary on the New Testament*, 1st American ed., trans. by A. C. Kendrick, vol. IV, New York: Sheldon & Company, 1860.

Parry, R. St. John, *The First Epistle of Paul the Apostle to the Corinthians*, The Cambridge Bible for Schools and Colleges, ed. by R. St. John Parry, Cambridge: The University Press, 1916.

Pinnock, Clark H., "The Case Against Form Criticism," *Christianity Today,* Vol. IX, no. 21 (July 1965).

Plummer, A., *The Gospel According to St. John, The Cambridge Bible For Schools and Colleges,* Cambridge: The University Press, 1923.

Roberts, Alexander and Donaldson, James (eds.), *Ante-Nicene Christian Library, The Apostolic Fathers,* vol. I, Edinburgh: T. & T. Clarke, 1876.

Robertson, A. T., *A Harmony of the Gospels for the Student of the Life of Christ,* New York: Harper & Brothers, [1950].

Robertson, A. T., *Word Pictures in the New Testament,* 6 vols., New York: Harper & Brothers, [1932].

Robertson, A. T. and Plummer, Alfred, *A Critical and Exegetical Commentary on the First Epistle of St. Paul to the Corintians, The International Critical Commentary,* 2nd ed., ed. by Samuel Rolles Driver, Alfred Plummer, and Charles Augustus Briggs, Edinburgh: T. & T. Clarke, 1963.

Robertson, James Alex., *Philippians, The Abingdon Bible Commentary,* ed. by Frederick Carl Eiselen, Edwin Lewis, and David G. Downey, Nashville: Abingdon-Cokesbury Press, [1929].

Sala, Harold J., *An Investigation of the Baptizing and Filling Work of the Holy Spirit in the New Testament Related to the Pentecostal Doctrine of "Initial Evidence",* unpublished Doctor of Philosophy dissertation, Bob Jones University, Greenville, South Carolina, 1966.

Salmond, S. D. F., *The Epistle to the Ephesians, The Expositor's Greek Testament,* ed. by W. Robertson Nicoll, vol. III, Grand Rapids: Wm. B. Eerdmans, n.d.

Sanday, William and Headlam, Arthur C., *A Critical and Exegetical Commentary on the Epistle to the Romans, The International Critical Commentary,* ed. by E. A. Briggs, S. R. Driver and Alfred Plummer, 13th ed., New York: Charles Scribner's Sons, 1911.

Schaff, Phillip, *History of the Christian Church,* vol. I, New York: Charles Scribner's Sons, 1887.

Strachan, R. H., *The Fourth Gospel, Its Significance and Environment,* 3rd ed., London: Student Christian Movement Press, 1941.

Strong, Augustus Hopkins, *Systematic Theology, Three Volumes in One,* Philadelphia: The Judson Press, [1907].

Thurneysen, Eduard, *A Theology of Pastoral Care,* trans. by Jack A. Worthington, *et. al.,* Richmond: John Knox Press, 1963.

Torrey, R. A., *The Person and Work of the Holy Spirit,* London: James Nisbet & Co., Limited, 1910.

Turner, George A., "A Decade of Studies in John's Gospel," *Christianity Today,* vol. IX, no. 5 (Dec. 1964).

Unger, Merrill F., *The Baptizing Work of the Holy Spirit,* Findlay, Ohio: The Putnam Publishing Co., c. 1962.

Walters, Orville S., "Have Psychiatry and Religion Reached a Truce?", *Christianity Today,* vol. X, no. 1, (Oct. 1965).

Warfield, B. B., *Counterfeit Miracles,* New York: Charles Scribner's Sons, 1918.

Weiner, Herbert, *The Wild Goats of Ein Gedi,* Meridian Books, New York: The World Publishing Company; Philadelphia: The Jewish Publishing Society of America, [1961].

Whiston, William, *The Works of Flavius Josephus, Antiquities of the Jews,* XIV, 10, Hartford: S. S. Scranton Co., 1905.

Winn. A. C., *The Acts of the Apostles, The Layman's Bible Commentaries,* ed. by Balmer Kelly, London: SCM Press, [1960].

Wood, C. T., *The Life, Letters, and Religion of St. Paul,* 2nd ed., Edinburgh: T. & T. Clarke, 1932.

Wordsworth, C., *The New Testament of Our Lord and Saviour Jesus Christ,* 7th ed., London: Rivingtons, 1870.